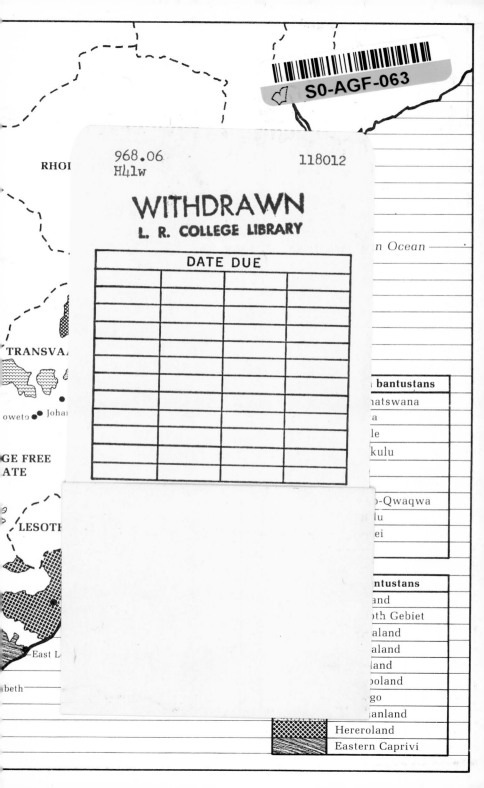

RHO

n Ocean

TRANSVA

oweto • Johan

GE FREE
ATE

LESOTH

East L

beth

bantustans

natswana

a

le

kulu

-Qwaqwa

lu

ei

ntustans

and

th Gebiet

aland

aland

land

ooland

go

anland

Hereroland

Eastern Caprivi

White Man,
We Want to Talk to You

DENIS HERBSTEIN

White Man, We Want to Talk to You

AFRICANA PUBLISHING COMPANY
A division of Holmes & Meier Publishers, Inc.
NEW YORK

First published in the United States of America 1979 by
AFRICANA PUBLISHING COMPANY
30 Irving Place, New York, N.Y. 10003

Copyright © 1979 Denis Herbstein

Library of Congress Cataloguing in Publication Data
Herbstein, Denis.
  White man, we want to talk to you.

  Bibliography: p.
  Includes index.
    1. South Africa – Race relations.   2. Soweto – Riots.   3. South Africa –
Politics and government – 1961–   I. Title.
DT763.H44 1979   968.06   78-11214
ISBN 0–8419–0455–3
ISBN 0–8419–0456–1 pbk.

PRINTED IN GREAT BRITAIN

Cry Rage! by James Matthews, from which the
quotation on p. 77 is taken, is published by
Ravan Press, Johannesburg

To ALL my fellow South Africans . . .

Contents

Preface

Though the reader will appreciate that I have little feeling of goodwill towards the Government of South Africa, it is none the less to that institution that I owe the writing of this book. At the end of 1975, after an absence of several years in London, I returned to South Africa as a foreign correspondent. At the end of my year's stay, I flew to Cape Town to see my parents. One morning, Captain Dippenaar and Sergeant Posthumous of the security police called at their home to serve papers expelling me from the land of my birth and upbringing. No reason was given. During the course of that dramatic year I had reported the Soweto uprising and other events for the *Sunday Times*, the *Guardian* and the BBC. Returning to England, I was angry enough to sit down and write this book.

My thanks to Mr Vorster's Government do not end there. For years I had written articles, both inside South Africa and out, lamenting the iniquities of apartheid. Now, piecing it together at my leisure, I have a much better understanding of how the system works, and whom it benefits. My previous writing was, clearly, too kind.

Normally I would have expressed my gratitude to those friends inside South Africa who, over the years, have given me a fresh insight into our country. They are all part of this book. Many are now detained or banned or are being harassed by the police. I see no reason to make life more difficult for them than it is already. I mention only two, Robert Sobukwe and Steve Biko. They are both dead.

The same restraints do not apply in England. Erica Flegg helped me with invaluable research, and challenged, argued and occasionally persuaded me to change my mind. Professor Julius Lewin, teacher of many generations of Witwatersrand

9

Preface

University students, subjected me to many a searching tutorial. Ronald Segal, who edited this book, never failed to encourage the journalist in me while despairing at my fragile capacity for watertight political analysis. All are forgiven and thanked.

Thanks also to Lyn Maree, for the use of her material on schools in Soweto; to Drake Koka, for his recollections of the uprising; to Basil Davidson, for casting a knowledgeable eye over the pages on the Angolan war. Others are mentioned in the text. Among those who are not, there are Jonathan Steele, Arthur Gavshor, Norman Kessel, Jane Henderson, Elaine Greene (agent–friend), and, that patient pair, Piers Burnett of André Deutsch and Michael Dover of Penguin. Finally, a word for the *Sunday Times*, without whose generous flexibility words would not have been put on paper. In particular, I gratefully testify to the old-fashioned courtesy of my news editor, Magnus Linklater.

London, April 1978

10

1. Soweto – the First Four Days

Wednesday 16 June 1976 is a cold winter's morning in Soweto, a South African township of a million, perhaps a million and a half, blacks. Teenage boys and girls, neatly dressed in school uniform, file out of their matchbox houses to join their school-mates in the dusty streets. It is not yet seven, but their parents have long since left to begin their working day in the homes and factories of white Johannesburg. The students are whistling, singing, chanting, greeting friends with the clenched-fist salute of black brotherhood, shouting '*Amandla Awethu*' – 'Power to the People'. Cardboard placards proclaim 'Afrikaans is oppressors' language' and '*Asingeni*' (We won't go in). They merge into one of several streams – from Orlando, Meadow-lands, Dube, Naledi – the élite of young African boys and girls who have managed, against all odds, to reach secondary school.

But today they are not going to their classrooms. Their destination is the Orlando football stadium, where they will hold a mass meeting to protest against the enforced use of Afrikaans as a medium of instruction for mathematics and social studies. They move from school to school, calling on those who are already inside to come out and join them. One stream is heading first for the Orlando West junior secondary school in Phefeni, where the 500 pupils have refused to attend classes since the middle of May. Another six schools in Soweto have been ordered by a white circuit inspector, Thys de Beer, to use Afrikaans.

Tension has been running high in Soweto for several months, culminating in an incident the week before, when a white security police lieutenant was trapped by angry schoolchildren at Naledi High as he questioned a pupil about a 'subversive' pamphlet. The lieutenant's car was burnt out and he had to be rescued by police reinforcements armed with tear-gas. Most of the marchers today are at schools where English is the sole medium of instruction, but they fear that they will be next on de Beer's list.

As the classrooms of one school empty, an irate black head-master telephones the police. A member of the South African Students' Movement, organizers of the protest, appeals to his 'brothers and sisters' to keep calm. 'Don't taunt the police; don't do anything to them. We are not fighting.' At police headquarters, Brigadier Schalk le Roux, divisional commissioner in charge of Soweto's racially-mixed police force, is surprised to hear from his chief security officer that a big march is taking place. Despite the incidents at several Bantu schools, he does not think that the situation is explosive. He sends 'a Bantu to the school to find out about the demonstration'.* But Bantu police-men are not welcome. 'Go and stay with your Europeans in town,' the students tell him.

Near Jabulani police station, a white man, thought to be a plain-clothes policeman, fires a shot at two students who are carrying a placard: '50–50 Afrikaans and 50–50 Zulu for Vorster'. A mile away, the largest group, numbering 10,000, but still growing, climbs up Vilikazi Street to the Orlando West school. They are excited, euphoric almost, at the success of their enterprise.

But now, screaming tyres and the revving of motor engines announce the arrival of ten van-loads of police reinforcements. There are nine whites among them, armed with revolvers, semi-automatic rifles and tear-gas. The show of strength, far from cowing the students, fuels their excitement. They taunt the police, wave their placards defiantly. They sing the national anthem of the black people: '*Morena Boloka Sechaba sa Heso*' (God bless our nation). The officer in charge, Colonel Johannes

---

*Bantu is the term for a group of languages spoken as far north as the Gulf of Guinea. The word -*ntu* simply means 'a person' (Bantu – people), but apart from its vagueness, the association with apartheid – and the fact that it was foisted on blacks by whites – makes it unacceptable as a description. The youth now refer to all 'non-whites' as 'black', but where necessary for purposes of clarity I have stuck to 'African', 'Coloured' and 'Indian'.

Kleingeld, does not have a loud hailer, and so cannot call on the students to disperse. Without warning, one of his men throws a tear-gas canister into the crowd, which retreats and, angry now, regroups.

More canisters are thrown, but the pupils hold their ground. Stones drop among the police. Colonel Kleingeld takes out his revolver and fires one shot into the crowd. Hector Petersen, thirteen years old and black, becomes the first recognized martyr of Soweto. No order is given, but the white policemen begin to fire repeatedly. Some students attack the police with stones, while others tend the dead and wounded. A seven-year-old boy is taken to a clinic, but he is dead on arrival. Colonel Kleingeld shoots an 'adult ringleader', Hastings Ndlovu, when, he claims, his life is in danger. By now Kleingeld is using his Sten gun because, he says, 'it has a more demoralizing effect than a pistol shot.' The students scatter into side streets, as still more police arrive.

Reports of the shootings spread rapidly through the township. The students surge up into Beverly Hills, past Uncle Tom's Hall, through the dried-up bed of the Klipspruit stream, breaking into groups, calling for recruits, bumping into children playing in the sand, shouting out the news to old ladies on their stoeps, overturning and burning cars, and hunting especially for the white Volkswagens used by officials of the Bantu Affairs Department (BAD). They attack anything or anybody who is of the Government; and if he talks Afrikaans so much the worse, for this is the language on the lips of the white policeman on a dawn raid – '*Waar's jou pas?*' (Where's your pass?) – or in the court which sends a man to gaol for not having a pass, or which expels him to a distant 'homeland'. But most of all, it is the language of the Government which framed the hated laws of apartheid.

A white WRAB (West Rand Administration Board) official is stabbed in many places, and left bleeding to death at the side of the road, draped in a poster with the words scrawled in blue ink: 'Beware! Afrikaans is the most dangerous drug for our future'. A black policeman is pulled from his van, his hands are locked together with his own handcuffs, and he is beaten.

13

Others are luckier. A British immigrant, Mrs Sylvia Carruthers, pleads from her surrounded car: 'I'm English.' She is allowed to go.

The area around Uncle Tom's Hall, not half a mile from Orlando police station, is like a war-zone. The students set up a road block, and question all who wish to pass. A driver, apparently white, is dragged from his car and beaten up, but his life is spared when the students realize that he is Chinese. Enraged groups of boys and girls attack, burn, loot, anything that has the stamp of white, and particularly of Government, domination: beer halls, bottle stores, post offices, administration buildings, the golf club house, even schools and libraries. Bakers' vans are stopped and the black drivers allowed to escape, but the bread is distributed to the people and the vans set alight. When the police arrive, the students protect themselves with a dustbin lid in one hand and throw stones with the other. At Orlando High School, the Eton College of black South Africa, the words 'Victory is certain – Orlando MPLA' are sprayed on to a classroom wall.

Meanwhile, back at the headquarters of the West Rand Administration Board, which runs Soweto for the Department of Bantu Administration, the chief director, Mr J. C. de Villiers, is enjoying a cup of tea with his boss, Manie Mulder (brother of the Interior Minister, Connie Mulder). An official interrupts them to say that 'there have been problems at a school again. Shooting has started and police dogs have been stoned to death.' By now Soweto is 'out of control'.

The ordinary police cannot cope. Casualties only serve to swell the ranks of the resisters. For the first time since it was formed five months before, the police anti-terrorism unit goes into action. A highly trained group of fifty-five men and three officers is led by the infamous Colonel Theunis Swanepoel, once chief interrogator of the security police. Wearing camouflage uniforms which give the impression that they are soldiers, the members of the task force sweep through the streets of Soweto. Swanepoel alone claims to have shot and killed five 'rioters', while his men add another nine to the list. There are less precise figures for the wounded.

Swanepoel, self-styled authority on communist guerrilla techniques, is known as the 'Red Russian'. He later explains how he dealt with 'a stone-throwing mob of more than 4000' in Orlando West. After firing warning shots, he saw one man standing in front of the crowd with arms outstretched and fists clenched. 'It was the sign resembling the horns of an ox, and I noticed the crowd had suddenly closed in on us, approaching in flanks from the left and right. I fired directly at the leader, who staggered back and vanished in the crowd, and then I fired at the "lieutenants" on both flanks.' Swanepoel explains that this 'ox-horn' sign is a 'well-known communist tactic', a method used in England and America.

It is two-thirty in the afternoon when the Minister of Bantu Administration and Development, M. C. Botha, introduces to the all-white Senate in Cape Town the second reading of his bill to give the Transkei Bantustan its constitutional 'independence': 'Today is also a day of hope and vision for the future,' he says. 'We look forward to and cherish the hope that here beside us another autonomous and mature nation will flourish. Mr President, in all sincerity I want to express the wish and request that the proceedings that will now follow in this House and determine the fate of millions of people and various national groups in this country will be treated with the seriousness and dignity they deserve.' So saying, the man most directly responsible for the events of Soweto that day begins a discussion that he hopes will solve his country's 'black problem'.

But the promise of independence in the Transkei does nothing to allay the distrust of the demonstrators in Soweto. By mid-afternoon they have been joined by the unemployed thousands of the township, and a sprinkling of *tsotsis*.* Some 30,000 bitter blacks are in the streets. Police drop tear-gas from Alouette helicopters. But the perennial haze from tens of thousands of

*Mostly primary school drop-outs, aged fifteen to late twenties, who have adapted to the lawless life of the townships by thieving (with or without violence), *dagga* (marijuana) smoking and wearing racy clothes. The word could be derived from the Sotho '*motsu*' (sharp), perhaps referring to their traditional weapon – the thin wire that glides between the ribs in a fight. The pointed shoes and stove-pipe trousers were once known as 'zoot suits', and could have been transformed into *tsotsis*. To be contrasted with the genteel township middle class, the '*ooscuse-me*' (sing. *uscuse-me*).

coal fires and the shroud of smoke from the blazing buildings make pin-point accuracy impossible.

By early evening black men and women are streaming back home from their jobs in Johannesburg. They have heard reports of the shootings and are desperately anxious to learn the fate of their own families. At Inhlanzana railway station, commuters are met by a posse of police who look as though they are expecting trouble. They are not disappointed. As a huge crowd of Africans builds up, the police fire tear-gas, to which the commuters respond with bricks and stones. The parents of Soweto, for so long cut off from their better-educated children, have become part of the struggle.

In the darkness, police stand waiting for vans to pick up the corpses and dump them at the nearest police station. Only black newspaper reporters can move about Soweto now, but the police refuse to cooperate in giving any information about the dead. The official figure at the end of the first day is still only three: 'a young black, an old man and a black policeman'.

Rumours are rife in Soweto that night. Has not Colonel Swanepoel asserted that the Africans drag their casualties away from the scene of a shooting? ('It is an old Bantu custom,' he is to explain later, 'to remove the dead and injured from the battlefield.') Later, the 'official' figure for Day One will be twenty-five dead (including two whites) and 200 injured. The second white official to die is Dr Melville Edelstein, a sociologist, who, ironically, had warned the Government that because of its policies resentment was swelling in the black townships.

The Minister of Police, Justice and Prisons, James Thomas Kruger, tells the Press that there has been smouldering unrest in Soweto for the past ten days because of 'dissatisfaction with the curriculum'. At ten past eight, Nigel Kane reads the news in English on S A T V. The great mass of white South Africa sees the inside of a black township for the first time. The Johannesburg stock exchange takes the news of the rioting 'calmly', but in the city of London gold shares fall 75c to R1 50c, and Harry Oppenheimer's de Beers lose nearly 15c.

The pink night sky is a reflection of the burning landscape. Blacks roam the streets looking for prey: the beer halls, which provide much of the revenue to administer the apartheid township; the Administration Board offices, where the rent records are kept; the schools which instruct the hallowed tenets of Bantu Education, the white-owned blacks-only buses. At 2 a.m. Barclay's Bank International in Dube is burning fiercely. Members of the student movement's action committee meet to plan their response to the police shootings. The 'sell-outs' – black policemen and Government officials, urban Bantu councillors, security police informers, any black man or woman who works for the 'system' – lie low.

All whites have been evacuated, except for the handful who are hiding at the homes of friendly Africans, or the heavily armed policemen, racing through the streets in patrol vans and shooting at random. A convoy of fourteen Hippos, anti-riot personnel carriers, arrives from Pretoria. The army is placed on stand-by, and units of the Witwatersrand Command defend the Orlando power station on the border of Soweto. A ring of policemen, commandos, police reservists, cuts off South Africa's largest city from the rest of the world.

The headquarters of Mr Vorster's security operation, Orlando police station, has become a fortress. In one of the cells is Mrs Oshadi Phakathi, president of the YWCA and director of the Christian Institute in the Transvaal, who has been locked up after intervening on behalf of an arrested schoolteacher. 'Throughout the night,' she said later, 'we heard shooting in the streets and in the police station. In the cells next to ours, we heard police assaulting the inmates, who were fighting back. Then there would be a shot ... and the screaming stopped straight away. Then we heard a voice in Zulu: " *Izani nimkhipe, O se a file, ni mbulele*" (Come and take him out, he is dead, you have killed him ...). The door would open and close ... it happened all night and the next.'

Mrs Phakathi said that two girls, covered in blood, were pushed into the cell. 'They described how they had arrived in a van loaded with corpses and injured people. The corpses were dumped on one side, and the injured laid flat on their tummies with hands spread out, and then policemen walked on them till they died and were thrown into the pile of corpses.'

The late-night TV news in Afrikaans has an extensive coverage of the events, but fails to mention that the Afrikaans language is the immediate cause of the trouble. Already some whites are asking why all the early-warning signals were ignored. As early as January 1975, the African teachers' association had told Minister M. C. Botha that the policy of forcing Afrikaans in black schools was 'cruel and short-sighted'. But when the Minister was asked whether he had consulted the black people over the ruling, he replied: 'No, I have not consulted them and I am not going to consult them.'

Now, Deputy Bantu Education Minister Andries Treurnicht complains: 'In the white area of South Africa, where the Government provides the buildings, gives the subsidies and pays the teachers, it is surely our right to determine the language division.' And he asks: 'Why are pupils sent to school if they don't like the language divisions?'

By the end of the first day of the rebellion, however, it is clear that the Afrikaans-language issue is merely the pin of a hand-grenade that is packed with the many grievances of South Africa's urban blacks.

The next morning, *Die Beeld*, an Afrikaans newspaper supporting the Vorster regime, asks: 'Has our government really no effective weapon other than bullets against children who run amok?' A Nationalist* commentator likens the language dispute to the hated policy of Lord Milner when, after the Boer War, Afrikaans schoolchildren were forced to learn through the medium of both English and Dutch. As a black clergyman explains, black children feel that the 'language of the oppressor in the mouth of the oppressed gives tacit approval to the policy of apartheid'.

A picture of a Soweto schoolgirl carrying the body of a dying boy is splashed across page one of the world's newspapers.

*The Purified National Party was founded in 1934 by a group of Afrikaners under Dr Daniel Malan, who refused to follow General J. M. B. Hertzog's old National Party into a coalition government with General Jan Smuts's largely English-speaking South African Party. By the end of the Second World War, the Malanites drew majority Afrikaner support. They won power in 1948, and have ruled South Africa ever since. When the Hertzogites returned to the fold, it became the Reunited National Party. Afrikaans newspapers are invariably official organs of the Party.

Soon, another photograph – of a Bantu policeman firing into a crowd of Soweto blacks – will do the rounds. Normally, only the rare Bantu sergeant carries a revolver, but as trouble brews there is a wider distribution of arms to the 'black jacks' (as the Sowetons call them). On 16 June, with the police taken by surprise, the black jacks begin their training on the spot.

During the night, burnt-out hulks of motor cars have been pushed on to the railway line near Phefeni station, so that commuter traffic is disrupted. And as the PUTCO* buses dare not enter the township, many parents are forced to stay at home. Angered by the shootings, some join the protesters. For the deaths, far from dampening down the ardour of the students, have incensed them to further action. The 'Township' edition of the *Rand Daily Mail*, with first-hand accounts by trusted African reporters, is available in Soweto, bringing home the full extent of yesterday's violence. The people of Soweto now hear that it is the fault of 'agitators' and 'tsotsis'. And if the official death-toll is three, many have seen more bodies than that with their own eyes.

Early in the morning, men, women and children sack a beer hall in Naledi, in the far west of Soweto. When Brigadier Jacobus Buitendag of the South African Railways Police arrives on the scene with two van-loads of men, they are assailed by stones and beer bottles. They shoot the 'ring-leaders', but the crowd refuses to disperse. Buitendag is surprised that 'the people have enough Dutch courage to face shots fired directly at them'. He does not use tear-gas because, he claims, the wind is blowing strongly in the wrong direction. In all, the railway police kill five people at Naledi, and another three at the next station on the line, Merafi.

Thousands of schoolchildren report for classes, unaware that M. C. Botha has closed Soweto schools for the rest of the week. But the older students return to protest, rampaging through the streets in search of targets. More schools and government buildings are razed. There are no white motorists

*The privately-owned Public Utility Transport Company provides bus transport between the city and most Rand black townships.

about any more, for a white skin is a death warrant. Every black in a car must convince the students that he does not work for WRAB, then shout '*Amandla*' (Power) and give the clenched-fist salute. Otherwise, the car is set alight and its occupant beaten up. Students visit African shopkeepers and ask to see their trading licences. If there is white participation in the business, the shop is burnt down. They cross the Potchefstroom Road, which borders Soweto, and burn down half a dozen Indian stores.

There are now 1200 policemen in Soweto, operating from rebellion headquarters at Orlando police station. Many are raw, rural Afrikaner recruits; at seventeen or eighteen, no older than the town blacks whom they are hunting. Alouette helicopters land at the sports field across the road, ferrying canisters of tear-gas. Hippos patrol the streets with guns protruding from the steel windows. Any group of youths standing about on a street corner or walking on the pavement is fair game; the more so, if they are seen giving the black power salute. In Diepkloof the police fire without warning into a group of youths, killing three. A black student says: 'We will not go into our houses. The streets of this place are all we have and we insist on walking in them.'

Ten miles away, in a white Johannesburg suburb, a teacher discusses Soweto with his English-speaking middle-class pupils, aged between fifteen and seventeen.

Teacher: 'What do you think of the trouble in Soweto?'

Pupils: [above the hubbub, is heard] 'Shoot them', 'Kill them all', 'Teach them a lesson'.

Teacher: 'What was the cause of the riot?'

Pupils: 'Agitators', 'Terrorists', 'They don't want to learn Afrikaans.'

Teacher: 'What do you think about the Afrikaans-language issue?'

Pupils: 'It's one of our official languages, that's the law, so they must put up with it.' 'I'm Greek, but I have to learn everything in English.' 'Before we gave them schools there was no trouble. Now we are building schools for them and this is all the thanks we get. They should be left uneducated.'

Teacher: 'If you had to learn biology in Zulu, what would you do?'

Pupils: 'We'd do what we were told.'

Teacher: 'I hope you find a teacher, then, because I can't speak Zulu. Many Soweto teachers can't speak Afrikaans. They'd lose their job and so would I.'

Pupils: [all boys]: 'Well, they shouldn't kill people.' 'They are savages.' 'They are straight out of the jungle.' 'They are so stupid they burn their own buildings.'

A girl: 'We should feel sorry for the ones who didn't want to join in.'

A boy: 'Our girl [maid] told us that two small black kids killed their own mother because she wouldn't give the black power salute.'

Teacher: 'They were on strike, peacefully, for five weeks, you know, to try and get the authorities to talk with them. Nobody took any notice. It can't be very nice to have no say in the running of your own life.'

Pupils: 'We haven't either, no one listens to us.'

A boy: 'Why should we learn Zulu anyway, what use is it?'

Other pupils: 'Of course it's useful.'

The same boy: 'Useful for what? To talk with your garden boy?'

A girl: 'Very soon it might not be your garden boy, it might be your doctor.'

There is a rare moment of sympathy from white South Africa, as Witwatersrand University students take to the streets of Johannesburg carrying placards proclaiming: 'Don't start the revolution without us.' They are joined by black workers but very soon the march is broken up by a mob of whites, armed with chains and crowbars. Four students are taken to hospital; others are arrested.

Gunsmiths do a brisk trade. Mr Julius Garb, a dealer in Rosettenville, explains that 'it's hard to say whether the sudden surge is purely because of the Soweto disturbances. The hunting season has also just opened.' But at least Johannesburg is clean. The municipal dustmen, who collect the rubbish and sweep the streets of the city and its white suburbs, are housed outside Soweto – and so have no choice but to go to work.

Black nurses at Baragwanath Hospital, on the outskirts of Soweto, protest when armed police refuse to admit a youth with three bullet wounds. In their starched white uniforms they give the black power salute to the black protesters outside the fence. All but six of the medical staff are white, and they are finding it difficult to get through into the hospital. In Orlando East a shop is burnt out when the owner refuses to sell paraffin to students wanting to set fire to a nearby W R A B municipal office. The students are led by the shop owner's son.

In the afternoon the Diepkloof Hotel, Soweto's finest, is ablaze. Indeed, nowhere within Soweto's sixty square kilometres can calm be taken for granted. The situation, according to one police source, is 'under control in the circumstances', but General W. H. Kotze, head of the police anti-riot squad in Soweto, asks: 'Can it get worse? We have no contact with the rioters and they have no contact with us.' He calls for still more police reinforcements.

Back in the Cape Town Parliament, there are calls for the resignation of Minister M. C. Botha and his deputy, Andries Treurnicht. In the absence of a statement by Prime Minister Vorster, his Police Minister, Kruger, is left to carry the can. He praises the police for maintaining 'the greatest measure of self-control', in face of strong provocation. He entrusts the task of inquiring into the causes of the riots to an Afrikaans-speaking, Government-supporting judge, Piet Cillie. Kruger talks of Herbert Marcuse, and black power and Danny the Red. 'Why do [the students] walk with upraised fists?' he asks. 'Surely this is the sign of the Communist Party?' And he concludes: 'It is my task to preserve law and order.'

By the end of the second day, the official count is fifty-four dead, all of them black except for the two whites killed at the start of the uprising. Mrs Phakathi is told by a black policeman at the Meadowlands police station that on the Thursday, he and a colleague collected 176 corpses in one section of Soweto alone.

The police have begun to arrest 'agitators', holding them under the no-bail clause of the Terrorism Act. Manie Mulder, the white boss of Soweto, appeals to the youth of his fiefdom, 'as well as their leaders and elders', to realize that they will not resolve the issue at stake by vandalizing their assets. He says: 'Let us come to our senses and discuss the cause of the trouble.' The students appear to have won a small point.

The violence can no longer be confined to Soweto. In Alexandra, a black dormitory in the heart of the city's wealthy, white, northern suburbs, schoolchildren burn down administration offices and vehicles, and erect a road block under the banner: 'Why kill kids for Afrikaans?' At Tembisa, east of Johannesburg, 700 boys and girls march in orderly protest through the streets.

As night falls, student demonstrators in another West Rand township, Kagiso, are joined by adults on their way home from work. The police intervene, and five more Africans are shot dead.

Meanwhile, the bodies of the dead pile up outside the Orlando police station. There are not enough blankets to cover them. Black policemen have rounded up a group of twenty youths, who are led into the courtyard and made to hop for twenty minutes while the police hit them across their bodies with batons and rubber hoses. Under cover of early morning darkness, the youths are forced to load corpses into a mortuary van. White policemen watch the scene, unconcerned.

By Friday morning, white South Africa knows that it has a full-scale uprising on its hands. The 'unsettled conditions presently prevailing' persuade the (white) Housewives League of South Africa to cancel its planned week of protest against an increase in the price of milk. The rebellion roars through seven townships in the Johannesburg area.

The most serious incidents are in Alexandra, home of thousands of black women who work as domestics in white suburbia. Unlike Soweto, which stands on its own in the veld, this is a black enclave, where migrant labourers living in single-sex hostels can compare their dreary lot with that of their prosperous white neighbours. The students and residents come together to vent their anger on white-owned properties. As the Dutch Reformed church, bottle stores, beer halls, the sports club house, a school, Indian businesses are set on fire, smoke drifts across the white suburbs of Bramley and Lombardy West. White shop and factory workers are evacuated as Africans spill out of the township and burn and ransack white-owned shops. Police, rushed in from Pretoria, cordon off the township, diverting traffic to the near-by Louis Botha Avenue, one of the city's two main roads to the north. Terrified white families in houses only yards away from Alexandra's fence hear chanting, shouting and gunfire, and catch a whiff of tear-gas.

The white women's civil emergency brigades have been called out, but they are not as effective as they should be. The *North Eastern Tribune* reports later that 'some of the people who had been trained in the civil emergency units – and particularly those in "Cell J" who were nearest to the riot area – barricaded themselves into their homes. These women all said "my husband will not let me leave the house". They fried their fish and made their soup for the volunteer firemen, but they would not leave their homes to deliver it to the fire station. It was left to a few of the "brave ladies" to collect and deliver the foodstuffs...'

Colonel Swanepoel and his anti-riot unit are summoned. Swanepoel later explains why tear-gas was abandoned in favour of 'buckshot' as a means of 'quelling the riots'. 'They would taunt us, throw stones at us and urge us to throw tear-gas. They became very good at handling it. They would just move to the left or right and avoid the fumes. Only innocent bystanders and residents suffered.' Swanepoel claims that he and his men fired 979 canisters of tear-gas. 'In the end we had to find another method. We decided not to use R1 firearms which would send the death and injury rate soaring. Instead we chose buckshot, which can seriously injure a man at ten yards but is more of a discomfort at twenty yards.' At least twenty blacks die from gunfire in Alexandra that day.

Now four black universities, hundreds of miles apart, react in solidarity with the students of Soweto. At Turfloop, in the northern Transvaal near Pietersburg, 2000 University of the

North students gather on the football field and pray on their knees for the dead of Soweto. This time the police do not use their guns, but instead they chase students across the campus with batons and dogs. One student jumps to his death from an upper-storey window. The officer in charge, Colonel Marthinus van Zyl, a self-styled expert on 'Bantu' behaviour, doubtless recalling the numerous incidents of 'window-jumping' by victims of security police interrogation, remarks: 'It is a phenomenon I have often noticed among blacks. In fact, three students jumped from windows that day. One was unfortunate enough to land on his head.' 359 students are arrested.

At the University of Zululand, Empangeni, three hours by car from Durban, students drive out the white staff and burn down the administration block, the library and a church. In Durban itself, police arrest eighty-seven medical students from the 'non-white' (African, Coloured and Indian) medical school, as they march through the streets waving placards. In Cape Town, at the Coloured (mixed-blood) University of the Western Cape, the staff association affirms its solidarity with the children and people of Soweto and pledges support to free South Africa from 'racism and oppression'.

At this point, the Government publishes the long-awaited report of the Theron Commission on the future of the country's two million Coloured people. The two most important recommendations – Coloured representation in the white central parliament and the repeal of laws forbidding sex and marriage between Coloureds and whites – are immediately rejected by Mr Vorster. If the Government cannot make concessions on the Coloureds, who are culturally and racially part of the Afrikaner's own family, what chance is there of liberalizing the 'Bantu' policy?

In Soweto the burning has died down, if only because everything that symbolizes apartheid is already in ruins. The attacks are a mixture of idealism and thuggery: the students aim at political targets, such as government offices, while the *tsotsis*, the township hooligans and small-time gangsters, loot the bottle stores. If the students do go into bottle stores it is invariably to empty the liquor into the gutter. A puritanical streak runs

25

through the rebellion; whereas, early on Thursday morning, white policemen are seen carrying bottles of whisky from the looted stores to their 'pick-ups'.

The language of black consciousness is everywhere heard: '*Azania*' (the name for a black-ruled South Africa), 'the people', 'possessing what is rightfully ours', and always '*Amandla*' and the clenched-fist salute, which by now is rewarded with automatic arrest. The *tsotsis* also demand the salute, but only to see if their victim is wearing a watch, from which he is then smartly separated. They speak a gangster Afrikaans, as if to distance themselves from their fellow blacks.

Now, at last, WRAB officials agree to talk to Soweto 'leaders'. But the meeting with the normally compliant urban Bantu councillors and school-board representatives is stormy. These 'uncle Toms' are conscious that their actions could invite retribution from the students. They refuse to participate in reconstructing Soweto until basic grievances are met. They want Afrikaans removed, the police withdrawn from Soweto, and a multiracial commission of inquiry into the disturbances. Says the Rev. B. Phofolo: 'If you have a nail through your shoe into your toe, you do not go on polishing the shoe. Let's remove the nail.' The only student present, Walter Mazula, tells officials that the students will refuse to have lessons in Afrikaans until the Prime Minister begins to learn Zulu.

In Parliament, Mr Vorster warns that the police 'have orders to use all the means at their disposal without fear or favour to protect life and property'. Referring to his coming meeting with Secretary of State Henry Kissinger in West Germany, Vorster says: 'In case, as it appears to me, the idea exists that the Government would hesitate to take action because of my coming talks, they [the protesting blacks] will be making a mistake ... However important these talks may be, order in South Africa is more important to me than anything else.' Brigadier J. J. Visser, Assistant Commissioner of Police on the Witwatersrand, is pleased: 'I will have the support from above that I want. From now on we will use tougher methods.' The police announce that they will not publish further figures for dead and wounded until the riots have ended.

Justice Minister Kruger invokes the Riotous Assemblies Act to ban all public meetings for ten days. And two white Christians, Dr Beyers Naude, director of the Christian Institute, and John Rees, secretary-general of the South African Council of Churches, are ordered by the chief magistrates of Johannesburg to 'dissociate yourselves completely from the present unrest'. Later they are accused of 'polarizing the races', though in fact they are trying to bring representatives of the races together for talks. Chief Gatsha Buthelezi, chief minister of the Zulu Bantustan of Kwa-Zulu, arrives in Johannesburg to 'identify with the people of Soweto'. By nightfall, Soweto's official death toll is eighty-eight blacks and two whites, with another 1000 wounded. Mr Thys de Beer, the school inspector, advises the Government 'not to step down on the language issue'.

On Saturday, Minister M. C. Botha meets Johannesburg 'urban black leaders' and says that he has no authority to suspend Afrikaans, because both English and Afrikaans are entrenched as official languages in the constitution. His deputy minister of Bantu Education, Dr Treurnicht, is not present, but he feels that 'it is for the Bantu's own good that he learns Afrikaans.' (Three days later, Botha suspends the compulsory use of Afrikaans and Mr Thys de Beer is transferred to Kimberley. Four other Afrikaans education officials who have been directly implicated in forcing Afrikaans remain in their posts, despite black calls for their dismissal.)

Long queues wait outside the mortuaries, as parents search for missing children. The official death count rises to 109 but after visiting Baragwanath Hospital, Chief Gatsha Buthelezi says that the true figure is closer to 700. Justice Minister Kruger denounces the claim as 'irresponsible and unfounded', and makes some claims of his own. He says that the riots were 'definitely organized', and names 'black power movements' like the South African Students' Organization and the Black People's Convention. Answering criticism of the high death toll, he says that the police did not use rubber bullets because they make people 'tame to the gun'. Later, pathologists will find that more than half the rioters killed by police in Johannesburg were shot in the back.

On Saturday afternoon, Prime Minister Vorster flies off to West Germany for talks with Henry Kissinger. Their primary objective: to bring Ian Smith to his senses over the deteriorating racial conflict in Rhodesia.

Soweto, the police report, is 'calm but tense'.

2. The Doldrum Years

The uprising in Soweto revived memories of the shootings sixteen years before in the black township of Sharpeville on the fringe of the white industrial city of Vereeniging. The crackle of bullets then had reverberated round the world and made the name of Sharpeville a synonym for the tyranny of apartheid.

Sharpeville, like Soweto, did not happen in a vacuum. Since 1957, black South Africa was aware that a former British colony, the Gold Coast, had become Ghana, and that others in the French and British empires were working through a timetable towards independence. The state of emergency in Nyasaland heralded the demise of the ill-fated Central African Federation and raised a question mark over the future of white rule in neighbouring Southern Rhodesia.

White South Africa too was preparing for a constitutional change. In January 1960 Dr Hendrik Verwoerd told his all-white Parliament that there was to be a referendum to decide whether the country should become a republic. The blacks, who had not beeen consulted by Britain on the formation of the Union of South Africa fifty years earlier, were to be ignored once again. (The independent Union of South Africa had existed since 1910, but Afrikaners considered it a creation of the British and therefore tainted.) Into this strained atmosphere stepped the unlikely figure of a British Conservative Prime Minister, Harold Macmillan, to warn of a 'wind of change' that was blowing through the continent.

The wind of change had been gusting through South Africa for some time. Only a week before the Macmillan speech, nine policemen – among them four whites – had been killed by angry blacks, while on an illicit-liquor raid in Durban.

March saw the climax of an anti-pass-law campaign launched

by the then non-violent African National Congress. The pass laws were a long-established institution by which every African male of sixteen and over carried the hated badge of subservience, the reference (or pass) book. For half a century the African National Congress had represented the aspirations of the country's African people, but tensions within the movement led to a split and the formation of a break-away Pan-Africanist Congress. The PAC launched its own 'decisive and positive action' on the pass laws. Their president, Robert Sobukwe, told his followers: 'You will leave your passes at home, surrender yourselves at the nearest police station and demand to be arrested. "No bail, no defence, no fine," is to be the slogan; and when you come out of prison you must offer yourselves for arrest once again.'

At midday on 21 March 1960, Africans began to gather outside the police station in Sharpeville. They had stayed away from work, willingly or by persuasion. They were unarmed. During the morning a squadron of South African Air Force planes wheeled and dived menacingly overhead, but the Africans were not intimidated. They were expectant because they believed that a 'big boss' from Pretoria was coming to make a statement on the pass laws.

Their holiday mood was not dampened by the arrival of police reinforcements in Saracen armoured vehicles. When the police arrested the PAC leaders, the crowd, numbering some 6000 by now, pressed on to the fence around the police station. Lieutenant-Colonel Pienaar, in charge of the police, ordered his men to line up and load five rounds into their Sten guns. He gave no order to the crowd to disperse. Two white policemen opened fire without orders and fifty others followed suit, using service revolvers, rifles and Sten guns. The Africans turned and fled. The police reloaded and fired into their backs. In the double burst of gunfire that lasted no more than half a minute, sixty-nine Africans died, including eight women and ten children, while 178 were wounded. Pathologists found that only 30 police bullets had entered the bodies of the dead and wounded from the front, while 155 had done so from the back.

'This incident', white South African schoolchildren are now

told in their history textbooks, 'caused much bitterness among the blacks.' At the official inquiry into the shootings, Lieutenant-Colonel Pienaar was asked whether any useful lesson might be learned from Sharpeville. He replied: 'Well, we may get better equipment.'

For a few days it looked as though the anti-pass-law campaign had achieved its immediate objective. On 26 March the Commissioner of Police announced that 'in view of the fact that Bantus, as a result of intimidation, are so gripped by fear to carry reference books ... I have decided to relieve this tremendous tension and to prevent innocent and law-abiding Bantus from landing in trouble.' No Bantu would be asked for his pass, nor would he be arrested for not having one. On the next day the venerated leader of the African National Congress, Chief Albert Luthuli, burned his pass.

Events moved quickly. There were peaceful demonstrations, arrests by the thousand, strikes across the country, more blacks shot by the police, and on 30 March the Government declared a state of emergency. As it became known that their leaders were being arrested, 30,000 men and women gathered in the black townships of Langa and Nyanga and marched along the national road into the heart of Cape Town. Saracen armoured cars stood by as the mile-long procession came to a halt outside the Caledon Square police station, where the prisoners were being held, a short distance from the Houses of Parliament.

Unlike Sharpeville, where policemen and Government officials had been the only white witnesses, this peaceful protest took place under the gaze of ordinary whites. The police did not open fire. The marchers' leader, a young man called Philip Kgosane, received from a police officer a promise of an interview with the Minister of Justice to discuss the arrests. Satisfied, Kgosane asked the crowd to disperse peacefully, and the demonstrators left, walking the eight miles back to their homes. Early the next morning, police, soldiers and sailors cordoned off the townships and batoned the inhabitants back to work. The strike was over. The trusting Kgosane never got his interview. He too was detained.

A week later the Pan-Africanist Congress and the African

National Congress were declared unlawful organizations. It was the end of an era that had begun with black petition for reform and had reached the limits of peaceful protest and passive resistance. The day after the bannings, as if to emphasize the apocalyptic moment, an English-speaking white farmer fired two bullets into the face of Dr Verwoerd. The Prime Minister survived to commend the Almighty for having protected him. And by 10 April the Government had recovered enough of its poise to end its retreat over the pass laws. Africans not in possession of their pass books would once again be arrested and charged.*

In the week of Sharpeville, the United States Administration of John Kennedy, having publicly deplored violence in all its forms, expressed the hope that 'the African people of South Africa will be able to obtain redress for legitimate grievances by peaceful means'. The U N Security Council debated Sharpeville despite protests from the South African delegate, Brand Fourie, that the United Nations was not entitled to consider 'a purely local disturbance'. By nine votes to none (Britain and France abstaining), Council members agreed that the situation in South Africa could lead to international friction and if allowed to continue might endanger international peace and security. They called upon the South African Government to abandon apartheid and racial discrimination.

At that time South Africa was still a member of the sterling area, its currency fully convertible into sterling. Sharpeville came as a surprise to foreign companies, whose directors suddenly saw revolution looming. Within a matter of weeks, an estimated £750 million of foreign investment left the country. For the Government and the business community it was the most serious aftermath of the shootings. New exchange-control regulations were introduced; but these could not bring the money back. The veteran Afrikaner business chief Dr M. S. Louw warned that the country's economic future was partly dependent on foreign goodwill and capital. 'We will have to

*The state of emergency ended late in August and the last of the 1800 detainees were released. Some 18,000 others, including Sobukwe, had been gaoled for their part in the campaign.

convince overseas countries that we are able to solve our racial problems satisfactorily,' he said. That would take some doing. In a frank appraisal of the country's international standing, the Cape Town Nationalist daily, *Die Burger*, depicted South Africa as 'the skunk of the world'.

Talk of 'change', of a 'new deal', was in the air. A delegation of English and Afrikaner businessmen, employers of one and a half million Africans, handed a joint statement to the Prime Minister. The delegation asserted that, although agitators had fermented unrest, their actions had been aided by the existence of genuine grievances, including the pass laws, influx control and curfew regulations. Some influential members of the Dutch Reformed Church declared apartheid to be unethical and without any foundation in Scriptures. A group of Nationalist academics even suggested that the Coloured people be represented in Parliament by four Coloureds rather than four whites.

Dr Verwoerd diverted these requests to the waste-paper basket. Nationalists would have to stand like 'walls of granite' on the policy of separate development – if not for themselves, then for the sake of their children. The doubters within the ranks of Afrikanerdom were easily routed. The doubters outside didn't matter a damn. To prove his determination, it was now to be made compulsory for African women to carry the hated pass. Verwoerd did make one concession, however. He promised to reduce the size of the pass book.

The country soon returned to the habits of the days before Sharpeville. Even its expulsion from the Commonwealth in March 1961 was converted into a victory. Forecasting that foreign capital would soon flow back to South Africa, Verwoerd maintained that leaving the Commonwealth would not have a 'long-term bad effect upon the economy'. In that same month the five-year-long Treason Trial came to an abrupt end. Mr Justice (later Chief Justice) Rumpff was unable to find proof of a communist plot to overthrow the state. Leaders of the African National Congress and the Communist Party of South Africa, as well as ordinary liberals, were released. The outcome of the trial, which had received world-wide publicity, was a humiliating blow for the Government. Henceforward it would do everything to facilitate the 'legal' conviction of its enemies.

But now the forces of law and order were to face a direct challenge. *Poqo* (literally, 'pure'), which was allied to the Pan-Africanist Congress, and *Umkonto we Sizwe*, the military wing of the underground African National Congress, launched separate campaigns of violent resistance to white rule. Verwoerd needed a strong right arm to eliminate the 'agitation'. Soon after becoming Prime Minister he had appointed a 42-year-old solicitor, Balthazar Johannes Vorster, to the twin posts of deputy minister of education, arts and science and of social welfare and pensions. It was a significant choice, for Vorster had been a wartime general in the pro-Nazi *Ossewabrandwag* (the 'ox-wagon sentinel' – a name which invoked the Voortrekker period of Afrikaner history). The 'O B', as it was known, spent some effort in blowing up post offices and doing its best to hamper the country's war effort. Vorster was interned for two years but was never tried for treason, mainly because the wartime Prime Minister, General Smuts, was soft-hearted towards his fellow Afrikaners.*

Verwoerd, an unashamed admirer of Nazi Germany, refused to hold Vorster's war record against him. In October 1961, at a critical moment in his country's history, Vorster was promoted to Minister of Justice.

The new Minister did not take on his job unarmed. The basis of the country's security laws had been laid in 1950 with the Suppression of Communism Act. Communists, liberals, black nationalists, some practising white Christians, and even the occasional Afrikaner, had been excluded from holding public office, from their jobs and from the membership of political organizations and trade unions, with their movement severely restricted by a simple 'banning' order from the Minister of Justice. There was no appeal against this sentence of 'civil death'. The Riotous Assemblies Act (which went back to 1930) gave the same minister power to ban the holding of public

---

*But in a country where guilt by association has become a fact of life, it is relevant to recall that Vorster's brother Koot, a Dutch Reformed Church dominee, was gaoled for attempting to pass on to the Germans information about the wartime defences of the Simonstown naval base.

meetings for as long as he liked, without requiring the consent of Parliament.

In the months before the coming of the Republic, Vorster's predecessor, C. R. (Blackie) Swart, had piloted the 'no-bail' law through Parliament. The new measure armed the police with powers to arrest 'agitators' and hold them for twelve days without bail. Though soon overtaken by more draconian legislation, it was the basis for the arsenal of no-trial laws that followed.

Towards the end of 1961, *Umkonto we Sizwe* launched its first acts of sabotage with a series of bomb explosions in Port Elizabeth and Johannesburg. In response to this new threat, Vorster introduced the Sabotage Act, which gave him powers to impose house arrest and to prohibit anyone from writing or publishing articles. A full-blooded attack on Press freedom was embodied in a clause by which a deposit of £10,000 could be demanded of a newspaper publisher, on pain of forfeiting the money if the newspaper was subsequently banned. With this single piece of legislation Vorster demonstrated his determination to root out all opposition. Henceforward the cartoonists would draw him wearing jackboots with a revolver at his hip.

In 1963 he appointed an old friend, Hendrik van den Bergh, as head of the security police. Van den Bergh had been detained with Vorster at Koffiefontein during the war; though they now publicly recanted their pro-Nazi views, they still shared a belief in the virtue of strong-arm methods. This partnership of the Koffiefontein Two paved the way for a series of laws which transferred important aspects of the administration of justice from the courts to the security police.

The Sabotage Act had not stopped sabotage. *Poqo* was waging a low-level guerrilla war, in which several white people as well as black 'collaborators' had been killed. Vorster vowed to 'exterminate this cancer in our national life'. His ninety-day law empowered police officers to arrest without warrant any persons suspected of committing, or intending to commit, or having information about, certain political offences. They could be held for ninety days but, in fact, a number of detainees who were freed at the end of this period were immediately re-arrested under the same clause. The English-speaking-opposition, the United Party, supported the measure in Parliament. Only Mrs Helen Suzman, sole representative of the Progressive Party, opposed it. Hundreds of arrests followed in the wake of this law. A series of trials in large and small towns across the country destroyed *Poqo*, dispatching its warriors to Robben Island gaol for periods ranging from three years to life.

Then in July 1963 the security police raided a farm in Rivonia, near Johannesburg, and captured practically the entire high command of *Umkonto*, including senior leaders of the underground ANC and of the illegal Communist Party. It was a shattering setback for the liberation struggle. Nelson Mandela, Walter Sisulu, Govan Mbeki and, later, Braam Fischer, the Afrikaner leader of the Communist Party, were gaoled for life.

Still not satisfied, Vorster armed his security police with even more authoritarian powers. The ninety-day law was abolished, to be replaced by the 180-day law. Vorster, by then Prime Minister, added the Terrorism Act to his arsenal of security laws. Within the terms of section 6, any police officer from a lieutenant-colonel upwards could arrest without warrant, then detain for interrogation, any person whom he had reason to believe was a terrorist or was withholding information from the police relating to terrorists. The police could hold the prisoner until such time as he answered the questions asked of him. The definition of 'terrorism' included: causing substantial financial loss to any person or the state; embarrassing the administration of the affairs of the state; and obstructing or endangering the free movement of traffic on land, at sea or in the air. Once charged, it was up to the accused to prove his innocence beyond reasonable doubt. In theory it meant that a man who was pushing his broken-down motor car along the highway could be hanged if he could not show that he had simply run out of petrol. South Africa had become a place where unknown prisoners died in unnamed gaols on uncertain dates at the hands of the security police.

Yet without the 'peace' that these security measures brought, it is doubtful whether the outside world would have so confidently contributed to the impressive revival of the economy that marked the middle years of the sixties. Overseas capital, from Britain, the United States, Japan, Western Europe, formed an unspoken partnership with the security laws, allowing Verwoerd and, later, Vorster to speed up their programme of separate development.

The 1960s saw South Africa's gross domestic product more than double: from R5349 million to R11,635 million. The massive withdrawal of foreign capital that had followed Sharpeville was more than balanced by the massive reinvestment from 1965 onwards. Certainly, the new exchange-control regulations made it extremely difficult to withdraw foreign capital, but there were no restrictions on the repatriation of profits earned by these subsidiaries. And much of British and American investment in the economy during those years came from the reinvestment of these profits.

The foreign, particularly the British, contribution to the post-Sharpeville growth of the economy was especially important in the field of technology. A British economist, Professor John Suckling, has calculated that technological know-how, passed on by foreign parent companies to their subsidiaries, was the major factor in this growth during the fifteen years up to 1972. All the other factors combined – the expansion of the labour force, and increases in the domestic and foreign-owned capital stock – only played a secondary role. Quite simply, South Africa could not on its own have carried out the research needed to modernize its industry. It had neither the funds nor the technicians.

Armed with sweeping antidotes to dissent, and heartened by the confidence of the Western business community, Afrikanerdom pressed ahead with its ambitious programme. Dr Verwoerd had been the great white *induna* (chief) of the country's Africans since his appointment as Minister of Native Affairs in 1950. In contemporary Africa, however, the philosophy which produced the terms *apartheid* (apartness) and *wit baasskap* (rule of the white boss) was no longer acceptable. The new, more sophisticated Afrikaner ideologues initiated an overhaul of existing terminology. An official 'history' of the period now admits that the National Party committed a 'cardinal error' in using the word apartheid. 'The connotation of this word', the historian tells us, 'made it susceptible to distortion and it became the vehicle of opprobrium and criticism inside and especially outside South Africa.' So Verwoerd changed the name to 'separate development', and even, on occasions, to 'separate freedoms'.

The statutory basis for 'separate development' was laid down before the Nationalists came to power in 1948. The 11,000 Africans on the common voters' roll were removed in 1936, when a definitive limit of 13 per cent was placed on the tribal lands available to Africans. A war measure by the Government of General Jan Smuts had outlawed strikes by Africans, while the industrial colour bar had been a feature of factory, mine and farm for many decades. It was also General Smuts who initiated a 1923 statute prohibiting Africans from remaining in a white urban area for longer than seventy-two hours, unless they had been born there or had worked there for a long time. But it was left to the Nationalist Government, and to one man in particular, the ingenious (and Dutch-born) Dr Verwoerd, to fashion a new society for South Africa's blacks.

Verwoerd first showed his hand in 1951 when the Bantu Authorities Act established the framework for a system of so-called African local and regional government based on the tribal chiefs. Direct rule by white magistrate and black headman was replaced by indirect rule through the chief, who was now given greater powers than he had ever enjoyed in traditional society. The chiefs, understandably, were those who accepted the new dispensation. Those who did not lost the title, as did Chief Albert Luthuli of the African National Congress. Widespread resistance to the new authorities was evidenced by the Pondo Revolt in the Transkei. Bantu authorities were a vital link in the evolution of the new politic; though at the time Verwoerd denied that he would grant independence to these embryonic home-lands. That might have had him labelled as a 'communist' by his fellow-Nationalists.

While he waited to launch the next stage of his programme, Verwoerd instructed his officials to keep reminding Africans who lived in the 'white' towns that they should not expect to live there for ever. Destabilization involved tighter enforcement of influx control through the pass laws, the removal of 'black spots' from the cities to commuter townships on the outskirts, and the further division of these black residential areas on tribal lines, so that Zulu and Xhosa, for example, were kept apart.

In 1959, the year after he became Prime Minister, the Promotion of Bantu Self-Government Act carved up the Bantu areas of the country into ethnic (or tribal) national units. In these eight areas, totalling 13 per cent of South Africa's land mass, the Bantu were promised 'full rights to develop'. The whites, barely one fifth of the population, would continue to dominate in the remaining 87 per cent of the country. There was no territorial provision for the other two racial groups, though the Coloureds outnumber whites in the Cape Province, as do the Indians in Natal.

After Sharpeville, Verwoerd moved with greater urgency, admitting that pressure was being exerted on South Africa. The world had to be shown that there really was an alternative to naked *baasskap*, while his own supporters needed reassurance that they were not heading for the 'melting pot' solution allegedly favoured by white English-speaking South Africans. He launched the next phase of separate development: the formation of the 'Bantustans'.* The Transkei, the largest of the tribal areas, was granted 'self-government', with the promise of independence to follow. Ominously, the definition of a Transkei citizen came to include any African who, though living permanently outside the territory, was descended from tribes resident in the Transkei.

From the 1950s, the industrial boom had created an unceasing demand for black labour. Interference with the flow of workers from the tribal areas into white factories would have been a threat to the country's security; the more so, since Afrikaner industrialists were making important inroads into areas of the economy once almost entirely controlled by the English. But

---

*'A form of fragmentation we would not have liked if we were able to avoid it, thereby buying the white man his freedom and the right to retain domination in what is his country.'

Verwoerd had foreseen this eventuality. He forecast that there would be a period when the flow of Africans to the 'white' cities would increase to meet the demands of white employers, but that then the flow would slow down, stop, and finally go into reverse, with the Africans pouring back into the tribal areas.

Who can tell whether Verwoerd actually believed this fantasy? His disciples certainly did. The prognostication became the accepted dogma, reiterated throughout the 1960s by deputy ministers and Government MPs spellbound by the magical powers of their Canute. Verwoerd cited 1978 as the year when the cities would begin to whiten, with their African population down to 2,500,000 by the end of the century.

The solution to the 'Native question' would, thus, be brought about by a simple two-pronged programme. All Africans not required for the economy of white town or farm would be expelled to the 'homelands'. And, as a corollary, more job opportunities inside and near to these 'homelands' would supposedly turn them into viable economic units. In the decade following Sharpeville, 400,000 Africans were expelled from the urban areas through a process known as 'endorsing out'. By law, the only Africans allowed to live in the 'white' towns were 'borners', or those qualified by working there continuously for a period of at least ten years. They were the 'section-ten people', their rights strictly defined in a wartime statute. From 1964, wives and children were only allowed to 'qualify' if they had entered an urban area lawfully in the first place. At the same time it became virtually impossible for wives and children to enter these areas lawfully.

The policy worked more cruelly in the western Cape than elsewhere, as the city of Cape Town and the surrounding towns and farms were designated a 'Coloured labour preference area'. The Coloured people, who outnumbered whites and Africans combined in the area, were expected to take over Bantu jobs. The western Cape became a laboratory for the experiment of separate development. But an exodus of Coloured labourers from white farms and resistance by urban Coloured to doing 'kaffir work' (rough labour), led to an increase in the number of Africans in the area.

Relentless enforcement of the 'endorsing out' programme did, however, produce a radical change in the composition of the community. Family life was virtually destroyed as women, children, the aged and infirm, the unemployed – all of whom a cabinet minister called 'superfluous appendages' – were rooted out and dumped 600 miles away to the east, in the Ciskei 'homeland'.

The policy was enunciated in an administrative directive:

As soon as they [Bantu] become, for some reason or another, no longer fit for work or superfluous in the labour market, they are expected to return to their country of origin or the territory of their national unit where they fit in ethnically if they were not born or bred in the homeland ... No stone is to be left unturned to achieve the settlement in the homelands of non-productive Bantu ...

By the end of the decade, 85 per cent of the Africans working in Cape Town had become migrants. In the Langa township, notorious for its 'single men quarters', males outnumbered females by eleven to one. Endorsement out was also used extensively in other parts of the country, particularly in the black townships circling Johannesburg.

In the months leading up to the townships' rebellion in June, I visited the Langa Bantu Commissioner's Court to see the pass laws, which control the movement of black workers, in action. The court is in the middle of the township, next to the police station, which stands, like an enemy fortress, behind a high barbed-wire fence. After obtaining a permit to be in Langa from the government offices, I walked across to the court for the start of the day's proceedings. A thick-set white official dressed in a pale-blue, short-pants-and-shirt safari suit, with a comb stuck jauntily into his sock, barred my way. There were no facilities for the Press, he said. Insisting it was my democratic right to enter, I found a place on the bench next to the 'Bantu' sergeant. There were sixty-eight cases on the roll that morning, fewer than the daily average of eighty, though the figure sometimes rose to 250 after a successful pass offensive by the police.

The court house was a tatty, prefabricated building, with

holes in the walls and cracked lino on the floor. The white magistrate, Mr van Wyk, a thin, dark man with a pencil moustache, chatted in Afrikaans to the prosecutor, Mr Nudorf. At five past ten the sausage machine purred into motion. Nudorf called out the name of the first accused, the Bantu sergeant barked out a refrain and a young woman with a baby on her back entered the box. Only five of the accused were out on bail, and she was not one of them. Mother and child had spent the night in the cells. Nudorf read out the charges in Afrikaans: being in the Cape Peninsula without permission and not having a reference (pass) book. The black interpreter translated into Xhosa and held a brief conversation with the woman, who then nodded impassively. 'I plead guilty on both counts,' the interpreter said, at which Nudorf rose an inch from his chair, muttered 'Accept', and lowered himself back again.

Justice was being seen to be done. There were, however, no defence solicitors in court, though technically even pass-law offenders are entitled to legal aid. Details of the offences were not explained to the person in the dock. A plea of not guilty would have upset the magistrate and meant a few more days, possibly weeks, in custody for the accused. Bail was sometimes paid by a white madame or a company employer, but most Africans thought bail was the payment of the fine.

Mr van Wyk, his voice barely audible from the well of the court, bestowed the going rate on the woman in the dock – R20 or forty days on the first charge, R5 or ten days on the second. Another pass-law statistic – and her sleeping child – was led away by the sweating sergeant. A steady stream of men and women, mostly women, were processed through the system. When evidence was called for, it was not given under oath. One man pleaded guilty, then claimed that he was qualified to live in Cape Town. The prosecutor checked the pass book and found it in order. The man was released. He had spent two nights in the prison cells.

An elderly man stepped into the dock. He had come to Cape Town from the Transkei without permission, to seek medical treatment for a kidney complaint. Magistrate van Wyk, encouraged perhaps by the presence of a white spectator in court, told the accused to get a certificate from the medical superintendent of Groote Schuur Hospital and he would then be given an endorsement on his reference book to remain in Cape Town for the period of his treatment – the sentence, R20 or forty days, suspended for twelve months. A mother, a sleeping baby on her back and another one on her arm, pleaded guilty on both counts. The magistrate, no change to his expression, fined her R25 or forty days and R5 or ten days. A younger woman clutching a fistful of notes pleaded guilty, paid her money and left as if she was settling her telephone account at the post office.

The prisoners chatted at the back of the court, or coughed into dirty handkerchiefs, or tried to comfort a crying baby, or simply sat, resigned to the inevitable. When the murmured conversations grew too loud, the Bantu sergeant would shout out sternly, in a trilingual '*Tula, in die court.*' (Silence in court.) The sergeant was kept busy hunting out the waiting prisoners, 'Miriam', 'Sally', 'Amos'. If there was no response he would tell the magistrate: '*Sy's afwesig, edele agbare.*' (She's absent, your worship.) The absconder was never pursued – it wasn't worth the effort and he would probably be picked up sooner or later in another police raid. The sergeant was a man to be pitied, his obsequious attention to the whites matched by his officiousness with the prisoners. He did his job well, but neither white nor black gave him his due. It takes a lot to do the white man's dirty work.

The white official with the comb in his sock ambled in to collect the growing pile of paper work. In the quadrangle outside the court room a group of women who had paid their fines were yawning in the sun. They even shared a joke with the Bantu sergeant, who squeezed the arm of one of them.

At ten past eleven the session was over. In the space of sixty-five minutes Mr van Wyk had disposed of fifty-seven Bantu, and wasted precious minutes over a further eleven who had not turned up. Of those who were dealt with, thirty-seven were convicted and paid their fines, fourteen could not pay and went to prison, while six were discharged or acquitted. The court raised R700, a low sum compared with the R3000 on a 'good day'. The presence of a white journalist might have inhibited Mr van Wyk in his fining. If it were so, it was a serious matter, for money raised in the pass courts is an important source of revenue in the implementation of apartheid.

Dimbaza was the most infamous of the 'dumping grounds' to which Africans were 'endorsed out'. Many families had been sent there from Middelburg, a white farming community on the wrong side of an arbitrary line drawn down the middle of the Cape Province by a former Secretary for Bantu Administration, Dr Eiselen. In order to make the western Cape 'Bantu free', all Africans to the west of the Eiselen line would be moved eastwards, while Coloureds finding themselves to the east would have to return to their 'traditional' home. Whites stayed where they were. Some Middelburg Africans, finding no jobs at Dimbaza, returned to the farms as migrant workers, leaving wives and children behind. They were now called 'bachelors'.

The state granted families without a father or son to support them a monthly food ration valued at £1.32. Dimbaza was brought to the attention of the white population through the efforts of a white Anglican priest, David Russell, who lived for six months on the same rations as his parishioners. Russell managed to touch a raw nerve of the white middle class. One woman tried the diet out on her dog. 'I can only report', she wrote to Russell, 'that my beautiful animal now looks unkempt, thinner and that her constant foraging in refuse, accompanied by the pitiful inquiring look she gives me, keeps me constantly aware of your hunger and that of thousands of African families.' The Government was not moved.*

A further million were expelled from their homes on white farms. The bulk of these were squatters who did not work for the farmer though they sometimes paid rent. The removals effected a long-held ambition of the powerful (white) South African Agricultural Union, which complained that squatting withheld land from white farmers.

But it was the abolition of another category of farm dweller,

*Russell has since been separated from his congregation of black squatters outside Cape Town by a banning order and restrictive house arrest.

the labour tenant, which was most bitterly resisted. The tenant worked for a white farmer for a part of the year in return for the right to live on the farm and, usually, to keep stock and cultivate a plot. When the system was abolished in Weenen (Afrikaans for 'weeping') in Natal, former tenants refused to accept wages of R6 a month. They also rightly feared that as full-time workers they would be tied to the land for the rest of their lives. They were ejected – often their kraals were burnt down – and forced to sell their stock at low prices to a buying ring of local white farmers. As a result, thousands of Africans moved into squalid shacks on the outskirts of Natal's towns, or were dumped in the Kwa-Zulu tribal area.

The removals which caused particular bitterness were the excision of 'black spots' – African-owned or -occupied land surrounded by white farms. The Government insisted that no one would have to move against his will, but the widespread black resistance was met by a tough official reaction. Expropriating procedures were streamlined. If the land was communally owned, a Bantu Affairs Commissioner had only to call a public meeting and tell the tribesmen that the land was to be expropriated. When part of the Bakubung tribe refused to vacate their farm near Rustenburg, the Department of Bantu Administration demolished their school. The tribesmen were eventually 'persuaded' to leave after their leaders were prosecuted for 'occupying state land without permission'.

Removals were not always for purely ideological reasons. The Bakwena Ba-Magopa tribe lived on a large, well-stocked farm in the western Transvaal. The deed of purchase did not, however, include mineral rights. When diamonds were discovered there, the tribe was forced to move and white diamond diggers were allotted claims on the land. Altogether 100,000 Africans were expelled from these rural 'black spots' in the decade after Sharpeville.

Hundreds of thousands more, who lived in urban 'black spots', were pushed out to new dormitory townships, whence they commuted daily to the white factories and homes.

Another half million Coloureds, Indians and Chinese were forced out of the cities under the Group Areas Act. Some 40,000

45

whites also had to move, but they had the satisfaction of being able to voice their disapproval at the next general election.

Plans were also well under way to consolidate the widely scattered fragments of the 'homelands' into more viable units. Kwa-Zulu consisted of twenty-seven separate pieces of land while Bophutatswana had nineteen, spread over three different provinces of the Republic. A further half million people, including a few thousand whites, were earmarked for removal in this way.

And within the tribal areas themselves, the Government had started building giant townships just across the 'border' from white industrial areas. Landless, jobless people from remote regions of the reserves would be driven here in the hope of finding work. These served a dual purpose. They provided cheap labour for white industry and, because they were situated on the other side of an arbitrary Bantustan frontier, they lulled Government MPs into believing that the cities were being progressively whitened. Yet these black townships were often closer than the white suburbs to the city centre and its industrial quarter. In 1970, figures for the four largest cities bordered by 'homelands' (Pretoria, Durban, East London and Pietermaritzburg) showed that over 300,000 Africans were living within twenty miles of these cities, compared with 400,000 in the municipal townships.

The harsh fact was that after a decade of unparalleled harassment of the black people not one town or city in the country had a white majority. (Windhoek, in Namibia, is the only town in Africa with more whites than blacks.) Indeed, Africans living in the 'white' towns now numbered 5 million; or a million and a half more than at the time of Sharpeville.

The other prerequisite for the successful achievement of separate development was the creation of a large number of jobs in or near the reserves. The African could hardly be expected to give up working in the cities unless he could find adequate employment at home. The Government pinned its hopes on the border industries, encouraging white industrialists to relocate their factories in 'white' South Africa close enough to the 'homelands' for the workers to commute to work daily or, at worst, weekly. But business resistance was strong, and only

80,000 jobs were created in this way – no more than the number of work-seekers emerging annually from within the 'homelands' themselves. Often the financial incentives to decentralization were so generous that industrialists used the money to install highly mechanized factories, and so defeated the aims of the policy.

Still more sluggish was job creation inside the 'homelands', where fewer than 25,000 new employment opportunities at so-called 'growth points' were provided in a dozen years. Yet in 1954, in a comprehensive survey of the economy of the reserves, the Government-appointed Tomlinson Commission called for the provision of 50,000 new jobs a year to relieve pressure on the land. If agricultural betterment programmes were launched immediately, Tomlinson said, by the mid 1980s the reserves would support 10 million people, leaving 6 million in the white areas. But the African population had already reached 16 million by 1970, while soil erosion flourished and unemployment multiplied. Far from setting up a counter force to the economic magnet of the cities, the reserves were plunged into a more desperate poverty. Already an estimated 85 per cent of households in the Transkei, the most constitutionally advanced of the 'homelands', were living below the poverty datum line, while about 95 per cent of families had less than eleven acres of arable land, the minimum needed for a peasant farmer to make a living. Unemployment, admittedly difficult to calculate in a subsistence economy, was conservatively estimated at 20 per cent. Of those who did manage to obtain a job, six out of seven were employed in white towns or on white farms. A Government survey found that the contribution of migrant workers to the Transkei gross national income had increased from 48 per cent in 1960 to 68.5 per cent in 1970.

Yet figures tell only part of the story. A mission doctor who worked in Zululand for many years has described the lot of those left behind. The migrant worker

may be well fed; doubtless he is. He may be well cared for; doubtless he is. He may have some companionship of others like himself. Yet the food he eats cannot fill the bellies of his children, nor the blanket he sleeps under warm any but himself. His care, his love, his family loyalty cannot reach out to his wife, nor caress his children, nor extend to the grandmother who brought him up.

By the end of the decade, Minister M. C. Botha was suggesting that the 'ideal solution would be if we could succeed in due course in having all Bantu present in the white areas on a basis of migratory labour'.*

The labour bureaux are the final link in this elaborate chain which ensures an uninterrupted flow of black migrant labour to the white economy. A black male must by law register at his nearest bureau within a fortnight of his fifteenth birthday unless he is still at school. Throughout the rest of his life until the age of sixty-five he must continue to register within one month of becoming unemployed, unless he is exempted by the labour officer because he is a *bona fide* scholar or farmer, or has been allowed to be self-employed, or is, 'in the opinion of the labour officer', physically or mentally incapable of being employed. Theoretically there is a choice of seventeen different work categories. But the recruiting officer is under no obligation to take the work-seeker's preference into account. For a father to quibble about whether he wants to work in a quarry or as a domestic servant could mean hunger, even starvation, for his family. The white farmer is well looked after. A bureau might be closed for all categories of recruitment except agriculture, with the result that the labourer is paid a much lower wage than he would get elsewhere in the economy. Once a young black is given a work category, he can only get it altered with extreme difficulty. He could be stuck with it for the rest of his life.

Once registered, he is not permitted to leave the jurisdiction of the bureau to seek work. He must await the arrival of the recruiting officer, which can be days, weeks, even months. The

*Though a happy family man and an avowed Christian, Verwoerd set great store on migratory labour for blacks. It would 'benefit the Bantu', he once said, 'because the established business interests in the European towns will never permit the urban locations to grow up into fully independent Bantu towns, because such development would in any case be contrary to government policy'. Yet a commission of the Cape synod of the apartheid-supporting *Nederduitse Gereformeerde Kerk* in 1965 condemned migratory labour for the way it caused 'the complete breakdown of family life', adding with some foresight that it 'results in a spirit of grievance and bitterness against the whites . . . this is something of which we in our multiracial country must take thorough cognizance'.

Black Sash⋆ president, Sheena Duncan, has compared the occasion to a cattle market:

> Two hundred and fifty men line up ... He wants 184 labour units for the companies he represents. He walks along the line and beckons forward those he chooses. This one looks strong, this one looks young and teachable, this one is too old, that one looks too thin. This one says he doesn't want to work at R8 a week because he was paid R11 in his last job. He must be too cheeky. 'Get back in the line. I don't want cheeky boys.' Those who are not picked must wait, maybe weeks, maybe months, until the next recruiting agent comes. The 'cheeky' one won't argue next time ...

A copy of the signed (or thumbprinted) contract goes to all the interested parties, except the labourer himself. Not surprisingly, there are misunderstandings. Contracts permit advances to the worker for fares and food to be deducted from his pay packet, provided that he is left with R1 after thirty days' work.† The contracts are invariably for one year, after which the employer must discharge the worker and send him back to the tribal area. By breaking his stay in the town, the worker cannot qualify for permanent residence in the 'white' area, even if he works for the same firm year after year. As in so many other matters controlling the everyday lives of Africans, the labour bureaux regulations were simply gazetted by the Minister without any discussion in Parliament.

The tribal governments also form part of the system, for they depend heavily on fees levied for contracts of employment and monthly payments on each employed worker. Afrikaner ideologue, liberal English-speaking capitalist and black Bantustan politician all stand to gain from a system as near to slavery as makes no difference.

As the 'homelands' sank in a morass of joblessness, soil erosion, sickness and lethargy, Minister M. C. Botha forecast

---

⋆These hardy suburban housewives at first stood vigil outside Parliament protesting at apartheid laws, then opened advice offices to help urban Africans through the maze of laws which governed their lives. In March 1978, the Sashers – no doubt to the consternation of their husbands – passed a 'one person, one vote' resolution at their annual congress.

†South Africa decimalized its currency in 1961, at which time the Rand was worth ten shillings. Today there are approximately R1.65 cents to the £1.

that there would be no independence before the turn of the century. In June 1970, however, Vorster announced that economic viability was no longer a requirement for statehood. 'Each black state is free to come and tell Parliament that it wants to be on its own.' It was an admission that separate development meant 'separation' for the black man, and 'development' for the white.

If it was now becoming apparent inside South Africa that separate development was not to be the answer to the white man's problems it was contributing even less to relationships with the rest of the world. From the late fifties, as colonial possessions in Africa metamorphosized into numerous independent states, racial discrimination claimed the increasing attention of the United Nations and its associated bodies. Boycotts of South African sherry, fruit and cigarettes were commonplace in Western Europe and Britain. And though exporters simply removed the 'Made in South Africa' label from their products and trade in fact expanded, the implications of this new strategy set alarm bells ringing.

As early as 1957, Foreign Minister Eric Louw had pointed out that 'the territories to the north of the Limpopo are the natural markets for our large and expanding industries.' Economists, encouraged by Verwoerd, developed the 'co-operative sphere' theory, in which the states of southern Africa would be free to follow their own domestic policies while co-operating economically. This Capricorn common market would bring large areas of the sub-continent into South Africa's sphere of influence, with a place to be allotted, eventually, for independent Bantustans. South Africa offered superior technology, agricultural and engineering skills to harness the natural resources of the area, and expected in return new markets for her manufactured goods. But Africa refused to swallow the bait. The Organization of African Unity (OAU), with its most urgent priority being the overthrow of white rule in the south, was formed in 1963. It immediately recommended a ban both on the entry of South African ships into the harbours of independent black states and on overflying routes by South African aircraft. A year later it placed a total economic ban on South Africa; though never watertight this was effective enough to cause a diminution in trade with black Africa at a time when exports should have flourished.

South Africa's white-ruled neighbours, though occasionally attempting to distinguish their own race policies from that of apartheid, suffered from no such scruples. When Ian Smith declared the unilateral independence of Rhodesia in November 1965, white South Africa and, in particular, its English-speaking population rallied to his support. Verwoerd refused to enforce the sanctions demanded by a United States resolution, fearing that the weapon would one day be used against South Africa as well. The Nationalists never recognized the illegal regime but ensured its survival by allowing oil and other Rhodesia-bound strategic goods to pass through their territory. South African companies helped keep the economy buoyant by investing heavily in their Rhodesian subsidiaries.

The following year, a low-scale guerrilla war broke out in the north of South West Africa, as members of the South West Africa People's Organization (SWAPO) crossed from neighbouring Angola and attacked South African soldiers. The frustrated SWAPO had turned to violence after the International Court of Justice at The Hague decided on a technicality that it could not test the legality of Pretoria's administration. A year later, a joint guerrilla force of the African National Congress (South Africa) and the Rhodesian ZAPU crossed into the Wankie region of north-west Rhodesia. The ANC contingent was heading for South Africa and, though it was quickly neutralized, Smith asked for help. Vorster, Prime Minister since the assassination of Verwoerd in 1966, obliged with a contingent of para-military policemen. With the Portuguese army fighting liberation movements in Mozambique and Angola, the sub-continent seemed poised for a generalized war against white supremacy.

Vorster understood the need for counter-measures to check the advance of his enemies. He set up a new and highly secretive department, responsible to him alone, called the Bureau for State Security – with the apt acronym of BOSS. His old friend from the Koffiefontein wartime internment camp, Hendrik van den Bergh, was put in charge. BOSS's task was to evaluate intelligence acquired by the security police and the defence force. But it acquired wider notoriety by the way in which it proceeded to operate outside the borders of the country: white South Africa was about to take the struggle for survival on a trip abroad.

One of BOSS's earliest tasks was to organize a combined strategy with the Rhodesian and Portuguese allies. In July 1969, tripartite talks, aimed at 'closer cooperation' in the fight against the liberation movements, were held in Lisbon. First-hand evidence of joint planning became available in the days after the rebellion which toppled the Portuguese dictatorship in April 1974. Captured files at the headquarters of the Portuguese secret police in Lisbon included a series of telegrams between PIDE (the secret police) headquarters in Lourenço Marques (now Maputo), Luanda and Lisbon. These set up a meeting of the 'Pool' of security chiefs from the three countries at the Angolan capital in October 1971. South Africa was represented by General van den Bergh; Major Tiny Venter, then head of the security police; and a certain Captain Noppe, while Rhodesia's Mr A. M. Braes and Mr Esler, together with Portugal's security director, Vaz, and his feared deputy, Gomes Lopez, were also there.

In Britain, BOSS has harassed political exiles and infiltrated anti-apartheid organizations. But only occasionally, through the indiscretions of one of its agents, have the style and nature of the Bureau's work been publicly disclosed. This happened in the Moumbaris affair. Alex Moumbaris and his French wife, Marie-José, went to South Africa in 1973 on a holiday trip; though it is clear from the trial that followed their arrest that he was working for the London-based South African Communist Party. The couple were arrested by the police without publicity, separated, and held incommunicado for four months.

Two weeks after their arrest, Moumbaris's mother, a Mme Amiel, received a caller at her Paris flat. A South African in his late twenties, he spoke good French and told Mme Amiel that he was a friend of Alex's, whom he had just seen in South Africa, and that he was on his way to England to study. The mother, who had not heard from the couple for several weeks, was glad to meet the young man. He produced a letter in Alex's handwriting. It was unusually formal. 'The bearer of this letter', it read, 'is a man whom I met here and he has asked me if he can spend a couple of days at our place in London. I accordingly ask you to kindly give him the key of the house which I believe to be in your possession.' It seems that Alex was forced to write the letter by his captors. The unsuspecting Mme Amiel handed over the key, and the visitor hurried off to catch his plane to London.

Weeks passed and Mme Amiel heard nothing more from South Africa. Desperate for news, she and the mother of Marie-José went to London to see if they could find any clues at their children's flat in Clapham. The place was in a mess, with papers strewn about, drawers ransacked, food rotting. The women supposed that the visitor had found himself a girl-friend, lived it up for a few nights and forgotten to return the key. They did not go to the police.

Weeks before, in a Pretoria prison, Marie-José's interrogators had shown her a picture of her husband. 'You have been to my flat,' she shouted angrily at them. They laughed. Marie-José Moumbaris, by then eight months pregnant, was deported from South Africa in response to strong pressure from the French Government. In the subsequent trial of her husband and five others, papers produced by the prosecution were identified by Alex Moumbaris as having come from his London flat.

Marie-José Moumbaris wrote to the Conservative Home Secretary, Robert Carr, to say that 'there can be no doubt whatsoever that South African agents raided and ransacked my London flat, illegally removed documents from it, and placed these in the hands of the prosecution in the trial of the Pretoria Six.' She asked Mr Carr to institute an inquiry into the affair, urging him to protest 'in the strongest possible terms to the South African Government at the brazen criminal activity'. The inquiry was duly launched but the Commissioner of Police

53

could find no evidence to support the suggestion that the flat had been raided by South African agents.

In the meantime, South Africa's outward-looking policy had achieved some success. The springboard into Africa had been provided by the independence of the three former British high commission territories, Lesotho, Botswana and Swaziland, which had found it difficult to resist the powerful economic influence of their neighbour. By the end of the decade Pretoria had exchanged diplomats with the black state of Malawi; trade and technical cooperation had developed with the islands of Malagasy and Mauritius; and, according to Foreign Minister Muller, there were 'direct contacts' with many more African states that he preferred not to mention.

The stumbling block was the strategically vital Central African state of Zambia. When Vorster put out feelers, President Kaunda declared that the policy of apartheid, 'which, frankly, is the policy of oppression and exploitation', stood in the way of friendship.

But the summit conference of East and Central African states that met at Lusaka in 1969 adopted a manifesto that was couched in almost conciliatory language. The white rulers were told: '... we would prefer to negotiate rather than destroy, to talk rather than to kill ... If peaceful progress to emancipation were possible or if changed circumstances were to make it possible in the future, we would urge our brothers in the resistance movements to use peaceful methods of struggle, even at the cost of some compromise on the timing of change.' Of equal significance to the qualified acceptance of evolutionary change was the declaration by black leaders that white South Africans were as much a permanent part of the continent as the indigenous inhabitants.

Meanwhile, some African leaders were determined to 'dialogue', come what may; particularly after Vorster declared himself willing to discuss any subject, including internal policies, with other African heads of state. Chief among these was the Ivory Coast's Félix Houphouët-Boigny, who, convinced that there was no available force to defeat apartheid, split the annual OAU summit meeting in June 1971.

The high-water mark of Vorster's efforts was a first-ever state visit to South Africa by a black leader, in the shape of Dr Hastings Banda. Even though the Malawian, a recipient of much Pretoria aid, criticized apartheid in public, his visit was seen by the whites as a brilliant success. Banda's stately procession through the sacred ranks of Afrikanerdom was widely reported in the black Press, however, and made Africans wonder why they could not be treated on equal terms as well. Moreover, despite the ructions which dialogue was bringing to black solidarity, not one black state openly condoned apartheid, or showed the slightest sign of agreeing that the policy of separate development would solve the white man's problems.

As the Third World majority swelled at the United Nations, the race policies of South Africa were subjected to mounting challenge. But Pretoria could always rely on friends in the West. When in 1970 the Afro-Asians secured a two-thirds majority vote in the Security Council for mandatory sanctions against South Africa and Portugal because of their assistance to Rhodesia, the United States and Britain exercised their vetoes. These two Western countries did support a UN resolution calling for an arms boycott, but General de Gaulle refused to conform, and France became apartheid's armourer. South Africa's annual defence expenditure rose more than fivefold, to R257 million, in the decade, and the indigenous arms industry became a large-scale employer of black labour. Relations with Britain, which white South Africans had feared might deteriorate under Harold Wilson's Labour Government, remained satisfactory.

The hunt for skilled immigrants centred mostly on the British, who obliged with a third of the 350,000 white settlers who arrived during the post-Sharpeville decade. Trade increased between South Africa and the large 'Free World' countries, while Japan, whose pig-iron merchants were afforded red-carpet treatment, had by the mid seventies established huge trade links with apartheid.* The muscle of South Africa's vast mineral

*The stern face of apartheid did produce one almost comical moment. A few months before the Tokyo Olympics, a Japanese swimming team was prohibited by the Pretoria City Council from taking part in a gala at the municipal baths on the grounds that the visitors were not white. Then it emerged that the team was connected with the Yawato steel industry, which had recently concluded a large deal to purchase

resources even promoted contacts beyond the Iron Curtain. The Soviet Union used the Anglo-American's Central Selling Organization in London to market its diamonds.

The one area where international boycotts succeeded was on the sports field. It infuriated sports-mad white South Africa, for whom the victory of their Springbok teams reinforced the belief that the white man was born to rule. The absence of black South Africans from the Rome Olympic Games in 1960 became, under African insistence, an occasion for the International Olympic Committee to apply pressure. By 1964 hopes of continuing the 'traditional' whites-only selection procedures had receded so far that a 'mixed' team was tentatively chosen after racially-separate trials. It proved, however, to be too little too late. South Africa has been out of the Olympics ever since.

Unconcerned by white rugby fans' growing disquiet at the prospect of South Africa's isolation, Verwoerd told New Zealand not to include Maoris in their touring team. 'We expect', he noted piously, 'that when other countries visit us they will respect our [customs] ...' The All Blacks refused to send an all-white team. But rugby is to the Afrikaner what pelota is to the Basque, and Vorster, under pressure from the mainly-Afrikaner rugby world, changed the rules soon after becoming Prime Minister. There have since been tours to South Africa from New Zealand, but none in the reverse direction. Vorster's own lack of 'respect' for his country's 'customs' was quietly forgotten. But that was rugby, and rugby was a special case.

In 1968, the Cape Coloured cricketer Basil D'Oliveira, who had emigrated because of the lack of sporting opportunities for blacks, was chosen as a replacement for an English touring side about to visit South Africa. Vorster cancelled the visit and accordingly personalized apartheid for many British people previously indifferent to calls for a sports boycott. How, they asked, when they saw D'Oliveira on their television screens, could this lightly tanned man be a threat to the security of South Africa?

The normally conservative Marylebone Cricket Club, which

iron ore from South African producers. The Japanese were found to be 'honorary whites'.

controls cricket in England, announced in 1970 that tours between the two countries would not be resumed until cricket was integrated at club level. When, some years later, Vorster did allow black cricketers to tour, it was once again too little and too late. More-radical voices were by now calling for the resumption of international competition to be contingent on the abandonment of apartheid.

Once the Afrikaners had achieved their republic – and the English, who voted almost to a man against it, saw that life would continue much as before – Verwoerd began to woo the other language group. Two English-speakers were invited into the Cabinet. But it was the business boom that did most to win the English over. Profits of 18 per cent and more were a reliable and widespread feature of the late 1960s.

Verwoerd was a complex ideologue, and the politically neutered English found it difficult to identify themselves with him. To them, he was the mad doctor with a strange scheme to hand over chunks of the country to the blacks. Vorster, with his pragmatic approach, his attachment to golf and his ability to tell a good story at club dinners, worked wonders. The success of his excursions into black Africa further endeared him to the English.

The reverse side of achieving white solidarity was the discouragement of any expressions of solidarity across the colour line. The banning of the liberation movements in their entirety had attracted so much adverse publicity for South Africa in 1960 that Vorster was loath to use it again to silence his liberal opponents. Instead, he relied on banning particular leaders of the small multiracial Liberal Party, which by then had declined into a pressure group without elected representation. Then, with the Prohibition of Improper Interference Act 1968, racially mixed political parties were declared unlawful. As a result, the Progressive Party, whose only member of parliament was Mrs Helen Suzman, went all-white. The Liberal Party gave up the struggle and disbanded.

'By 1970,' an Information Department history declared sadly, 'there was no indication that South Africa's policy was accepted or even fully understood by the world at large ... Despite a resilient economy and bright prospects for the future,' this official version continued, 'South Africa entered the seventies in a serious and reflective mood. Conscious of the need to adjust to changing conditions in a manner that would not endanger the heritage of centuries of Western endeavour in South Africa, the country faced critics, detractors and enemies, determined at all costs to choose its own time and own methods of political development towards the ideal of general participation in the government of the country.'

By now, however, the plea to 'give us more time' seemed to be inhibiting, rather than contributing to a solution. Dr Erich Leistner, an economist with the pro-Government Africa Institute in Pretoria, estimated that by the turn of the century South Africa would have 29 million blacks, of whom 9 million at the most could be absorbed by the tribal areas. 'A black tide of vital statistics is threatening to swamp and finally to drown the policy of separate development,' complained a correspondent in a Durban newspaper. The white birth-rate was dropping, and at 13.4 per 1000 in 1968 was less than half that of the Coloured population. (There are no official figures for the African rate of population increase, but it is certain to be much higher than that of the whites, despite the much higher infant mortality rate.) *Die Oosterlig* newspaper in Port Elizabeth wrote that 'birth figures in South Africa are also political figures ... if something drastic is not done, the whites will be involved in gradual genocide.'

Unpatriotic Afrikaner mothers were not the only formidable obstacle to the success of Mr Vorster's plans. Another was the condition of the black proletariat. The period saw the beginnings in London and New York of pressure on American- and British-owned companies to improve pay conditions of workers in their South African subsidiaries. Even the Interior Minister, Theo Gerdener, warned that '... such gigantic differences in living standards as we have to do with in South Africa can ... lead to murder and violence because the less privileged of the two can no longer tolerate the apparent wealth, ease and prosperity of his neighbour.' Gerdener complained that white living standards were unrealistically high, and suggested that white salaries should be 'virtually frozen' until the wage gap was narrowed.

The alarm signal came, unexpectedly, from South West Africa when, late in 1971, many thousands of Ovambo migrant workers across the 'white' south of the territory went on strike for better conditions. The hand of the liberation movement SWAPO was evident from the determined way in which the stoppages spread. The workers faced criminal prosecutions for breach of contract but were instead sent back to their Bantustan (to be replaced, in some cases, by white schoolboys earning R109 a month, compared with the minimum cash wage of R8 25c for a black worker). Despite the heavy Government crackdown, the strikers did win some minor concessions: in particular, greater flexibility in changing jobs, if the employer behaved unreasonably. They had demonstrated that black migrant workers could unite and withstand considerable intimidation.

Six months later, Johannesburg's African PUTCO bus drivers, who earned R30 a week, struck for wage increases of up to 150 per cent. The company offered 2 per cent. Africans are not recognized as 'workers' under industrial laws, and it is accordingly illegal for them to take industrial action. The 300 drivers were arrested at a sit-in at their depot, but were released after a demonstration by fellow-drivers outside the John Vorster Square police headquarters. In the end they won increases of about 30 per cent.

The most impressive demonstration of black industrial strength came with the wave of strikes by Africans and Indians in and around Durban during 1973. In all, some 60,000 workers were involved in action for higher wages and better conditions at 150 factories. They too won concessions which resulted in an increase of some R6 million to the annual wage bill.

Labour unrest also spread to the mines, this time with fatal consequences. One night in September 1973 the police were called to Harry Oppenheimer's Western Deep Levels gold mine at Carletonville, in the western Transvaal, to deal with demonstrating migrant workers. They shot eleven dead – 'in the execution of their duty', as the white magistrate found at the subsequent inquiry. The workers had been demanding higher wages for a month, and there had been no effective channel of communication for their grievances. The need for a trade union was never more eloquently illustrated. The shootings led to a deterioration in relations with the Lesotho Government, which declared a national day of mourning for its five citizens killed at Western Deep. In South Africa's black townships, 'Carleton-ville' was added to 'Sharpeville' in the pantheon of black martyrs shot to sustain white supremacy.

Though different in their causes and nature, these and other strikes were a sign that African workers were becoming increasingly restless. The 1970s did see relative improvements in black wages, though the absolute gap continued to widen. In the decade up to 1974, the white–black ratio declined from 12:5 to just under 11:1. It was a narrowing largely attributable to a continued shift in the economy from dependence on mining and agriculture to industry and commerce, where black workers were generally better paid. But even in the gold mines, where at the end of the sixties the wage ratio was 20:1, the average annual African wage rose from R350 in 1973 to R565 the following year and then to R948 in 1975. The mining industry was more than compensated by the rocketing price of gold, which enabled revenues to reach new heights.

Larger pay packets also reflected the gathering movement of blacks into semi-skilled and even skilled jobs, because there were not enough whites to satisfy the demands of the economy. By 1970, the manpower shortage on the railways had become so acute that over 1000 Africans were 'temporarily employed' on work normally performed by white graded staff: mainly as flagmen, trade hands, shed attendants and stokers. Another 12,000 Africans were in jobs formerly held by unskilled and ungraded white railworkers. Other Africans were doing the same job that white 'shunters' had done, but were described as 'train marshallers', and paid a suitably low wage. The trains functioned as well as ever.

White trade unionists were satisfied as long as the job had been racially declassified, and white and black did not work together on equal terms. They were suspicious of employers who cut the rate for the job, as happened occasionally with African bricklayers. Africans were allowed to do construction work reserved for whites provided that they used tools other than those normally given to artisans. Far from breaking down the barriers of job reservation, these trends merely meant that the colour bar floated upwards. White workers continued to enjoy the plums of the economy; the more so, as fewer were now doing semi-skilled jobs.

It was not the migrant workers who benefited from this process, but the black urban 'insiders', or, in the words of a Government minister, 'temporary permanents'. More knowledgeable in the ways of the city and available for training in new skills, they were in many respects closer to the white townsmen than to their cousins from the countryside. Industry came increasingly to depend on them. Having invested time, money and effort in training it found the normal high turnover among unskilled workers uneconomic. At the same time, both Government and management appreciated that this influential but underpaid sector of the black workforce carried the seeds of future industrial unrest.

And indeed, the life of the black worker hardly improved in the wake of these well-publicized wage rises. They were accompanied by sharp jumps in the price of consumer goods, and the cost of food rose alarmingly – by over 16 per cent in the year ending March 1973. As blacks spent a substantially larger proportion of their incomes on food than did the whites, the worth of their new pay packets soon seemed much like that of the old. It was the white supermarket owners and furniture dealers who apparently prospered; black shopkeepers in Soweto were restricted in the type of goods that they were allowed to sell. It is possible, therefore, that wage increases during the first half of the seventies, far from stilling black frustration, merely fired it. Demands for political change are more likely to be made by people with rising economic expectations than by those whose daily life is fully occupied in the grind of keeping alive.

Pretoria's grip on the far-flung corners of the country was being tested in South West Africa. For half a century the territory had been governed as a virtual fifth province: its whites elected to the central parliament by whites, its blacks subject to the full rigours of racial discrimination. Now there were warnings that it might become the pass through which the assault would come to overthrow apartheid in South Africa itself. The Ovambo strike followed only a few months after an advisory opinion by the International Court of Justice at The Hague confirmed that the United Nations had acted lawfully in terminating the mandate. There were sporadic outbreaks of violence in Ovamboland, as SWAPO attacks spread from the Caprivi Strip in the far north-east of the territory. In February 1972, the government decreed emergency regulations in an attempt to snuff out SWAPO's influence.

Later that year, the UN Secretary-General, Kurt Waldheim, visited South West Africa in the hope of preparing the ground for self-determination. But Vorster had already begun to carve up the territory into Bantustans on the South African model. The popularity of this policy was reflected in the embarrassingly low 2.5 per cent poll for the elections to the Ovamboland legislative council in July 1973. Later in the year the UN general assembly voted overwhelmingly to reaffirm the legitimacy of the 'struggle for liberation from colonial and foreign domination and alien subjugation by all available means, including armed struggle'. By now the territory was becoming widely known by its new name of Namibia, after the Namib desert that stretched along the Atlantic seaboard. SWAPO, which had thought up the name, now called itself the South West Africa People's Organization of Namibia.

The outward policy experienced another set-back when the new government on the island of Malagasy (Madagascar) suspended the agreement for economic cooperation with South Africa. Zambia continued to import some R55-million worth of goods from South Africa each year (mostly machinery for the copper mines), but Kaunda and Vorster were still not talking to each other. There were headaches for Pretoria on the war front. By mid 1973, South African para-military forces and pilots flying Super Frelon helicopters were openly in action against Zimbabwe guerrillas, who were infiltrating across the north-east border as the Portuguese failed to contain Frelimo forces in the north of Mozambique. Frelimo opened a new front near Cabora Bassa, with the avowed aim of sabotaging construction of the huge dam being built to supply power to South Africa.

Back home, well-laid plans for the black 'homelands' were running into difficulties. The black leaders had begun to behave independently of their masters. Chief Gatsha Buthelezi, chief minister of Kwa-Zulu, was one of the most persistent critics of Government policy but most of the tribal leaders profited from their immunity as clients of Pretoria to attack Bantu Education, the industrial colour bar, the pass laws and even separate development itself. They refused to ask for 'independence' until their claims for large tracts of land in the white 87 per cent of the country had been met. Buthelezi included seventeen 'white' towns in the outline of his fractured territory. Tribal chief ministers held a summit meeting at Umtata in November 1973 to frame a programme of minimum 'demands', and call for the creation of 'one black nation, not weak tribal groupings divided along ethnic lines'.

Their outspokenness helped fill the vacuum left by the banning of the liberation movements in 1960. They were not in any sense the heirs to that tradition. But for a while theirs was the only audible African political voice. Any claim they might have had to being the real spokesmen for the country's 18 million Africans was seriously challenged by a new force in the cities: that of black consciousness.

3. Black Consciousness

1968 was a year of unprecedented student radicalism in France, Britain and the United States. In South Africa too, black students at tribal colleges clashed with white authority, and then made a crucial decision to leave the multiracial National Union of South African Students (NUSAS) and found their own union instead. At the time, the birth of the all-black South African Students' Organization (SASO) was only of passing interest to the outside world, but very soon it became the spearhead of a confident political movement based on 'black consciousness'.

The Afrikaans universities had also once belonged to NUSAS, but its multiracialism had so disturbed them that they had broken away to form a separate racist organization. When Afrikaner Nationalism came to power, mixing was strenuously discouraged. Blacks were excluded from the 'open universities' of Cape Town and the Witwatersrand, and sent to Zulu, Xhosa, Sotho, Coloured and Indian tribal colleges. NUSAS and the mixed University Christian Movement were prohibited by the state from operating on these campuses. Then, in 1968, eight years after the founding of the Sotho college at Turfloop in the northern Transvaal, its student body voted to affiliate to NUSAS. The white college authorities duly refused permission, prompting demonstrations by the students and the arrival of the police to seal off the campus. The acting rector of the college, an Afrikaner, Professor F. G. Engelbrecht, advised the students to form their own separate organization.

By that time, black students were themselves increasingly resentful of the dominant role played by whites in multiracial organizations. Their feelings came to a head when African students attending the NUSAS congress in 1968 had to be accommodated separately in an African township. It was not the fault of the organizers, but blacks now claimed that they were wasting their time in relying on the altruism of a few ineffectual white liberals. The radical posture of the University Christian Movement had frightened off many white students, leaving a black majority. At its conference that year a group hived off into a 'black caucus' which discussed the need for a black student body. The result was the South African Students' Organization.

At its first congress, in 1969, the students were still unsure of their new role. The conservatives among them argued that race separatism played into the hands of the Government, while 'middle-of-the-roaders' warned that SASO would not long survive and should be accordingly careful of breaking old ties. The radicals though still critical of NUSAS bided their time and continued to recognize it as the sole student body.

The caution did not last long. At its second conference SASO withdrew recognition of NUSAS as a national union, believing that 'the emancipation of the black peoples in this country depends on the role the black peoples themselves are prepared to play ... aware that in the principles and make-up of NUSAS, black students can never find expression for aspirations foremost in their minds.'

SASO's 1970 policy manifesto elaborated the new militancy based on black awareness and pride. To start with, a fresh perspective was given to what the white man called 'the black problem'. 'The white man must be made aware one is either part of the solution or part of the problem', the manifesto declared; concluding that, 'because of the privileges accorded to them by legislation and because of their continued maintenance of an oppressive regime, whites have defined themselves as part of the problem.'

Excluding whites from the struggle did not imply 'anti-whitism', but merely 'a more positive way of attaining a normal situation in South Africa'. The manifesto emphasized that 'South Africa is a country in which both black and white live together and shall continue to live together', but that in order to achieve these aims, 'personal contact with whites, though it should not be legislated against, must be discouraged especially where it tends to militate against the beliefs we hold dear.' SASO was later instrumental in expelling NUSAS from the Southern African Students Union, which represented students in the sub-continent. NUSAS had by this time conceded that SASO was the only organization that could effectively represent black students.

The vehicle for this psychological and physical liberation of the black man was black consciousness. SASO defined it as 'an attitude of mind, a way of life', exhorting the black man to 'reject all value systems that seek to make him a foreigner in the country of his birth and reduce his basic human dignity'. He must 'build up his own value systems, see himself as self-defined and not defined by others'. 'At the heart of this thinking,' wrote a founder of SASO, 'is the realization by blacks that the most potent weapon in the hands of the oppressor is the mind of the oppressed.' Once the black man, through this process of 'conscientization', was made aware of the nature of his oppression, he had taken the first step towards his own liberation. Africans, some of them in the tribal legislatures, gave up their Western names and began to call themselves Nyameko, Mokethi or Sabelo.

The movement was not restricted to students, but spread through an intricate network of voluntary organizations – cultural, sporting, church, educational, cooperative and workshop. The one obvious gap was a political party. Since the banning of the liberation movements in 1960, legal black political activity had been limited to parties based in the tribal areas. The Government encouraged Chief Kaiser Matanzima's Transkei National Independence Party, for it fell four-square within the framework of separate development. But now, as the SASO students started to graduate from their universities, they realized the need for an off-campus political organization.

In 1972, a conference of 100 African, Indian and Coloured delegates met near Pietermaritzburg to launch the Black People's Convention (BPC), a 'political movement' for all black people who could not reconcile themselves to working within the framework of 'separate development'. Though BPC did not elaborate a coherent strategy, it did express unequivocal opposition to apartheid and an outright rejection of Bantustans, separate Coloured and Indian councils, Bantu Education and other segregated institutions.

The term 'black' now included Coloured and Indian, as distinct from the Africans-only policy of the Pan-Africanist Congress in the early sixties. 'Black' replaced the 'non-white' (or 'non-European') favoured by whites – though black radicals still mockingly described 'moderate' blacks as 'non-whites'. In their lighter moments they called the whites 'non-blacks'. No longer would the black man be seen in negative terms. A reporter from the liberal *Rand Daily Mail* was thrown out of a SASO conference because his newspaper used the term 'non-white'. The *Mail* quickly changed the description to 'black'.

But this principle of black solidarity involved papering over deep racial divisions. Coloured and Indian students and school-children were attracted by black consciousness, and even some 'sell-out' Coloured Labour Party members talked of a 'black front' with Africans and Indians; but it did not go much deeper than that. Historically, Indians and Coloureds had been cast adrift between the two major races, to view both with equal trepidation. The harsh treatment meted out to the two smaller groups by the Nationalist Government had done much to alienate them from the whites. But this did not mean that they were willing to throw in their lot with the Africans. Hindu and Moslem Indians and Afrikaans-speaking Coloureds would find it difficult to fit into the same 'black culture' as rural and even de-tribalized urban Africans.

Nor were all Africans allowed to join these 'black' organizations. Bantustan leaders, even an outspoken critic of apartheid like Gatsha Buthelezi of Zululand, could not belong to BPC or participate in its discussions. A black schoolteacher was acceptable but not an inspector in the Department of Bantu Education. The black middle class was also reprimanded for not making efforts to further the cause of black liberation.

White liberals were dismayed to find themselves consigned to the other side, along with Afrikaner nationalists. Indeed, they were considered the biggest obstacle in the way of black unity. If John Vorster was despised for heaping all manner of misery on the black man, then Alan Paton and his liberal followers were attacked for telling him how he should respond to such treatment. 'Not only have they kicked the blacks but they have also told him how to react to the kick,' complained one of the founders of SASO, Steve Biko. Henceforward, blacks would disregard white counsels of moderation which had got them nowhere in the past. As blacks withdrew from multiracial organizations, an anguished Alan Paton asked whether the white liberal should leave South Africa, keep silent for ever, go north and be trained as a guerrilla fighter, or just lie down and die. But the black radicals were no longer interested in supplying an answer; though some were aware of the danger. 'History has charged us with the cruel responsibility,' said one black leader, 'of going to the very gate of racism in order to destroy racism ... to the gate [but] not further.'

When Justice Minister James Kruger blamed the Soweto rebellion on an 'alien imported ideology ... Black Power', he was deliberately ignoring the basically 'made in South Africa' elements of black consciousness. The clenched-fist salute and the cry 'Power to the People' did have their origins in the United States of the 1960s (though tribal leader Kaiser Matanzima claimed to have introduced the Black Power salute to South Africa as the symbol of his national independence party). But the symbolic resemblances belied a fundamental distinction. Blacks would never be more than a minority in America and so Black Power there was limited to asserting the black personality in a racially mixed society. South African blacks, on the other hand, were the natural majority, and their own commitment to Black Power was a credible preparation for the day when they would take over the government of the country. Although black consciousness ideologues have drawn on the ideas and writings of Black Power, they are more usefully seen as the heirs to a tradition of cultural nationalism in Africa itself, ranging from 'negritude' to the philosophy of African socialism and African

humanism. Even Dr Hastings Banda, a 'sell-out' in the eyes of
BPC, was quoted approvingly as saying of his own Malawi:
'This is a black man's country and the white who does not like
it must pack up and go.'

An important component of black consciousness is 'black
theology', a 'study of disinheritance and liberation from the
perspective of people who are oppressed because of their
colour'. The profound relevance of black theology in a country
where church-going plays an important role in the life of the
people, was not lost on black radicals. They accused the South
African Christian churches of being 'one of the most powerful
instruments in making possible the political oppression of black
people'. While the white colonists were busy robbing the
blacks of land and liberty the white churches were busy, however unconsciously, undermining the black will to resist.

They did this by teaching the black that he lived a heathen and
barbarous life. His only salvation lay in conversion to Christianity, which meant rejecting his traditional dress, authority,
social organizations, marriage customs, medicine and much of
the indigenous culture. Salvation lay not just in Christ but in
the white man's civilization so that the black was persuaded to
believe himself inferior. The very language of the Church
underlined this feeling. 'Black' and 'evil' were interchangeable
terms, while the prominence given in Christian teaching to the
'nobility of servitude' provided a further moral buttress to his
exploitation. BPC lumped the English Churches – Anglican,
Catholic, Methodist, Presbyterian – together with the
Government-supporting Dutch Reformed Church. Nor were
the black priests spared, for they had imbibed this alien creed
at the white-run theological seminaries; singled out were the
upper-crust black priests who 'hobnob with the whites and
ignore the needs of the masses'.

Black theology was not anti-Christian, but sought to 'relate
God and Christ once more to the black man and his problems.
It wants to describe Christ as a fighting god, not a passive god
who allows a lie to rest unchallenged.' A black Catholic priest
explained that 'we have accepted Christ, who has been brought
by the white man. But we do not accept what the white man

says about Christ. We are going to find out for ourselves what Christ has to say to us.'

Black theology certainly succeeded in making organized Christianity more political. One group of churchmen, IDAMASA (the Inter-denominational African Ministers' Association), had been in existence for half a century, when it was won over, in 1972, to black theology. Its 1000 members suddenly acquired an interest in experimental farming, school syllabuses and the problem of inter-tribal fighting. The potential was enormous. There were 3000 independent churches, which attracted the support of at least a fifth of the African population.

These all-black churches were by tradition even less socially aware than their Protestant and Catholic counterparts, but there had been striking examples of resistance to the state's authority. When in 1906 every African over the age of eighteen in the province of Natal became liable to pay a poll tax, many tribesmen refused. In one incident, two policemen were killed while attempting to deal with the insubordination. The two leaders of the rebels were prominent members of an Ethiopian Christian sect, the African Congregational Church. Their excuse for not paying was that, as Christians, they were not subject to the chief's authority. Both men and a dozen of their followers were subsequently hanged. If independent church preachers ever began to inject a note of black consciousness into their stirring Sunday sermons, the political outcome could be explosive.

By 1972 SASO had become the undisputed spokesman for the country's black students, claiming, not without justification, a membership of 8000 that was still growing. The figure equalled the total enrolment at the tribal colleges, though there were technical students, trainee teachers and even some non-students among the members.

If black consciousness spread like wildfire through the tribal colleges, the Government almost seems to have arranged matters with that in mind. The campuses were, with the exception of the Indian college in Durban, dumped in the bush miles from the large population centres. Here, far away from Western liberal traditions, the state prepared to fashion a respectful Bantu technician equipped to serve the needs of white South Africa. But the very opposite happened, and an entirely unexpected strain of outspoken young men and women emerged. The reasons, in retrospect, are clear. Most of these students came from 'white' towns, where they kept in touch with developments elsewhere in Africa and the Third World. Not only were they sophisticated, but in a school system where only one in 750 obtained university entrance qualifications, they also represented a tough intellectual élite.

As enrolment at tribal colleges grew, so did the proportion of students from working-class homes. They knew first-hand of the appalling conditions under which their parents lived and worked, but they could also understand the working of the apartheid system, with their own allotted roles in an exploiting white economy.

At one time, blacks at the 'open' universities or at Fort Hare had been drawn largely from a mission-educated middle and lower-middle class. Liberals, some black and many whites, had hoped that if the blacks could acquire sufficient education they would help to make, by earning their own admission, a multi-racial democracy. But then separate development got under way. The new out-of-town black locations destroyed what little social contact had existed between black and white; the blacks were put through separate educational systems and even given their own 'countries'. No longer did anyone, least of all the students at Turfloop, Fort Hare and Ngoye, dream the old dreams.

The segregated campuses were in the hands of illiberal Afrikaner academics, and the rectors, appointed by the Government and usually belonging to the Afrikaner *Broederbond* secret society, would get in touch with the local security police at the first sign of trouble. There were some black lecturers, and a rare black professor. But they were paid less than the whites, drank their tea in separate staff rooms and joined their own staff associations; there was even a system of separate white and black senates and councils. Their treatment at the hands of shopkeepers and police in the near-by white towns reminded them that they were still blacks. The students themselves considered their education inferior to that given at the white universities, indeed, their degrees were not accepted beyond the borders of South Africa. Their hostility was heightened by the knowledge that they were profiting from the very Bantu Education that they so loudly denounced. Of course, they had little choice, other than to forgo the chance of higher education altogether (or to enrol for a course by correspondence at the University of South Africa).

The man who brought S A S O to national prominence was Abraham Tiro, a former mine worker and past president of the Turfloop students' council. Tiro was chosen by his fellow students to speak on their behalf at graduation day in April 1972. It was an unusual occasion: headed by the chancellor, Dr W. M. Eiselen (one of the architects of apartheid), and the white rector, professors, council and honoured guests filled up so much of the hall that some black parents, who had travelled long distances to see their sons and daughters graduate, were unable to find places.

Tiro began his address by recalling the assurance of Prime Minister Vorster that no black man had ever landed in trouble for fighting for what was legally his. 'Although I don't know how true this is,' said Tiro, 'I make this statement my launch pad.'

Tiro called for a system of education common to all South Africans. 'What is there in European education which is not good enough for the Africans?' he asked. 'In theory Bantu Education gives our parents a say in our education but in practice the opposite is true. At this university, students are forced to study the philosophy of education through the medium of Afrikaans. When we want to know why, we are told that the senate has decided so. Apparently this senate is our parents.'

Why, he asked, was a black man 'unceremoniously kicked out of the [campus] bookshop? Apparently, this is reserved for whites. According to policy, Van Schaiks [a Pretoria firm of publishers and booksellers] has no right to run a bookshop here. A white member of the administration has been given the meat contract to supply the university – a black university ... and why were white students given vacation jobs at this university when there are students who could not get their results due to outstanding fees ... does the administration expect me to get a vacation job at the University of Pretoria?

'Right now our parents have come all the way from their homes only to be locked outside. Front seats are given to people who cannot even cheer us. My father is seated there at the back. My dear people, shall we ever get a fair deal in this land? The land of our fathers.

'The system is failing because even those who recommend it strongly, as the only solution to racial problems in South Africa, fail to adhere to the letter and the spirit of the policy ...

'The challenge to every black graduate in this country lies in the fact that the fault of all wrongful actions in South Africa, restriction without trial, repugnant legislation, expulsions from schools, rests on all those who do not actively dissociate themselves from and work for the eradication of the system breeding such evils.'

Tiro, looking over the heads of the white audience, ended his address: 'Let the Lord be praised, for the day shall come when all shall be free to breathe the air of freedom which is theirs to breathe and when that shall have come, no man, no matter how many tanks he has, will reverse the course of events.

'God bless you all ...'

Three days later the all-white disciplinary committee expelled Tiro, and he was escorted off the campus. When a petition for his reinstatement was rejected, the students began a sit-in protest in the main hall. The rector suspended the student council and banned all meetings. The students still refused to attend lectures, so the entire student body of more than 1100 was expelled, and police – with riot sticks and dogs – were called in from the town of Pietersburg to see them off the campus. But, despite police taunts, the students would not leave. It was only when food and water supplies were cut off and access to the toilets denied them that they returned to their homes. The campus was sealed off by the police.

The students were later offered readmission if they signed a form accepting Tiro's expulsion, the suspension of the S R C and of the constitutions of all black committees on the campus, including SASO. They were advised by the SASO national president to return so as 'to continue the fight for educational justice', but not to respect the conditions. On returning they found that twenty-two SRC and SASO members had not been reinstated. Half the student body turned round and went home. When lectures resumed for the remaining students, police were on hand to see that there was no more trouble.

By now black students were protesting in solidarity across the country. The angriest reaction was in Bellville, at the Coloured college ten miles from Cape Town. Here too lectures were boycotted as students complained of white control. The Government issued urgent regulations banning from the campus all organizations not expressly approved by the authorities, along with any pamphlets or statements that did not have the consent of the rector, Professor N. Sieberhagen. Accusations by four Coloured lecturers that the college administration was collaborating with the security police were speedily justified. The rector summoned the police to terminate a visit by SASO president Jerry Modisane, who was arrested and fined for trespassing. The college was temporarily closed.

SASO was also seen off the campus at the Indian college in Durban. Again, black consciousness leaders were suspended and classes boycotted. The Government had added insult to injury by appointing Senator Owen Horwood, the only English-speaker in the Government and a brother of Mrs Ian Smith, to the post of chancellor of the college. At Fort Hare – the eastern Cape university which had been forced to exclude all black students who were not Xhosa-speaking – the rector, Professor J. M. de Wet, called in the police to break up a boycott of classes. The local SASO chairman was arrested by the security police. By mid June, 160 students had left the campus. At a fifth tribal college, in Zululand, students carrying placards in support of their colleagues at Turfloop disrupted a graduation ceremony.

The two months of protests that followed the expulsion of Abraham Tiro amounted to a virtual state of insurgency in the black colleges. The widely scattered black campuses united under the leadership of SASO. Signs of black solidarity were especially apparent at the Coloured and Indian colleges, and because many students lived in the 'white' cities S A S O's influence spread into the townships, where the South African Students' Movement was formed in Soweto by high school pupils.

Yet if the Government was alarmed it certainly did not show it. All that the white public knew of these events came from an occasional short paragraph in a newspaper, reporting the arrest or expulsion of black students at a distant college. Only when white Cape Town university students, focusing attention on events at Turfloop, were pursued by baton-wielding police into the sacred precincts of the city's St George's Cathedral and beaten up beneath the altar, were the grievances given headline treatment.

The Government waited until the beginning of the academic year in March 1973 to act. After receiving the interim report of a parliamentary commission of inquiry into the activities of N U S A S it banned seven English-speaking student leaders and a lecturer under the Suppression of Communism Act. English-speaking white South Africa, normally critical of its radical students, reacted angrily. The bannings were debated in Parliament, and the Prime Minister received a delegation of principals from the four English-speaking universities. Within days, eight black student leaders, among them S A S O president Modisane and former presidents Steve Biko and Barney Pityana, were also served with five-year banning orders.

White public reaction was muted, while the Afrikaner rectors of the tribal colleges, far from leading a protest delegation to the Prime Minister's office, were overjoyed. When the bannings were debated in Parliament, Minister of Justice Piet Pelser was asked why the students were not instead being tried in court. That, he explained, would only 'give them a platform'.

But S A S O, far from being cowed, simply replaced its leadership from the reservoir of willing recruits. Within months, seven student successors to the banned leaders, including the newly appointed S A S O president, had themselves been banned, and three of the original eight were given prison sentences for contravening their banning orders. Harassment by the security police and the banning of anyone showing the slightest sign of leadership became automatic policy.

Some of these students fled the country. Among them was Abraham Tiro. In February 1974, in Gaberones, capital of neighbouring Botswana, he was killed by a parcel bomb. The parcel bore Swiss postmarks, and had apparently been posted by a university organization in Geneva. The director of the organization denied, however, that he had sent a package to Tiro. As all mail from Europe to Botswana passed through Johannesburg, suspicion turned on the South African security police. Tiro, the Botswana Government declared in a statement, 'had incurred the displeasure of certain powerful circles in South Africa'.

By 1973, black consciousness had become the motivating force of various voluntary organizations throughout the major cities. Some of these had been specially created, but often a well-established society was penetrated by SASO or BPC and underwent a sudden and drastic revision of its attitudes towards blacks. The switch usually took place at the annual conference, helped along, if the 'Uncle Toms' were uncooperative, by verbal 'strong-arm tactics'. This new awareness was both the cause and the outcome of a remarkable blossoming in the 'culture of liberation'. At one period in 1974, fourteen 'black' plays were attracting enthusiastic audiences in the cities and villages; with most of the theatre groups refusing to play before white audiences.*

The search for the authentic black experience gave rise to a black drama liberated from the inhibitions of Western theatre. 'From theatre that spoke of their ills and tribulations, there evolved theatre that spoke to black people about ways and means of changing their situation.' Coloured, Indian, African and mixed groups produced new plays written about South Africa or injected fresh meaning into established works. Anouilh's *Antigone*, dealing with moral conflicts of life in occupied France,

---

*This 'black' theatre did not include the musical *Ipi Tombi*, which has been rapturously acclaimed in London and New York. Black theatre critics saw it as a cheap commercialization and a ridiculous abasement of the proper tribal dance and musical patterns.

was performed by the Theatre Council of Natal (TECON). It was freely adapted to local conditions – complete with simulated hangings, newsreel film of slum housing, and a chorus of black women.

The People's Experimental Theatre (PET) in the Johannesburg Indian township of Lenasia produced *Shanti*, written by an African vice-president of the BPC, Mthuli Shezi. Its theme was a love affair between an African boy and an Indian girl, partly set in a guerrilla camp. Even before his play was staged, Shezi had become a martyr of black consciousness when mysteriously he fell under a train after an argument with white railway officials over their 'unacceptable' treatment of some black women passengers.

There was no bar to 'black' theatre written by whites. In the Port Elizabeth African township of New Brighton, Winston Ntshona and John Kani collaborated with the white playwright Athol Fugard in writing and producing the widely acclaimed *Sizwe Banzi is Dead*.

An annual 'Black Review' appeared for the first time in 1972, detailing events in the black community. Whites were ignored, except in so far as their actions or opinions impinged on black people. *S'ketsh*, an arts review for blacks, reported the new cultural fervour. A Music, Drama, Arts and Literature Institute (MDALI) was formed in Soweto, but it folded after participants in a black arts festival were arrested and harassed by the security police.

A new poetry of protest and lament was born, reflecting the mood of black consciousness. Magazines like *Ophir*, *Bolt*, *Classic* and the SASO newsletter published the writings of young blacks. A Cape Town Coloured, James Matthews, wrote in his book of poetry *Cry Rage!*:

> It is said
> that poets write of beauty
> of form, of flowers and of love
> but the words I write
> are of pain and rage.

The book was banned by the South African Government after the first edition of 4500 copies had almost sold out.

Gibson Kente, whose musicals were progressively influenced by black consciousness, ran into trouble with his *Too Late* (it followed another musical *How Long*) which parodied education and religion, and hit out at the inhumanity of white officials. The play was first banned by the Publications Control Board, then cleared, following a court appeal. But it was effectively silenced when a number of government-run Bantu administration boards refused permission for its performance in township halls. Others suffered more heavily for their art. Nkutsoeu Matsau, secretary of the Sharpeville youth club and a BPC member, was gaoled for five years under the Terrorism Act for publishing a poem called 'Kill, Kill'.

The Black Community Programmes (BCP) were an ambitious attempt at instilling awareness among the peasants in the tribal areas. Their clinic at Zenampilo, near Kingwilliamstown, in the eastern Cape, was an early exercise in community medicine, where expectant mothers were instructed in child care and birth control methods.* In its first six months, 2500 patients visited the clinic. There were signs that self-reliance and pride in black effort were being generated in one of the most debilitated parts of the country. But a massive extension of the programme was needed if it was to have any general and lasting effect on the population.

Black Community Programmes also set up several cottage industries, manufacturing leather goods and Xhosa cloths, in the destitute areas of the eastern Cape. The purpose of the project was twofold: to ward off starvation and at the same time to encourage peasants to exploit their natural resources. It is easy to find parallels here with the work of Gandhi and his disciples among the peasants of India, but in South Africa, once the projects show signs of success, the Government intervenes. Steve Biko, who launched BCP in the Kingwilliamstown area, was banned in 1973.

In their critique of Western values, black consciousness writers attacked private enterprise, individualism, the 'Coca-Cola and hamburger society'. Their solution, according to the aims of the Black People's Convention, has been the achievement

*Its two doctors, both African women, were banished by the Government in 1977.

of 'African socialism' through 'an equitable economic system based on black communalism, the philosophy of sharing'. This economic credo is both contradictory and vague; lost somewhere between the idyll of tribal life and the ruthless struggle for survival in the 'white' cities. Public discussion of socialism is hampered by the disapproval of the security police, but the radicals did express minimum socialist demands: nationalization of the mines, redistribution of the land, abolition of the industrial colour bar.

The most tempting target of all for the exponents of black consciousness remained the black workforce. SASO set up a black workers' council in 1972, stressing the need to 'conscientize them about their role'. The patronizing language reflected the deep gulf between student and worker. After the strikes in Durban in 1973, several new 'black awareness' trade unions were formed under the umbrella of the Black Allied Workers' Union (BAWU), but they made slow progress. One reason was that Coloured and Indian workers were chary about exchanging what few rights they had under the official system, for no rights in a 'black' union. Black workers who did join a union were soon dispirited by the absence of any improvement in their pay and work conditions.

The understanding grew that the interests of the workers could not be limited to the factory floor: they extended to the ghetto, to the crowded commuter bus and train, to the absence of amenities for black workers in the towns, to the influx control laws, to the lack of adequate schooling and the consequent prevalence of illiteracy.

At one stage students played with the idea of getting jobs in factories – both to 'conscientize' the worker and to educate themselves. The project, known as Edu-ploy, came to nothing. But growing belligerence led to a strike for equal pay with whites by ten African doctors employed by the Johannesburg city council. As clinics in Soweto faced closure, the council gave in to the demands. It was a rare victory for the principle of equal pay for equal work.

The successful ten-year struggle by Frelimo, culminating in the defeat of Portuguese colonialism in neighbouring Mozambique, was watched with relish by black South Africa. SASO and BPC organized a series of rallies to mark the establishment on 25 September 1974 of a Frelimo transitional government. They sent missionaries to Lourenço Marques to obtain Frelimo speakers. A white businessman cabled Justice Minister Kruger to warn that if he did not ban the Durban rally thousands of whites would act on their own to see that it did not take place. On 24 September Kruger responded to this manifestation of 'public opinion' with a month-long prohibition on all black consciousness gatherings.

On the day, several thousand Durban blacks gathered outside Curries Fountain stadium, which was cordoned off by the police. When they began a march on the city, chanting 'Viva Frelimo' and punching the air with their clenched fists, the police turned Alsatian dogs on them. Some forty blacks were arrested, and as many fled the country. At first it seemed as though the charge would relate only to holding an illegal meeting. But soon afterwards the decision was taken to stage a slow political trial against black consciousness.

After being held four months in solitary confinement under the Terrorism Act, twelve blacks were charged. Led by Muntu Myeza, president of SASO at the time of his arrest, they climbed the steps of the Pretoria magistrates' court from the cells below, defiantly singing, '*Ashikhathali noma siyabotshwa* ... we do not care if they arrest us ... we are determined on liberation ...' They gave the clenched-fist salute and turned their backs on the white magistrate to greet friends and relatives.

Eventually, after a false start and a separation of trials, seven African and two Indian leaders of BPC and SASO, all in their twenties, were charged with conspiracy to transform the state by unconstitutional, revolutionary and/or violent means. Other allegations, some of which went back to the founding of SASO in 1968, included denigrating whites and representing them as inhuman oppressors of blacks; eulogizing people convicted 'of terrorism, subversion, sabotage and communism'; discouraging foreign investment in the South African economy; and – curiously, given the content of Bantu Education –

'portraying historical events in such a way as to cause, discourage or further feelings of hostility by blacks towards whites'. Not one charge involved a covert or overt act of violence, though the Frelimo rally produced an alternative count of 'provoking the police to use violence'. Under the Terrorism Act, the minimum sentence was five years; the maximum, death.

The evidence contained over 100 pages of poems, speeches, manifestoes, and even a resolution calling on Coca-Cola and IBM to withdraw from South Africa. The prosecution cited a poem which went:

> To weep is a waste of glorious time.
> Time to grab arms,
> And aim them at
> The blue-eyed enemy
> Lurking in the bushes.

And, in addition, a magazine article which declared: 'Hitler is not dead, he is likely to be found in Pretoria'; a play which portrayed the shootings at Sharpeville as 'deliberate mass murder by whites'; and an SASO resolution, influenced by black theology, which noted that: 'Christ was a revolutionary ... who had joined the Essenes [an Israeli revolutionary movement], worked in close collaboration with the Zealots [an Israeli guerrilla warfare unit] against the Romans.' The students had resolved to look at Christ as 'the first freedom fighter' and instructed their black theology agency to correct the interpretation of Christ's mission that had been 'atrociously perverted and distorted by white imperialists in their selfish and repressive aims'.

The trial of the SASO Nine got under way in Pretoria's Palace of Justice in August 1975. By then, Mr Vorster had recognized the Frelimo Marxist revolutionaries as the legal government of independent Mozambique. On 25 September the surly prosecutor, Cecil Rees, was persuaded to blow out the candle on a cake that marked the first anniversary of the men's detention. Nine months later, when the schoolchildren of Soweto rebelled against the imposition of Afrikaans, the SASO Nine were still on trial.

Black consciousness was not stunted by the repression. On the contrary, the township people, though not necessarily belonging to its organizations in any large numbers, admired the defiance and resilience of the young leaders. On the other hand, the diffuse base of the movement seemed to hinder the formulation and implementation of a unified political strategy. If the vacuum left by the bannings of the Pan-African and African National Congresses was to be filled, it had to be by an organization that was willing to take direct political action against the Government. But the black consciousness policy of withdrawal was pre-political. SASO's manifesto specifically urged that 'before black people join the open society they should first close their ranks, to form themselves into a solid group to oppose the definite racism that is meted out by the white society, to work out their direction clearly and bargain from a position of strength.'

And, by the mid seventies, there remained gaping holes in the support which black consciousness could claim from the black community. Migrant workers, farm labourers, Bantustan residents had never heard of it. In the cities, the leadership and much of its overt following were drawn from the educated élite. Yet its potential was enormous. And the Government, mindful of Afrikanerdom's own historical struggle, understood that revolution began in the minds of men. Mr Vorster's dilemma, however, was that the more apartheid was imposed, the more these dangerous ideas flourished. And they flourished more dangerously in that area of South African life which placed special emphasis on the inferior status of black people – education.

4. Education for Slavery

In 1941, when it still looked to Afrikaner nationalist intellectuals as if Nazi Germany would win the war, a young professor at the university college of the Orange Free State wrote:

One of the outstanding achievements of this volk is that in the midst of an overwhelming barbarism, it succeeded in remaining white. This achievement can be ascribed to its Christian way of life, and secondly to its racial feeling in terms of which there is a clear and natural dividing line between the races which must not be crossed. We must continue to build along this road in order to ensure the continued existence of white civilization in South Africa and the white character of the Afrikaner volk ... The relationship between white and non-white will be that of Christian guardianship ...

The man who wrote those words, Dr Niklaas Diederichs, is today President of the Republic of South Africa.

In the classrooms of South Africa these concepts are strictly enforced through Christian National Education (CNE), which provides the basis for the division of schools and universities into 'Bantu', 'Coloured', 'Indian' and 'National' (or white). CNE has its roots in the Afrikaner's struggle against the English invader for the survival of his language and homeland. To this day, though Afrikaans is spoken by a large majority of the whites and by almost every Coloured, English remains a feared and formidable enemy. White children are forced to attend either English- or Afrikaans-medium schools, in accordance with the language spoken at home. And thus there is shaped a true nationalist, imbued with 'love of one's own, especially one's own language, history and culture'. As a result, English-speaking children, mouthing concepts drummed into them by textbook and teacher, with reinforcement from press, radio and television, and a year of national service in the army, find little difficulty in using loaded terms like 'Bantu', 'separate development' and 'communist' (for African nationalist).

Nowhere are the misplaced ideals of Afrikaner nationalism seen to better effect than in the working of Bantu Education. The programme for educating Africans was prepared by the Institute for Christian National Education established by the *Broederbond* cultural organization F A K (*Federasie van Afrikaanse Kultuur Vereeniginge*). The Institute's manifesto recommended that 'native education should be based on the principles of trusteeship, non-equality and segregation; its aim should be to inculcate the white man's view of life, especially that of the Boer nation, which is the senior trustee . . .' and it added: 'Only when he has been Christianized can he and will he be truly happy and secure against his own heathen and all kinds of foreign ideologies which promise him sham happiness ... we believe that he can be made race-conscious if the principle of apartheid is strictly applied in education just as in his church life.'

When the manifesto was published in February 1948, it was widely seen as a crude left-over from national-socialism, fit only to gather dust in a Pretoria cupboard. Within three months, however, the Nationalists had won the general election; and one of the signatories to the manifesto, Dr E. G. Jansen, was appointed Minister of Native Affairs. When the Transvaal congress of the party formally approved its contents, Christian National Education began its career as official dogma.

Before Afrikanerdom launched its new deal, however, there was a final commission of inquiry under the reliable back-room boy Dr Willem Eiselen. Significantly, he reported that Africans who had given evidence showed 'an extreme aversion to any education specially adapted for the Bantu'. These feelings were ignored. The terms of reference ensured: 'the formation of principles and aims of education for natives as an independent race, in which their past and present, their inherent racial qualities, their distinctive characteristics and aptitudes, and their needs under ever-changing social conditions are taken into consideration'.

On the language of instruction, Eiselen recommended that the vernacular should be used for the first eight years, and then gradually be extended to secondary schools and even training institutions. The African was to learn Afrikaans and English only 'in such a way that [he] will be able to find his way in European communities; to follow oral or written instruction; and to carry on a simple conversation with the Europeans about his work and other subjects of common interest'.

Piloting the Bantu Education Bill through Parliament in 1953, Dr Verwoerd clarified its purpose in a celebrated statement:

My department's policy is that education should stand with both feet in the reserves and have its roots in the spirit and being of Bantu society. There, Bantu education must be able to give itself complete expression and there it will be called upon to perform its real service . . . There is no place for him in the European community above the level of certain forms of labour . . . for that reason it is of no avail for him to receive a training which has as its aim, absorption in the European community . . . until now he has been subject to a school system which drew him away from his own country and misled him by showing him the green pastures of European society in which he is not allowed to graze.

And he added: 'I will reform [Bantu education] so that natives will be taught from childhood to realize that equality with Europeans is not for them. Race relations cannot improve if the wrong type of education is given to natives.'

For more than a century this 'wrong type of education' had been provided almost exclusively by the mission schools. But they were certainly not hotbeds of radical thought and practice, as Verwoerd implied. On the contrary, their tolerance of segregated schooling and the paternalism of their teaching methods had attracted a great deal of criticism from radical educationists. What Verwoerd resented was the way in which they prepared the African intellectually for some place in a common South African society.

A minority of African children, mostly in the Cape, were in schools administered by the white provincial administration. But the provinces did not object to surrendering African education to the central government in pursuit of the new policy. African and liberal educationists, however, rejected Bantu Education. One African, Dr D. G. S. M'Timkulu, said that Africans 'seek for integration into the democratic structure and institutions of the country. To them one of the most effective ways of achieving this is by education – an education essentially no different from, or inferior to, that of other sections of the community.'

The African National Congress organized a boycott of the new system, with some success in the Johannesburg area and the eastern Cape. Dr Verwoerd countered by warning that he would not readmit absentees. The 7000 children who stayed away on the opening day of Bantu Education, 25 April 1955, were removed from the school register, and 116 'surplus' teachers were sacked. The boycott collapsed.

The 5000 state-aided mission schools were the prime target of the state take-over. Curricula and teachers now had to be approved by officials in Pretoria. It became illegal to run a school which was not registered, and registration was solely at the discretion of the Minister. On that basis the churches were left a choice: to hand over control of the school to the state or to retain control, but with the life-giving subsidy for teachers reduced to 75 per cent. Verwoerd warned that the teachers' subsidy might not last for ever. Soon after the final date for choosing had expired, the teachers' subsidies were reduced to half, then a quarter, and within three years were stopped altogether. The churches needed an iron nerve and a ceaseless flow of funds to survive.

The Dutch Reformed Church willingly handed its schools over to an educational policy that it had itself significantly promoted. The Catholic Church resisted most strenuously but its resources were inadequate. By 1974 fewer than 400 African mission schools remained, and all but a handful were Catholic. There were 12,000 Bantu state schools: the historic role of the Church in educating the country's blacks had been successfully extinguished.

In line with the (white) view that parents should play an 'organic' role in the education of their children, control of community schools, which housed the bulk of African children, was handed over to the people. But in effect, 'control' has meant the hard work of running the schools, without any say in the formulation of policy. Each school has a committee, partly elected by parents, which is responsible to an area school board; and this in turn employs the teachers, maintains the schools and investigates complaints. The Government can accordingly boast that 80,000 parents and teachers are involved in the administration of Bantu Education. In this way the deficiencies of the system can conveniently be blamed on the Africans themselves.

But after two decades of Bantu Education, the top fifty officials, the great majority of the regional directors and inspectors, and all but one of the permanent secretaries to black ministers of education in the tribal areas, are white. Every important decision remains in the hands of the cabinet ministers, who rule by regulation without reference to Parliament, in a wide variety of activities covering the registration of schools, syllabuses, media of instruction, and conditions of service for teachers. As school boards would learn over the use of Afrikaans, any recommendation which conflicts with official policy is rejected out of hand by white officials.

Government ministers said much about the need to improve African schooling, and they even set up a separate Department of Bantu Education in 1959 to show that they were in earnest. Behind this concerned façade, however, ran two constants of white Nationalist policy: African education should not develop at the cost of white education, and the African community should shoulder a proportion of the financial burden. Only in the topsy-turvy world of South Africa is the poorest racial community called upon to contribute to its own education, while the three other groups get it free from the state. The churches had raised large amounts of money towards the costs of black schooling, but with the hand-over of schools to 'the people', private charity was officially discouraged.

When the state took over African education it immediately pegged the amount of money available out of the general revenue at R13 million, with the balance to come from 'Bantu tax'. The improvement of African education was made dependent on African earnings, which were severely restricted by the industrial colour bar and, to a large extent, by poor education. Today, Department officials are fond of reminding visitors to South Africa that the African pays R36 million in taxes, while

Bantu Education costs R59 million, and 'we make up the difference.' The calculation ignores the substantial share of the national income that accrues to the state from indirect tax paid by Africans on items like cigarettes and liquor, or from the fines that Africans pay for contraventions of the pass laws. It ignores, too, the contributions of African parents to their children's education. And it ignores the wretchedness of the reward that Africans have received for their labour in building one of the richest countries on the continent.

Certainly, the number of pupils, teachers and buildings has grown substantially. But the quality of education, unsatisfactory as it was under the churches, has deteriorated disastrously. Figures for 1975 show that it cost R41 a year to educate an African child, but R621 for a white. If account is taken of the estimated 30 per cent of African children who get no education at all, the white-to-African ratio on expenditure rises from 15:1 to almost 22:1.

In the new townships, African parents subsidize the cost of lower primary school buildings (which accommodate two thirds of African schoolchildren) through an education levy added to their house rentals. The amount varies from 20c a month to 38c in Soweto, where the shortage of schools is particularly grave. And the school boards have to raise half the capital towards the building of secondary schools in both urban and rural areas, as well as find the money from parents to pay the salaries of privately hired teachers for whom there is no money from the national budget. At one time every sixth teacher was being paid in this way. Furthermore, African children must pay school fees, though white, Coloured and Indian children do not.

For the first two decades of Bantu Education, every African child had to buy his own textbooks and stationery though class readers were very occasionally supplied in the primary classes. (Parents with high-school children may have to pay up to R40 a year for books.) In the mid seventies the Department began a long-term programme to supply free textbooks. Some classes were given a good supply of books; the next year it was down to a trickle; and in 1976 the flow had all but ceased. Teachers complained of chaos in their classrooms, with five pupils for every textbook. The Government, blaming 'spiralling costs', announced that the free-book programme had been extended from three years to five. 'We are not cutting back,' explained an official, 'rather, we are taking a long time to go forward.'

The erection of high schools in the urban areas is assiduously discouraged, while there are none at all on the white farms. Future black leaders are expected instead to attend boarding schools in the appropriate Bantustan, where they might confirm their tribal affiliation. Thus, though the majority of the country's Africans live in 'white' South Africa, there are twice as many children at high schools in the tribal areas as there are in Soweto, Langa and other 'white' areas. Boarding school fees add R100 and more to the cost of educating a child.

There is a further unnecessary expense. The school uniform, that relic of British tradition, is not compulsory in African schools – indeed, the Department discourages it – but in the scramble for a classroom place, the child wearing the school blazer and tie is less likely to be turned away on the first day of the year than the one who comes in ordinary clothes.

One of the early actions of the Nationalists on coming to power was to curb the grant for school feeding, then 2d a day for children of all races. As Bantu Education was launched, African school boards were given the choice of using their funds either for school feeding or for the extension of educational facilities. The Department was in no doubt as to what choice should be made. It promised to contribute an equal amount again if the money was spent on new classrooms. But if the school boards still preferred the provision of meals, then it was up to the headmaster and his school committee to buy and prepare the food. The posts of school-feeding organizers were abolished. Private school-feeding schemes proliferated, but they were dependent on the limited charity of white liberals. Tens of thousands of African children who left home without breakfast now had to wait until the evening for their first meal of the day – or satisfy their hunger with Coca-Cola and crisps.

In its efforts to show the world that the welfare of the Bantu is dear to its heart, the Department encouraged the enrolment of more pupils than the classrooms could hold, or the teachers could teach. While the number of African children at school increased fivefold in a quarter of a century of Nationalist rule, the erection of buildings lagged behind at half the rate. Yet building is done on the cheap. Apart from the financial contribution of the parents, huge savings are made through the relaxation of job reservation to allow African building workers on school sites, where they receive a fraction of the wages paid to whites. The buildings are of the barest brick, with no ceiling to ward off the roar of the summer rains pelting down on the corrugated iron roof. Inside, children may be sitting four to a desk intended for two, or kneeling on the floor and using their wooden benches as desks. Electric lights are a luxury. The absence of electricity at home sometimes drives a child out of doors at night to do his homework under a street lamp.

Nor is every school of the brick-and-iron variety. A recent survey revealed that more than a quarter of the registered schools in Soweto were mere 'shadows', without four walls and a roof to call their own; providing lessons in churches, halls, tents, classrooms borrowed from other schools, or simply under a eucalyptus tree. And all of this is to be compared with the standard white model of assembly hall, library, science laboratory, audio-visual equipment, sports field and central heating in the classrooms (for a Johannesburg winter at 6000 feet above sea level).

At the storm centre of Bantu Education are the teachers, tossed about in the conflicting currents of racist ideology, ambitious parents and bursting classrooms. They have to enforce unpopular measures, teach a slanted curriculum, perhaps conduct lessons in Afrikaans. And they are woefully unprepared for the task. Fewer than one teacher in nine has a school leaving certificate, and barely a thousand – out of 68,000 teachers – are graduates. Women teachers outnumber men by almost two to one, in line with a decision by Dr Verwoerd to save money in teacher training and salaries.

So desperate is the need for staff that virtually every teacher-training college student passes the examination at the first try, to go straight into a class of anything from fifty to ninety pupils (the teacher–pupil ratio was 1:40 in 1950, and today is 1:53).

The size of the classes rules out individual attention or pupil participation and makes marking homework a sisyphean toil. The teacher, understandably, resorts to dreary 'chalk and talk' and sets factual, easy-to-mark homework, so that the dull child is left behind and the bright one is bored.

Furthermore, a teacher can count himself lucky to have only one session a day. The space and staff shortage is so serious that nearly a million children, out of 3,700,000, are taught in double session, or as African parents call it, 'hot seat'. In the first four years of schooling – sub-standards A and B and standards one and two – the same teacher takes two sets of classes a day. Pupils use the same desks and books, but the normal course of four and a half hours is reduced to three hours. The strain on teachers, with classes of fifty in quick succession, is reflected in the particularly poor results of the second group.

For all that, African teachers are miserably rewarded – receiving half to a third less than their white colleagues (the 900 white teachers in African schools are, of course, on white salary scales). In the absence of a large professional class, the schoolteacher is a leader of his community, yet he cannot maintain an appropriate standard of living on his salary. He is subject to the humiliating harassment of pass searches and, unlike teachers of other race groups, requires the permission of the Bantu commissioner if he wishes to teach in another 'white area'. It is not surprising that teaching is a last-resort profession for a bright African school-leaver; and that for a disturbing number of those who do find their way into the classroom, drink provides an easy relief.

A Government minister has explained that 11,000 additional teachers and classrooms, costing R14 million in salaries and R37 million in classrooms, would be needed to abolish 'hot seat'. Yet for many years private help in the building of schools was forbidden. This was highlighted by the blocking of an Anglo-American Corporation grant to a Soweto secondary school. In the resulting storm of criticism, the Department issued a circular declaring that donations would be allowed, subject to ministerial approval. The Johannesburg newspaper the *Star* launched a 'T E A C H' fund to raise money for African school-building and equipment. The money from T E A C H, and from business firms, has already provided classrooms for 2300 junior high school pupils in Soweto and the West Rand.

Perhaps the most deprived area of Bantu Education is the school on the white farm. Here, teachers without any qualifications predominate. Indeed, most of them are recruited locally, in line with a suggestion from Dr Verwoerd that this would serve 'to combat the dangers of unsuitable teaching'. All the farm schools are primary only, and the rare child who wishes to proceed further must go to a boarding school in the tribal areas. The white farmer is wary of allowing an education which might tempt his slave labour to search for a better life in the towns.

Thus, a curriculum was devised which would include 'the basic idea of teaching the child in order to fit him for farm work'. The first Bantu Education Minister, Mr Willie Maree, described farm-school teaching as:

A training in the normal activities of the farm, in order to encourage a feeling of industriousness on the part of these children, and ... to sharpen in their minds the fact that education does not mean that you must not work with your hands, but to point out to them specifically that manual labour on a farm is just as good a formative and development level as any other subject is ... If there is any farmer who has a farm school and who wishes to make use of the school children under the supervision of the teacher to assist with certain farm activities, this can be arranged in a proper manner ...

Unlike Bantu Education in the 'white' towns, there is no African school board to supervise farm education. It is entirely in the hands of the white farmer. He has total control over whether a school should be established, over which children should attend, and over the appointment and dismissal of teachers. A child from an adjacent farm may only be enrolled with the written consent of both the owner of the farm on which the school is built and the owner of the farm on which the child lives. If just one farmer objects to the building of a local school, the authorities will veto the plan. In the face of such obstacles, it is the African parents who build most of the schools themselves. Today, every third African school is on a white farm and together farm schools are responsible for a tenth of the total enrolment.

There is no better illustration of the way in which quality has been forsaken for quantity than the drop-out figures. Two thirds of all Africans at school are in the first four classes. Their brief taste of education provides no more than the first inklings of literacy. Children continue to drop out at such a rate that only 6 per cent of those who enrol in the sub-standard classes actually get into secondary school. The reasons are varied: the high cost of schooling; the need to increase the family income; restrictions on the building of secondary schools in the towns; or simply failure in the primary school exams through hunger or because of the absence of light, warmth and a quiet place for doing homework. It is a feat of endurance for the one African child in 500 who reaches the final year at school and, even more so, for the one in 1100 who succeeds in his matriculation.

Just before the Soweto uprising, the Government announced plans to spend R102 million on the extension of television to blacks. The expected operating cost of R40 million a year is over half the Bantu Education budget. Yet very few Africans can afford a set, and few houses in Soweto have electricity. Economists pointed out that the money would be just enough to launch a four-year programme of free universal education for Africans. A public opinion survey in Soweto at the time showed that 500 out of 522 Africans interviewed preferred education to television. Student placards called for 'more schools, no TV'. However, this overlooked the propaganda value attached to television, if used in the 'right' way by the Government.*

The extended use of the mother tongue and of Afrikaans as languages of instruction provoked the special anger of African parents and educationists. In the mission schools the African child had been taught in the vernacular for no more than four years, after which English (and occasionally Afrikaans was progressively introduced as the medium of instruction, with the change-over completed before the end of primary school. Bantu Education halted this, and set in motion a process of

*In 1975, a deputy minister estimated that compulsory education and a reduction of the teacher – pupil ration to 1:30 required 97,000 additional teachers and classrooms, costing an extra R126 million in salaries and R330 million in classrooms – less than the increase in South African's defence budget for 1977.

determined retribalization. From 1959, the African was taught in the mother tongue throughout the eight years of primary school, and then in both English and Afrikaans at high school. This ideologically based attempt at social engineering was of course educationally unsound. With his knowledge of English undermined, the black child would be cut off from his brothers in Africa, and even from other tribes in his own country, for whom English is the lingua franca.

In urban areas, where tribal affiliations have been weakened by intermarriage and long separation from the tribal areas, the townships are none the less being divided up into ghettoes within ghettoes. Tswana, Zulu, North Sotho children go to tribal schools administered by tribal school-boards. For some years North Sotho children happily attended the Bathokwa lower primary school in Atteridgeville, near Pretoria. Then, wide-awake officials discovered that the building was in a Venda-language area. The 500 Bathokwa children were kicked out and 'temporarily schooled' at another North Sotho school, while their buildings were handed over to the Vendas.

When educationists complained that it was absurd to teach through the medium of tribal languages that were incapable of reflecting Western concepts, departmental committees were ordered to create new Bantu terminologies. The Eiselen commission had recommended that mother-tongue instruction should be gradually extended through secondary school into the training colleges, and there is no doubt that some Afrikaner ideologues still hanker after the day when the African can receive his entire education without recourse to a world language. The mainstream of Department thinking, however, understands that as blacks take on more sophisticated jobs, proficiency in the language of the employer is a necessary evil.

The real feelings of African parents were revealed in the tribal areas, most of which were given their own education departments under a black minister at an early stage of their constitutional development. The rapid decline in the standard of written and spoken English since the introduction of Bantu Education in the Transkei led to fears that the language would soon develop into a local patois. With the closure of many church schools staffed by English-speaking whites, the teaching of English fell largely into the hands of Afrikaners and unqualified Africans. A Transkei commission on education (1963) described the practice of suddenly and simultaneously imposing two additional languages as the media of instruction in the first year of secondary school as 'a linguistic burden unique in the history of education'. Religion, music, physical education and other non-examination subjects continued to be taught in the mother tongue, with the remaining subjects divided up equally between the two official languages. The Transkei opted out of Bantu Education altogether, reverted to the old system of four years' mother-tongue instruction, and gave parents the subsequent right to choose between English and Afrikaans. Every school chose English. Today, all the tribal areas have English as the exclusive medium of instruction from the mid-primary classes, and Afrikaans has been relegated to an ordinary subject. Whatever the criticisms of the Transkei as a puppet state of Pretoria, its government has tried to improve schooling by devoting a quarter of its impoverished budget to education.

The tribal chief ministers proposed to Mr Vorster that if Africans in 'white' South Africa were indeed citizens of the Bantustans, they should be allowed to follow the educational practices current in the Transkei and elsewhere. In 1975, the Department made a substantial climb-down by reducing mother-tongue instruction in its schools from eight to six years; at the same time, primary schooling was itself reduced by a year to seven years, so bringing it into line with the education systems of the other race groups.

When Dr Verwoerd warned that there was no place for the African in 'white' society above certain forms of labour, he purposely did not stipulate the level. If the economy is in recession and there are enough whites to do the skilled jobs, then the four-year drop-outs, with enough English (or Afrikaans) to 'follow written or oral instruction', will be adequately educated. In times of expansion, particularly when European immigrants cannot be found to fill the semi-skilled jobs, then the Verwoerd level floats upwards. Today, the shortage of skilled manpower, particularly in the manufacturing sector, has led to a mushrooming of industrial training centres in 'white' areas.

The new schemes, established by state, local authority or industry, are an object lesson in how the floating colour-bar serves the white economy. The Department of Bantu Education has several industrial manual-training centres in urban residential areas where a boy about to enter secondary school gets an hour's basic training a week in woodwork, metalwork, welding, building practice, punch-card and computer operating or similar subjects. After that, he can elect to do a practical junior certificate course, and spend more time at the training centres.

The Department also runs training centres in white factory complexes to serve the needs of industry. Sites are provided by industrialists or the local authority, who then cover the running costs. The centres provide basic scholastic training, together with courses in motor and machine maintenance and service, fork-lift operating, woodwork and machining, and similar semi-skilled jobs no longer filled by whites.

At the summit of Bantu Education are the so-called 'bush colleges' where an intellectual élite is being prepared for the leadership of independent tribal areas. Like so many other examples of the 'traditional' South African way of life, ethnic education at university level is a recent invention. Afrikaner nationalists objected to the presence of blacks at the 'open' universities of Cape Town and the Witwatersrand, though student mixing at these institutions, in general, went no further than the lecture theatre and debating hall. Black medical students were not even allowed to dissect white cadavers.

In 1960, under the curiously titled Extension of University Education Act, Africans were barred from the open universities and sent to three ethnic colleges. Zulus and Swazis had to register at the University of Zululand; Sotho, Tswana, Tsonga and Shangaan, at the University of the North, Turfloop, in the northern Transvaal; while Fort Hare, in the Ciskei, which since 1916 had accepted Indian, Coloured and the occasional white student, in addition to Africans, now became an exclusively Xhosa college.

Bantu Education stamped out the liberal traditions of Fort Hare overnight, introducing an authoritarian regime reminiscent of a Victorian boarding school. Students now required the permission of the hostel superintendent each time they left the college precincts. No student society could be formed, no meeting held, no student magazine or pamphlet circulated without the permission of the rector. If a student wished to receive a visitor to the campus he required the consent of the rector or 'his duly authorized representative', and then only on express conditions. When police activities on the campus triggered off disturbances at Fort Hare, further regulations were gazetted. Students have now to apply annually for 'permission to report for registration', and then produce a testimonial of good behaviour from a minister of religion or a (white) Bantu commissioner. Even if the student complies with the good conduct conditions, the rector may still refuse to readmit him. Contravention of the regulations often leads to expulsion by a disciplinary committee under the rector. And each time the students react more stringent controls are introduced.

The African lecturer at a bush college is in a more trying situation than the teacher in a Bantu school. To begin with, he is in a minority. White professors and lecturers, invariably Afrikaners, predominate – except for the most modest post of junior lecturer, which is filled by Africans. The white is employed by the college council. The black comes directly under the Department of Bantu Education, is subject to civil service regulations and the disciplinary code of the college; is held guilty of misconduct if he publicly criticizes the Government. He is, needless to say, paid substantially less than his white colleague.

The subordinate status of their black teachers has been a constant source of student resentment. Despite their wariness of all things white, African students would still prefer to attend mixed universities. Until such time as that happens, however, they insist that their colleges be staffed by blacks. In 1977, Professor W. M. Kgware replaced a white rector at Turfloop to become the first African in charge of a university. Professor Richard van der Ross, a Coloured, has been rector of the Cape Town Coloured University since 1975. Both appointments achieved apartheid's aims in education.

97

The Government is proud of its Bantu universities. The figures show that in fifteen years, enrolment quadrupled to 8000. But the great majority of those enrolled are either doing diploma courses or are studying by correspondence at the University of South Africa. A mere 442 Africans graduated in 1973 (latest figures). Enrolment at the country's eleven white universities in 1974 was almost 100,000.

If education prepares a person for a decent and well-remunerated job, then Bantu Education can be seen to have failed dismally. Nowhere is the racial imbalance of South Africa more cruelly illustrated than in the professions (architects, lawyers, engineers, scientists, doctors), where whites outnumber Africans by 36,000 to 200. In 1973 there was one African engineer and one African dentist in the whole country. There are no engineering or dentistry courses at the tribal colleges. A prospective student needs the consent of the Minister of Bantu Education to do a course at an 'open' university. Engineering applicants have been refused on the grounds that there were no employment prospects for such Africans – this, at a time of desperate under-development in the tribal areas.

The system has been notably wayward in producing African doctors – barely 200 in the last decade and a half. The total of sixteen African medical graduates in 1974 compares with 580 from the five white medical schools. Medical training is not yet ethnic. Coloured, Indian and African study together at the Non-European faculty in Durban and there are also a few Africans enrolled in the faculty at the University of the Witwatersrand. But plans exist to establish separate African, Coloured and Indian medical, dental and veterinary schools. In mid 1976, the Government jumped the gun and announced that no more Africans would be enrolled at the Durban medical school, though not a brick had been laid at the new medical school in the Tswana tribal area near Pretoria. When protests from all races persuaded the Minister to postpone his decision, it was a rare example of common sense, if not compassion, triumphing over ideology.

We have seen how Bantu Education has been devised as an assembly line for the production of black labour units that are politically rooted in the tribal 'homelands'. The process is institutionalized in the under-education of the African child, through poor teaching, overcrowded classrooms, empty bellies and early drop-outs. Furthermore, to make sure that he knows his place in society, he is confronted with syllabuses and textbooks which project the white man's vision of the world.

Africans, as well as Indian, Coloured and white schoolchildren, get a version of history which tells how the shiftless 'Bantu' waged incessant war on the hardy white settlers, concerned only to till the soil and tend their flocks. And then, when the fighting stopped, the 'Bantu' settled happily into their 'traditional' – and shrunken – areas of the country. The Minister of National (white) Education has explained that this presentation of the National Party's policy in the school syllabus 'is put in perspective as forming part of the development history of our policy relating to peoples'.

The writing of the textbooks is largely in the hands of reliable Afrikaners, many of whom are working or retired school inspectors. And even they have to be careful. A textbook now in use was returned to the author three times by the Department of Bantu Education before the chapter on separate development was considered acceptable. If textbooks are good business for government officials, they are even more lucrative for Afrikaner publishing houses, which have won a large slice of the market from the well-established English firms. African control of their education does not extend to publishing textbooks. Perskor controls several undertakings in the African book business. Its board of directors includes the former Minister of Bantu Education M. C. Botha, as well as Interior and Information Minister Connie Mulder, and former cabinet colleagues Ben Schoeman, Jan de Klerk (National Education), Dr Hilgard Muller and Marais Viljoen. Perskor also publishes *Bona*, an educational magazine distributed free to African schools by the Department of Bantu Education, which buys 250,000 copies a year.

Nasionale Pers, the rival Afrikaans publishing house, also produces textbooks, as well as the official educational monthly *Bantu*. On its board of directors are Deputy Prime Minister

99

Piet Botha, National Education Minister Piet Koornhof and Labour Minister Fanie Botha. So powerful is the influence of these firms that their books are even sold in the neighbouring black state of Botswana. And now that the Department has launched a programme of free textbooks for African high school pupils, cabinet ministers will doubtless reap even greater dividends.

The selling of separate development is the preoccupation of the social studies course, a compound of history, geography, civics and elementary economics. The children must recognize the legitimacy of the 'homeland' system in order to pass their exam. They are obliged to use words like 'nations', 'Bantu' and 'homeland', when the only home that they know is their particular township. Little is done to make their present situation intelligible. The existence of the townships, which happen to be an integral part of 'white' South Africa, is studiously ignored. No mention is made of the banned liberation movements, or of the imprisoned leaders. The pass laws, overcrowded trains, economic exploitation: none of these is explained, unless it is absolutely unavoidable.

The social studies textbook written by Schoeman and Prior pictures on the cover the chief ministers of the eight Bantustans, giving the impression that they are the true leaders of the African people. 'There are many different nations in South Africa', the chapter on civics teaches. 'It is natural that these people will be proud of that which is their own.' The 'these people', it should be remembered, are sitting right there at their cramped desks and reading this bizarre account of their tribal patriotism. The chapter on the Bantustans admits that it has been difficult for the 'older folk in the homelands' to get used to new ideas. However, say Schoeman and Prior, 'the new citizens of the homelands, especially those who like yourselves have been to school and have learned these new ways, are going to make the task so much easier in the future.'

The Afrikaner makes no bones about his intention to control Bantu education. The social studies textbook for Forms 2 and 3 (by van der Merwe, Gerber and Strydom) explains why it was necessary for education to be taken out of the hands of the missionaries. 'If you pay for anything, it is logical that you would want to have some authority over whatever you have paid for. If a man has already paid his *lobola* [bride price], he, and no longer her father, has a say over the wife.' The passage also provides an incidental insight into the way tribal practices are encouraged by officialdom.

The books are often carelessly translated from Afrikaans into English. The preface to *New History Form III* (by van der Merwe and Strydom) states: 'This book is presented with due deference at the instigation of many supporters to continue service rendered in a previous series.' All the textbooks reveal a hopeless misunderstanding of everyday life for black people. Schoeman and Prior present imaginary extracts from the diary of an African girl driving with her father across South Africa. 'Follow her journey in our atlases and in our imaginations', African pupils are told – which is all that they will ever do, for even if they could afford the trip, many of the amenities are for whites only. Swimming 'in the sea near Muizenberg' would invite heavy fines and possible imprisonment for going on to a white beach. The girl and her family have lunch in Bloemfontein; they would be lucky to find a restaurant for blacks in Afrikaner-dom's most bigoted city. And the visit to the Voortrekker Monument near Pretoria would have had to be on a Tuesday, the only day in the week when it is open to blacks (and closed to whites).

This inability of the textbook writers to get inside the skin of their readers is apparent not only in social studies. A domestic science book lists the giving of instructions to the black maid as one of the household chores. There are other insidious themes running through the textbooks. Chief among these are descriptions of the natives as uncivilized, warlike and untrustworthy; the superior worth of white civilization; and the depicting of the black man as a passive being, for whom things have to be done by the generous whites. The whites 'came from Europe and brought with them the skills which enabled South Africa to become a wealthy industrial nation'. When the Dutch first settled at the Cape in 1652, they met up with the Hottentots, who were 'not reliable and caused much trouble'.

The interpreter, a man called Herrie who had learnt some English from passing ships, was 'untrustworthy and cunning ... he would trade cattle for goods the Dutch were offering, then steal back the cattle at night.'

The impression is given that slaves lived an idyllic existence and that it was cruel of the British to set them free. The textbook says that they were 'well treated compared with ... other colonies and countries. Van Riebeeck made their children go to school and he tried to convert them to Christianity.' But slaves were black, and so came the French Huguenots, 'whose importance lay mainly in the fact that they strengthened the white population'. After the British colonized the Cape, Governor George Grey 'realized that the Colony would develop only if more whites settled in the country'. So the colony was 'further enriched by 6000 British immigrants'.

Not every white man was welcome, however: Dr John Philip of the London Missionary Society 'sided with the Hottentots and other non-whites against the white farmers'. His book *Researches in South Africa* abounded with untruths and distorted ideas. It contributed much towards giving a wrong picture of racial relations in South Africa to the outside world. He also advocated 'equality of all people irrespective of race or colour'. Not surprisingly, Dr Philip is one of the few whites in South African history to be viewed with any sympathy by blacks.

And Dr Philip's behaviour was as nothing compared with a predecessor in the London Missionary Society, Dr van der Kemp, who had married a Hottentot and 'believed that he had to descend to the same level as the Hottentots before he could improve their way of life'. But these aberrant missionary do-gooders were the exception, and van der Merwe willingly admits that 'the honour must therefore go to the missionaries as the first people who were responsible for the education of the Bantu.' The view ignores the well-developed techniques, formal and informal, for the passing on of knowledge in tribal society. It maintains 'civilization for you began when we (the white men) arrived.' In most cases, the very opposite was true, and Western practices were the ruin of indigenous culture.

The most serious mutilation of the truth concerns the 'simultaneous arrival' and the 'open land' theories, which are held to provide white South Africa with the moral basis for separate development. According to the first, the migrating southern Bantu tribes crossed the Limpopo River (on the northern border of present-day South Africa) in the fourteenth century; yet there is meticulously substantiated evidence of black smelters at work on the Melville Koppies, in the heart of present-day Johannesburg – and in the gold fields – as early as A.D. 450, or more than a millennium before the arrival of the first whites. Nevertheless, the Department of Information maintains that the Bantu crossing of the northern border coincided with the arrival of the Dutch at the Cape. Patience Strong, the English writer of children's fiction, paid a fleeting visit to South Africa in 1975 and then related that the Bantu 'came after the Dutch and the British' – which would have been after 1795!

The second theory is that various parts of the country were empty and so fell to the rightful possession of a particular race or tribe. In a section headed: 'How most of the land fell into the Europeans' hands', van der Merwe explains that the Dutch trekked eastwards from the Cape without coming across any Bantu until 1770. 'The entire territory between Cape Town and the Fish River therefore became the legitimate possession of the Europeans by virtue of first occupation.' And today the Fish River is the western boundary of the Ciskei Bantustan. Liberal historians, however, long ago confirmed that Africans were living to the west of the river well before the arrival of the Dutch. The Xhosa had been so long in the region that their language had incorporated several click sounds from the near-by Hottentots.

Indeed, the white concern to draw historical frontiers with the Bantu tribes overlooks the presence of these same Hottentots and Bushmen in the western Cape long before it became a refreshment station for ships of the Dutch East India Company. When the early settlers were not making war on the Hottentot men, they were seizing the women as concubines. The expulsion of the Hottentots from their grazing lands, along with their reduction through drink and European disease, is one of the darkest chapters in South African history. Darker still, the case of the Bushmen, who, like the Aborigines of Tasmania, were all but exterminated in an act of deliberate genocide.

And so, in the words of the historian, the land continued to 'fall'. The Voortrekkers found the present Orange Free State 'almost completely uninhabited', while the rest of the province was gained in exchange for cattle from a native chief. Likewise, says van der Merwe, the Transvaal was virtually uninhabited, having been rendered barren by the Zulu wars of expansion. All the Voortrekkers had to do was to defeat the Matabele King Mzilikazi and 'take possession of the Transvaal by reason of conquest'. The Zulus were recognized by the Voortrekkers as the owners of Natal, so that when their chief, Dingane, ceded land to Piet Retief, it was 'in terms of a properly-styled and signed document'.

'We notice, therefore,' says van der Merwe, 'that a very large portion of South Africa fell into the hands of the Europeans by virtue of first occupation, conquest or purchase.' In this way, African schoolchildren learn that they have no right to live in the 'white' areas, and that the inexorable logic of history, rather than the government in Pretoria, decrees the establishment of their 'nations' in their 'traditional' 13 per cent of the country.

Nor, the textbooks remind their readers, should the benefits of the white man's intervention be overlooked. Van der Merwe claims that it saved the smaller Bantu tribes from further extermination by the Zulu King Shaka. Otherwise, 'there probably would have been a much smaller number of Bantu in South Africa today'. The other 'benefit' was that the Christian religion and education could be brought to the Bantu.

The discovery of diamonds sets the stage for further juggling with the facts of history. Indians had to be imported to work on the sugar plantations in Natal because the Bantu 'were not eager to leave their homelands'. Yet two pages later, van der Merwe relates that 'thousands of Bantu left their traditional homelands to work on the mines.' An important reason for this sudden change of heart is not disclosed. In fact, the colonial government imposed a head tax on every adult African male, who, in the absence of a cash economy, was unable to pay it, and so went off to raise the money in the mines. Such, indeed, were the beginnings of the migratory labour system.

The textbook explanation dwells on a different theme. Before the arrival of the white man, 'the Bantu had unlimited land'. He used wasteful agricultural methods. The women tilled the soil while the men were the soldiers and hunters. 'With the arrival of the white man, land became less plentiful.' The tribal wars were stopped, 'the Bantu population then increased notably and land became yet scarcer. It became necessary, therefore, for the Bantu to cultivate the land better. In this attempt they are assisted by the Government by word and deed. Yet this advice is not accepted by many Bantu and the following mistakes are still made . . .' Van der Merwe then lists the absence of fertilizers, the neglect of crop rotation, and overstocking. 'The result is that many Bantu find it difficult to make a living from farming . . . many men are compelled to leave their homes and seek work on the mines and elsewhere . . .'

The pass laws, the most loathed of all apartheid practices, are justified as being a protection for the black man. 'The people who are already permanently resident in the cities must also be protected so that they are not deprived of their work by new residents. It must also be seen to that the work of our people is not taken away from them by foreigners from across the borders.'

It certainly takes a lot to embarrass Mr van der Merwe, for whom the industrial colour-bar is apparently as fixed and unchanging a fact as the roundness of the earth. 'A serious shortage of skilled labour exists', he admits. And his solution (as the bright Bantu in the front of the class pricks up his ears): 'Attempts are at present being made to augment [*sic*] this shortage by immigrants from overseas.'

This version of South Africa's past and present is so improbable that teachers and children cannot take it seriously. Yet, they must pretend that they do, for unorthodox answers in their public exams bring failure from the hands of the whites who correct the papers. The high school pupils are faced with an enormous gap between what they know to be true and what they need to know in order to succeed. So they concentrate on learning as much as they can by heart.

Even before the Soweto language rebellion, there were signs that high school children were having problems in adjusting to the alien curriculum. While researching a thesis on Bantu Education, Ms Lyn Maree, a sociologist, was asked by a Soweto matric student whether he should use the terms 'Boers and Kaffirs', rather than blacks and whites: 'So they don't think we are politically motivated.' Another student told her that it was 'not wise to be too interested in history in South Africa'. Ms Maree, who visited high schools in the township in 1975 for her London University master's degree, found that pupils writing history exams sometimes ignored the South African half of the paper, in the hope that they would scrape through on the European section. It seemed that they were afraid of giving the 'wrong' version of their own history. Three out of four matriculants failed their history finals in 1974.

There can be few, if any, school systems as exam-oriented as that of black South Africa. Such is the shortage of classroom space that failure at whatever level means an end to the school career. In the junior certificate exam, a first- or second-class pass is needed for the advance to matric, while a third-class pass allows entrance to a teacher-training college. Once in the final year the African's chance of obtaining a school-leaving certificate is considerably less than that for the other racial groups. Success depends not so much on his own ability but on the needs of the economy and the space available at the universities. The present matriculation pass rate is an improvement on the early years of Bantu Education when it dropped to 18 per cent.

Lessons are earnest affairs, rarely presenting problems of discipline for the teacher. Pupils know better than anyone the sacrifice that their parents have made to keep them in school. After attending lessons in several Soweto high schools, Ms Maree remarked that they were so boringly presented they would have caused a riot in many English schools. 'But the children did not fidget or make a noise and most of them seemed to be paying careful attention.' If the teacher did not arrive, a pupil would come to the front and conduct a revision lesson with the help of the class.

Ms Maree found a high degree of political awareness in the classroom. It was far in advance of a comparable group of white seventeen- and eighteen-year-olds (though Africans, because they start school later, are sometimes in their twenties before they matriculate). At the time that she was visiting one school – for obvious reasons it cannot be identified – Mr Vorster was attempting to persuade the Rhodesian white leader, Ian Smith, to release an imprisoned African nationalist. The pupils asked Ms Maree why Vorster 'meddled in Rhodesia when things are so horrible here'. The Prime Minister had recently asked the world for six months in which to make important changes. 'What will he do next?' they asked her. 'I replied by asking them when the six months would be up. With one accord the class told me.' It is safe to say that very, very few white children would even have bothered to ask the question, let alone know when Vorster's time was up.

The French Revolution was a firm favourite. Ms Maree reports a teacher as telling the class how much could be learned by studying the history of other countries: 'It gives us strength and courage to carry on and try,' he said. In one revealing exchange, another teacher asked his class what the word 'political' meant. 'When you are against the law,' said one pupil; and 'the people who are excluded from government,' said another.

The thesis includes a collection of essays by final-year pupils at one school on 'What I think South Africa will be like in fifty years' time'. The essays have several surprising characteristics in common. Though they are nearly all overtly political, and include vigorous attacks on apartheid, there is remarkably little expression of race hostility (though this, it should be remembered, was a year before the Soweto uprising exacerbated anti-white feelings). Not one accepts 'separate development', and hardly any mention the 'homelands'. With one exception, they all anticipate that in half a century from now, South Africa will be a non-racial democracy, with blacks represented in the central parliament and all the races sharing in common prosperity.

They are immensely patriotic, proud of South Africa's achievements and its wealth, and predict that it will be one of the most powerful countries on earth. They are also aware that they live in a highly repressive society, with a big prison population, detention without trial, and gaoled liberation leaders. Their knowledge of events in southern Africa and farther afield is better than that of most white South Africans, for the good reason that these are of burning importance to them.

Opinions expressed in the essays indicate that the slanted curriculum is not succeeding in turning young Africans into docile Bantu. If the events of Soweto a year later are any guide, the very opposite is happening. No education system in the world can persuade a black child in a South African city today that the life he lives in and out of the classroom is an illusion. Long before the uprising, pupil resentment was erupting in periodic violence. In 1972 police arrested a total of 300 schoolchildren on charges which included arson and public violence. The following year, 116 pupils at Cofimvaba high school in the Transkei were convicted in court after stoning the principal's house, overturning a police car and looting the tuck shop. They were protesting at the failure of the authorities to supply school uniforms that had been paid for two terms before. The twenty-three children under the age of fourteen were discharged, but most of the others were caned. If Dr Verwoerd, in the early fifties, blamed rising black opposition on missionary education, what would he say about the huge escalation of classroom violence since then?

We cannot know for certain what effect Bantu Education is having on the attitudes of African children. Inevitably, the great majority who leave school after fewer than half a dozen years must be influenced by the strong dose of tribalism. The longer they stay on in school, however, the more they see through the façade. They leave as bitter, determined young men and women. They know a great deal about the white man – his language, his history and customs, the inconsistencies between his Christian belief and his Machiavellian practices, his fears of the black man.

In this way they are well armed, unlike whites of their own

age, who do not wish to understand African languages; who cannot glean from radio, television or newspaper what the black man is really thinking; who look upon Africa north of the Zambezi as a barbarous hinterland peopled by a succession of Idi Amins and black 'terrorists'.

When the state took over black university education in 1959, Professor Z. K. Matthews, the foremost African academic of his time, resigned from Fort Hare. 'Education for ignorance and inferiority is worse than no education,' he said. That point of view gained special currency after the Soweto uprising, when thousands of black children sacrificed a year – and possibly their final chance – of education, by refusing to write end-of-the-year examinations. Yet that very education appears to have played a cardinal role in influencing the attitudes of the rebel youth.

Now they have turned on their parents, accusing them of collaboration with their white masters. Teachers are asked by worried fathers: 'What are you doing to our children? They won't listen to us any more.' When a group of whites from the moderate Progressive-Reform Party asked a Soweto headmaster if they could meet his matric students to find out what they were thinking, he told them: 'They consider it a waste of time. The only whites they are ready to talk to are Nationalist politicians – they are the ones we will have to settle with.'

The rejection of white liberals shows the influence of black consciousness in Soweto high schools, where the South African Students' Movement has been recruiting for several years. The interplay of black consciousness and Bantu Education is of paramount importance in shaping the political maturity of black youth. The real education of South Africa's black schoolchildren only starts when they have seen through the system, when they learn how to reject it, while using it for their own purposes.

As Wilkie Kambule, headmaster of Orlando High, said in June 1976: 'We have a large number of boys and girls in the higher classes and they are wasting their time. The only thing they are preparing for is to change this country.'

5. From Lisbon to Soweto

Early in the morning of 25 April 1974 a group of left-wing officers in the Portuguese army overthrew the fascist regime of Marcello Caetano and ushered in a new era of decolonization in southern Africa. By the time that Mr Vorster awoke from his night's sleep, it had become clear that he could no longer rely on his principal allies to maintain white supremacy. Mozambique and Angola, which once kept independent black Africa at arm's length from South Africa, would soon be run by governments of 'terrorists'.

The South African Government, though disturbed by the sudden change, did not panic. It must have known from intelligence reports that Portugal, the poorest country in western Europe, could not indefinitely prosecute colonial wars on three fronts thousands of miles apart. Whites persuaded themselves that there was no real parallel between metropolitan Portugal and the Republic of South Africa. The Portuguese fighting-man derived no benefit from his years of toil and bloodshed under the African sun. He wasn't defending his homeland or his family; all he was doing was filling the coffers of the banks and the trading companies. If the war ended, he would go back to Europe, where his right to a home was not in dispute. The white South African soldier, on the other hand, was defending a way of life from which he derived very visible benefits. If the war were lost, the English-speakers might find a haven in the West, but the Afrikaner, his links with Holland long broken, would have nowhere to go.

Portuguese officers, stimulated by the ideological grit of their black adversaries, had gone back and launched a revolution at home. It was unthinkable that this could happen to the white South African. None the less, as a precaution, the South African army later appointed commissars to watch over the ideological orthodoxy of its national servicemen.

This was how white optimists saw the end of the Portuguese empire. Its defect was that it completely ignored the black man, to whom it didn't much matter whether it was a colonial Portuguese, a first-generation Rhodesian Englishman or an Afrikaner with roots going back to the seventeeth century who was denying him rights in his own country.

The pragmatic Mr Vorster took stock of the new strategic relevance of Rhodesia, which had once combined with Mozambique to provide an all-but-impenetrable barrier to guerrilla infiltration of South Africa from the black north. Now the guerrillas had hundreds of miles of common border with South Africa through a friendly Mozambique. The real danger, however, was in a sharpened racial conflict in Rhodesia itself, with hostile black governments on nine tenths of its borders. One glance at the map showed Rhodesia as a giant boulder balancing precariously on top of South Africa. Mr Vorster, untroubled by arguments of kith and kin with the 'English' of Rhodesia, decided that Mr Smith would have to be replaced by a black government acceptable to South Africa. In August 1974, barely three months after the Lisbon *coup*, the Rhodesian leader flew to Cape Town to hear that his country was no longer vital to the defence of the white south.

Mr Vorster's feelings for the rebel leader oscillated between the cordial and the frigid. They were best when the two men were watching a rugby match, worst when Mr Smith was considered to be standing in the way of a 'settlement'.* But in general, there was no particular affection between Afrikaner and white Rhodesian, especially since the referendum half a century before in which the Rhodesians had voted two to one against joining the Union of South Africa. If Afrikaners did have strong feelings for UDI, it was because they knew that Rhodesia was a trial run for South Africa itself.

Officially, South Africa was at pains to insist that it did not

*There was a family connection between the two governments. Mr Smith's wife was the sister of Senator Owen Horwood, South Africa's finance minister and the token English-speaker in the otherwise all-Afrikaans cabinet.

interfere in the internal affairs of Rhodesia. Unofficially, it had kept the regime alive by disregarding the international call for sanctions. Now, Mr Vorster proceeded to play a delicate game in which he pressurized Mr Smith into making concessions to his black nationalists, while at the same time he was seen by his own electorate to stand by him. The means he employed were of a brutal simplicity. Rhodesia had no arms industry of its own. Much of the military hardware required for its anti-guerrilla war was manufactured in South Africa, or passed through there on its way north. In his blunt, deliberate style, Mr Vorster reminded Mr Smith of this dependence.

Arthur Grobbelaar, general secretary of the Trades Union Congress of South Africa, told his Rhodesian colleagues squarely that 'while your country has until now acted as a buffer zone in blunting terrorist incursions from black Africa, your importance to South Africa for that purpose has now declined.'

The white public knew little of what was going on, particularly that Mr Vorster was outsmarting his devious ally in deviousness. In Parliament on 10 September, Foreign Minister Muller was denying 'most vehemently that the South African Government is interfering in the internal affairs of Rhodesia'. Less than a month later, a State Department official in Washington was telling a congressional sub-committee that South Africa 'may even one day accept [black rule] in Rhodesia'.

If Rhodesia was feeling the chill winds of Vorsterian pragmatism, South Africa itself was under no less pressure from its Western friends to amend apartheid. With the Vietnam War out of the way, foreign ministries and newspaper editors could devote more time to the world's next flashpoint. A Portuguese delegate at the United Nations emphasized the isolation of his recent ally: 'We are happy to be able to erase the shame which consisted of seeing the name of Portugal beside those of countries which persist in imposing inhuman and anachronistic racial discrimination through minority hegemony.'

At the end of October 1974, the Security Council debated an African resolution calling for the Republic's 'immediate expulsion' from the United Nations. On 23 October, the Prime Minister called eight of his cabinet colleagues, the Leader of the Opposition and the diplomatic corps to hear him deliver a major policy statement in the Senate. Southern Africa had 'come to the cross-roads', he said. The choice lay between peace on the one hand or an escalation of strife on the other. No specific promises were made about apartheid, but the speech was considered conciliatory enough for President Kaunda to speak of 'the voice of reason for which Africa and the rest of the world has been waiting'.

The next day, in New York, South Africa's UN ambassador, Pik Botha (since become Foreign Minister), entered the crucial debate which would bear heavily on his country's future in the world body. 'I do not deny', he said, 'that unsavoury and re-prehensible incidents between black and white do occur in South Africa, incidents which no civilized man can defend, incidents which I cannot condemn too strongly.' Never before had a senior spokesman of apartheid made such frank admis-sions about his country – not, at least, in public. 'I want to state here today very clearly and categorically,' Botha continued, 'my government does not condone discrimination purely on the ground of race or colour. Discrimination based solely on the colour of a man's skin cannot be defended.' Then he made what seemed to be a momentous promise: 'We shall do everything in our power to move away from discrimination based on race or colour.'

There was one cautionary note for those hoping to see a rapid end to apartheid. Ambassador Botha admitted that, 'I would mislead you if I imply that this will happen overnight. There are schools of thought, traditions and practices which cannot be changed overnight. But we are moving in that direction. We shall continue to do so.'

When the resolution was voted, Britain, France and the United States exercised a triple veto for the first time in United Nations' history. A week later, speaking to his constituents in Nigel, Mr Vorster publicly thanked the three Western powers for preventing the expulsion. And he added: 'Give South Africa six months' chance. I ask no more than that. Then they will be amazed at where the country stands in about six months' time.' The speech seemed to imply that his errant Republic would put its house in order as speedily as possible, and so cease to be an embarrassment to its allies.

After his Senate speech, Mr Vorster had contacted President Kaunda, believing that the two countries had a 'key role to play' in the solution of Rhodesia's problem. The response was positive. Virtually overnight, Mr Vorster was promoted as an acceptable figure in the West, while his diplomats discussed with the leaders of Zambia, Botswana, Tanzania and Mozambique ways of bringing the stubborn Smith to his senses. Even before the 'give us six months' speech, Mr Vorster had flown to the Ivory Coast for talks with President Houphouët-Boigny. Later, he paid a call on President Tubman in Liberia.

Fellow Afrikaners, dismayed that their leader had actually slept in the house of a black president, were comforted to hear that he had found a bible on the table at his bedside. President Jean-Bedel Bokassa of the near-bankrupt Central African Republic sent an official mission, including two cabinet ministers, to South Africa to seek financial aid. They discussed a hotel project in the capital, Bangui. The outward policy was alive and well again, under the new name of 'détente'.

The more that détente burgeoned into a beautiful friendship between Vorster and Kaunda, the more South Africa interfered in Rhodesia's affairs (and the more insistent became the denials that this was so). There could be no talk of a settlement in Rhodesia without the participation of the two nationalist leaders, Joshua Nkomo and the Rev. Ndabaningi Sithole, who were both in detention. In December 1974, South Africa and the front-line black governments persuaded Mr Smith to free the two men so that they might attend a conference in Lusaka. Though the meeting came to nothing, the settlement initiative was by no means dead. Foreign Minister Hilgard Muller called in at Lusaka later and met the black nationalist leaders who 'happened to be passing through at the time'.

South Africa's interfering non-interference came out into the open over the affair of Mr Sithole. The nationalist leader had returned to Rhodesia in March and was redetained just as he was preparing to leave for the Organization of African Unity meeting in Dar-es-Salaam. Kaunda sent a message to

Vorster stressing the vital role of Mr Sithole in détente. Dr Muller and his veteran Secretary for Foreign Affairs, Brand Fourie, flew to Salisbury at once for urgent talks with Mr Smith. The black leader was released. It was 'not a decision to which the Rhodesian government readily agreed', Mr Smith said frankly, but 'we were assured that to do so would sufficiently assist the course of détente.'

For Zambia, a major obstacle to a solution was the continued presence of South African para-military policemen fighting with the Rhodesian security forces. Mr Vorster, recognizing the dual merit of encouraging détente and discouraging Smith, proceeded to extricate himself from the entanglement. The 2000 policemen were in Rhodesia at the invitation of Mr Smith, and that could not be deemed 'interference'. To pull them out unilaterally, however, would undoubtedly be so. At first, Mr Vorster said that the police would be withdrawn 'as soon as violence stopped' (18 February 1975). But in April, with no immediate prospect of an end to violence, the police were ordered back to their camps within Rhodesia. By the end of August the last of them was back home. The official explanation was that the policemen had initially been sent to intercept South Africa-bound guerrillas as they crossed the Zambezi River. No such infiltration had taken place for some time.

The Rhodesian soldiers shrugged it off. The 'japies were no bloody good at fighting terrs anyway', they said. Mr Vorster continued to arm white Rhodesia. President Kaunda welcomed the withdrawal of the police as a step in 'lessening the areas of difference between the two countries'.

Mr Vorster was rewarded for his efforts with a conference in a railway carriage on the Victoria Falls bridge linking Rhodesia and Zambia. It was the most concerted attempt at settlement in the decade since UDI. Mr Vorster met President Kaunda, even stepping into Zambia for a stroll. Mr Vorster breathed heavily, but unavailingly, on Mr Smith. Later, in a television interview, Mr Smith claimed that it was not his fault. 'If this new initiative had not been taken by Mr Vorster and the four northern presidents we would have had a settlement by now.'

The South African cabinet, the Afrikaans Press, the whole

white nation it seemed, were appalled at this slur on the honourable intentions of their leader. The anger simmered for a while, and then Mr Smith was called to Pretoria. After four hours of 'candid discussions' with his mentor, Mr Smith issued an apology to Mr Vorster 'for any embarrassment caused by my remarks', and declared: 'there was no inference that Mr Vorster has in any way attempted to interfere in Rhodesia's internal affairs'. The Rhodesian delegation once again expressed their high appreciation of Mr Vorster's efforts to promote a more favourable climate for a peaceful solution.

The impact of these strange comings-and-goings depended on the colour of your skin. The intervention on behalf of Mr Sithole captured the imagination of the politically minded blacks. They saw through the charade quickly enough. Why, they asked, could not Vorster release Mandela and Sobukwe in South Africa and talk to them about a 'settlement'? The white rationalization was that Rhodesia, by opting for a constitution that would one day – even if it was thousand years away – lead to majority rule, was already an integrated society. What difference did it make if the Prime Minister helped to contract the time period for achieving black rule. South Africa? on the other hand, had chosen 'separate development', and could never become integrated.

White South Africans saw Vorster as a Merlin, whose magic wand would let them have the external cake of détente while they ate the internal cake of race privilege. A poll in the Johannesburg *Star* showed that the former *Ossewabrandwag* general had become white South Africa's best-loved figure.

Mr Vorster showed an equally deft diplomatic hand over the accession to power of the Marxist government in Mozambique, whose border was barely 200 miles from Pretoria. He quickly assured Frelimo that he would not interfere in their domestic affairs, and claimed to have received assurances in return that Mozambique would not be used as a launch pad for sabotage against South Africa. Before independence in June 1976, right-wing settler groups in the capital, Lourenço Marques, made several armed attempts at their own brand of UDI. The South African Government refused to intervene, ignoring pressure from its own large Portuguese community to do so. Officially, 25,000 refugees crossed into the Transvaal, but many more failed to register at immigration offices. Eager as South Africa was for white settlers, only Portuguese with skills to offer were given work permits. The rest had to return to Portugal – or perhaps call in at one of Johannesburg's mercenary recruiting agencies, to find 'work' in Rhodesia, and later, in Angola.

Samora Machel, the Frelimo leader and first president of Mozambique, did not abandon his determination to destroy apartheid. For the time being, however, it suited his purpose to remain unadventurous in his dealings with South Africa, while not disappointing his fellow revolutionaries. Diplomatic relations were not established between Pretoria and Maputo, the new name for Lourenço Marques,* and it was Oliver Tambo of the banned African National Congress, and not a member of Mr Vorster's Government, who represented South Africa at the independence celebrations.

But Mr Tambo would not yet be allowed to send his guerrillas across the border. After a dozen years of war, the Mozambique economy was in no condition to resist reprisal raids by white commandos. And Mozambique relied heavily on its apartheid neighbour to provide foreign exchange and support its economy. By long-standing agreement, much of the rail traffic from the industrial areas of the Transvaal went through Mozambique ports. And, as skilled Portuguese fled the country, South African technicians were in demand to keep Maputo and Beira open. The dam at Cabora Bassa, which was nearing completion, would sell much of its power to South Africa.

But it was the 100,000 black Mozambicans working on the Witwatersrand gold mines who were of greatest immediate economic importance. By traditional arrangement, 25 per cent of each labourer's wage was deferred, and paid to the Mozambique government in gold, calculated at the official rate of 42 dollars an ounce. The gold was then sold at the market rate, the labourer was paid on his return the quarter of his wage owed to him, and the rest went into the state coffers.

*It had been changed briefly to Can Phumo, thought to be an early anti-colonial hero, but later established as a pro-Portuguese collaborator.

White South Africans believed that they had come rather neatly out of the predicament of Mozambique independence. The only real hardship was that they were no longer welcome in 'L M'. Those whites who were allowed in on business still checked into the town's best-known hotel, the Polana, where the cautious barman was once heard to ask a white customer: 'What will you drink, comrade boss?'

For the black man and woman in South Africa, the coming of an independent black state was not altogether new. It had happened in Swaziland, Lesotho and Botswana. What was new was that this government had got there by force of arms; and having done so, had turned its back on the West. There can be no doubt that the example of Frelimo encouraged the black youth of Soweto in their efforts to liberate themselves from white rule.

Across the southern continent, in Angola, South Africa found it more difficult to adjust to the perils which followed the end of Portuguese power. Quite suddenly, this part of Africa began to intrude menacingly into the life of the white south. Now, as Portuguese soldiers withdrew, S W A P O guerrillas could leave their camps in Zambia and install themselves in southern Angola, within striking distance of Namibia.

S W A P O's support in Ovamboland had been proved by the success of its boycott call in the 1972 elections. As a result, the Government, through the Ovambo tribal authority, proceeded to make life uncomfortable for the liberation movement. S W A P O was not (nor is today) illegal, but its leaders and members were increasingly subjected to harassment by the security police throughout Namibia. They were held without trial, gaoled and tortured, often by electric-shock treatment.

In Ovamboland, under the state of emergency, the police and the tribal executive ruled as they wished. The tribal courts tried men and women simply because they belonged to S W A P O. They fined them, deprived them of their right to work in the south (there is virtually no employment in Ovamboland), flogged them. On one occasion, an Anglican schoolteacher was brought before Chief Minister Eliphas and a crowd of tribesmen to be flogged on his bare buttocks with the rib of a makalani palm branch. A leader of Demcop, a minor political party also opposed to white rule, was publicly flogged on his bare buttocks. One man was flogged thirty-one times for refusing to resign from SWAPO. He lost consciousness half-way through. Minister of Bantu Affairs M. C. Botha refused to intervene on the grounds that flogging was 'an old custom of the tribe'. The floggings continued until they were outlawed by the Bloemfontein appellate division in February 1975, well over a year after Lutheran and Anglican bishops had commenced legal proceedings against the tribal authority.

In the meantime, some 2000 SWAPO members had crossed the border into Angola to get away from the combined terrorism of white soldiers and black chiefs. They included many educated Ovambo teachers, nurses, church workers, policemen and members of the SWAPO youth league. Some were found places in schools and colleges around the world, others joined the guerrillas. But their departure seriously depleted SWAPO leadership in Ovamboland.

The collusion of Chief Eliphas and the chiefs of the two other tribal areas on the northern border, Okavango and the Caprivi Strip, helped the Government to proceed with its policy of divide and rule. In the 1960s, the Odendaal Commission had devised a system of Bantustans for Namibia on the same basis as that in the Republic. Again, the aim was to retain the vast bulk of the land in white hands, and to provide a sufficiency of cheap black migratory labour. The fragmentation of the country had an additional relevance in Namibia – the three northern Bantustans would provide a buffer against incursions from Angola and Zambia. Once they had been given 'self-government', their 'chief ministers' could invite the South African police and army to defend the borders.

Early in 1975, a second general election in Ovamboland saw a miraculous increase in polling from 2·5 per cent to 55 per cent; and victory for Eliphas's Independence Party, despite SWAPO's boycott call. Government, chiefs and radio had staked their all on a result which would prove the people's addiction to Bantustans. The election was held under a state of emergency, with the army in full control, and the S W A P O leadership no longer there to encourage defiance of the mighty organs of state. Observers were not allowed to witness the polling. There were widespread reports of vote-rigging and intimidation, with army patrols visiting villages to see who was voting. White lawyers who later visited the Bantustan seeking evidence to have the elections declared null and void found that their key witnesses were 'unavailable'. No case was brought.

In December 1974, the Security Council condemned South Africa's 'continued illegal occupation' of Namibia. Six months later, as the Council met once again to consider its next step, Foreign Minister Muller told U N Secretary-General Kurt Waldheim that South Africa's presence in Namibia was not that of an occupation force, but as an administering power which was there with the consent of and at the wish of the people. The Security Council was not impressed. The Afro-Asians tabled a motion calling for an immediate and mandatory arms embargo against South Africa. The motion was vetoed by Britain, the United States and France – on the grounds that the situation in South Africa was not a threat to world peace.

Mr Vorster's solution was the Turnhalle Conference, attended by delegations from each of the eleven 'tribes' (including the whites) designated by Pretoria as 'the true and authentic representatives of the inhabitants of South West Africa'. 'All options are open,' Mr Vorster told them. They might, if they wished, even choose a unitary state. Clearly, however, the ethnic nature of the conference indicated that a Bantustan solution was what South Africa had in store for them. Only the white, Coloured and Kavango delegations represented the majority of their tribes. Some delegates were hand-picked by white officials at a football match; there were allegations that the Damaras represented a minority grouping in their tribe which had been encouraged by the South African Bureau of State Security (B O S S); while many of the others, including a Bushman delegate, were on the payroll of the Government. S W A P O, which condemned Turnhalle as a device to perpetuate white rule, was not invited. It would not have come anyway, for it was a national, and not an ethnic organization.

Meanwhile, in southern Angola, the Portuguese had withdrawn from the border, making it easier for SWAPO to infiltrate across the Kunene river into Ovamboland. White soldiers, chiefs and their wives, tribesmen who were considered collaborators with the regime, were now direct targets for assassination. In August, Chief Eliphas, a hated symbol of South Africa's presence, was gunned down by unknown assailants. A headman, his wife and seven tribal policemen were killed in October, as SWAPO demonstrated its contempt for the Turnhalle Conference.

On 17 October, Defence Headquarters announced that South African troops had made a reprisal raid into Angola, destroying two SWAPO camps and killing seven guerrillas. Six days later, a column of 1200 South African troops crossed the border near the town of Pereira d'Eca, and the ill-fated invasion of Angola was under way.

Hopes for a peaceful transition to independence in Angola were hampered by one disastrous obstacle – the splintering of the nationalist struggle into three mutually-antagonistic movements, deployed on different fronts, and fighting with differing motivations. In Portugal's two other African colonies, Guinea Bissau and Mozambique, the dominant liberation armies were close to victory at the time of the Lisbon *coup*. In Angola this was far from the case.

The armed revolt against Portuguese colonialism had begun in February 1961, with an attempt to free political prisoners from Luanda's São Paulo prison. The attack failed; and the vengeance of the colonials was bloody in the extreme. The episode was a prelude a month later to an armed revolt by the Union of Angolan Peoples (later to become the Angolan National Liberation Front, or the FNLA) under Holden Roberto. It drew preponderant support from the northern Ba-Kongo, whose fellow tribesmen had recently won independence in the neighbouring French and Belgian Congos. But the revolt was put down with such savagery that as many as 300,000 people fled into the (Belgian) Congo, and the Front's effectiveness as a fighting force was much reduced.

Roberto's nationalist credentials were enthusiastically

accepted by most of black Africa; in addition, the movement received limited aid from the United States (the Central Intelligence Agency kept Roberto on a retainer), as well as, in time, arms and instructors from the People's Republic of China. Indeed, it was the sole recipient of aid and recognition from the Organization of African Unity until as late as 1971, when the Popular Movement for the Liberation of Angola (MPLA) was granted this status as well.

The MPLA had its roots in Luanda, where, in the fifties, followers had been imprisoned and sometimes shot by the police. Its supporters had taken part in the February 1961 attack on São Paulo prison. The MPLA leader, Agostinho Neto, a paediatrician, sometime leader of the Portuguese communist youth movement and escapee from detention in Portugal, launched a separate guerrilla campaign, first in the enclave of Cabinda, and then on the eastern front near Zambia.

Progress was slow, for the area of combat was sparsely populated, but the MPLA's socialist teachings did attempt to win support outside the narrow confines of tribalism. The popular movement received some arms from the Soviet Union, and at one stage from Peking as well. It also had a military training camp in Brazzaville, in the Congo Republic, organized by the Cubans.

The third movement, the National Union for the Total Liberation of Angola (UNITA), was the brain-child of Dr Jonas Savimbi. While Roberto's foreign minister, Savimbi had perceived that the FNLA was steeped in corruption, a pawn of the Americans, and no longer a fighting force. He founded UNITA in 1965, basing it almost exclusively on the Mbunda tribe in the south and west of Angola. Although small, the movement appears to have had bases deep inside the country and, like the MPLA, to have administered 'liberated areas'.

UNITA received some aid from Peking, but claims to have managed on arms seized in battle from the Portuguese and in clashes with the rival liberation armies. It was not well known abroad, and few foreign observers entered its territory; apart from Savimbi, it only really surfaced as a third force after the Lisbon *coup*. There is convincing evidence that, from at least

1972, UNITA were in collusion with the Portuguese army, who gave them arms to be used against the MPLA.

Not surprisingly, military successes were rare for all three movements, so that in 1972 Portugal was able to divert several thousand troops from Angola to the more active Mozambique front. Then came the *coup*, and each movement claimed to represent the people of Angola.

When the Portuguese army stopped fighting, the MPLA, though strong in ideological discipline, was significantly weaker in weapons than Roberto's National Liberation Front. The MPLA's ally, the Soviet Union, perhaps the more eagerly because of setbacks suffered in the Middle East, perceived Angola as an opportunity to establish a foothold in an area which had suddenly acquired immense strategic importance.

The American people, for their part, were in no mood for a foreign adventure that smelled ominously of another Vietnam. And this almost certainly encouraged Cuba to send troops to help the MPLA. In the first Cuban-authorized account of the war (see the *Washington Post*, 10–11 January 1977), the Colombian author Gabriel Garcia Marquez wrote of Castro's belief that the Ford Administration would think twice about intervening openly:

It had just freed itself from the quagmire of Vietnam and the Watergate scandal ... It had a president no one had elected. The CIA was under fire in Congress and low-rated by public opinion. The United States needed to avoid seeming – not only in the eyes of African countries, but especially in the eyes of American blacks – to ally itself with racist South Africa. Beyond all it was in the midst of an election campaign in Bicentennial year.

So United States intervention, like that of Russia, Cuba and South Africa, had to be clandestine. Secretary of State Henry Kissinger claimed the Russians began to exploit the situation as early as the autumn of 1974, through shipments of 'some arms and equipment to the MPLA'. However, personnel attached to the State Department's Africa Bureau claimed that Soviet escalation only began 'after our own decision to increase significantly the United States involvement'. There is, of course, no similar information coming out of the Kremlin. But the Russians had been aiding the MPLA intermittently for a decade, and it is difficult to draw the line between continuing aid and an increase amounting to an intervention in the internal affairs of a foreign country.

The White House, relieved of the need to support fascist Portugal in its colonial wars, now turned to Holden Roberto, the man whom it had been subsidizing for just such an eventuality. In January 1975, CIA funds, to the extent of 300,000 dollars, began flowing to the FNLA leader. It was the very month when the Lisbon generals were attempting to defuse the bitter rivalry between the three movements at a conference in Alvor, Portugal. The leaders agreed to set up a provisional government which would integrate their military forces into an Angolan army and hold elections prior to independence in November that year.

It was the cue for thousands of heavily armed FNLA guerrillas to leave Zaire and northern Angola and flood into Luanda. By late March they were involved in the first of a series of bloody clashes with the MPLA. With his men outnumbered, Neto asked Russia for more aid. And the Russians obliged.

The civil war broke out on 8 July, as the MPLA drove the two other 'armies' out of Luanda. The governments of Zambia and Zaire asked the United States for assistance. A high-level Administration review board, the 'Committee of Forty', headed by Dr Kissinger, decided on a substantial increase of aid to both the FNLA and UNITA. By early autumn the United States was flying in to its allies several million dollars of military equipment a month, which was channelled through Kinshasa's Ndjili airport, and then flown on to airfields that were in the hands of Roberto or Savimbi. The UNITA leader received 'several hundred thousand dollars in covert black box funds from the CIA'. The American Government also gave Zaire's President Mobutu (Roberto's brother-in-law) funds to buy arms from various European countries, especially Belgium, for use against the MPLA.

From August, Russia was able to step up arms deliveries to the MPLA – infantry weapons, machine guns, bazookas and rockets. One source estimates that Neto received 110 million dollars' worth of Soviet arms in 1975, or twice the amount that he received in all fourteen years of anti-colonial warfare. By the middle of October, less than a month before independence, the MPLA controlled all but four of Angola's sixteen provinces.

In his articles, Marquez explains that contacts between Cuba and the MPLA had been 'very intense' for a decade. In May 1975, Neto met a Cuban commandant in Brazzaville and requested military aid. In mid July, Marquez says, a week after the outbreak of the civil war, the MPLA again asked for aid. Fidel Castro then approached 'a leftist member of the junta in Lisbon', Colonel Otelo Saraiva de Carvalho, to arrange Portuguese permission for the aid. Carvalho, then on a visit to Havana, 'promised to see to it but his answer had not yet arrived'. Marquez continues:

When the Cuban troopship *Vietnam Heroico* arrived in Puerto Amboim at 6.30 a.m. on October 4, and the *Cora Island* arrived on the 7th and the *La Plata* at Punta Negra on the 11th, they docked without anyone's permission – but also without anyone's opposition.

The Cuban instructors were met by the MPLA and immediately set up the four training centres ...

Unfortunately, Marquez does not detail the number of 'instructors', their role or their fire-power. An American source put the force at about 200. All we know is that 'training centres' were set up in strategic areas of the country.

From across the 800-mile border, the South African Government watched with increasing alarm. Its immediate concern was to counteract the build-up of SWAPO forces, though in the long term it would also need a black regime which could be persuaded to make life difficult for guerrillas. If Angola, unlike Mozambique, was not a captive of the Republic's economic magnet, there was still room for exercising influence. By 1975, trade was going up in leaps and bounds, though it was weighted heavily in South Africa's favour (wheat, fruit, pharmaceuticals, and the prospect of selling mining machinery; in exchange for coffee). A small band of white South African cattle farmers in the south around Serpa Pinto and Silva Porto indicated the attractions of this virtually unexploited land. Or, as a commercial attaché at the South African consulate in Luanda told the author:

'The Portuguese had this fantastic country for 500 years and they did bugger all with it.' (The consulate offices, like those of France and some other Western countries, were in the Presidente building, Luanda's tallest. It was part-owned by President Mobutu Sese Seko of Zaire – providing yet another pressing reason for his brother-in-law to take over the country.)

Had the MPLA been the sole victor in the anti-Portuguese war, the South Africans would have had little choice but to come to terms with them. But, unlike the situation in Mozambique, there were other, non-Marxist, organizations willing to invite South Africa in, rather than see the MPLA take over the country. And if the two other movements hated each other with some intensity, they did have one allurement: they were ready and willing to allow continued Western exploitation of the country's natural resources.

Pretoria, taken by surprise at FRELIMO's swift accession to power in Mozambique, now had more time to prepare for a different dénouement in Angola. Once the MPLA showed signs of gaining the upper hand, Pretoria began to woo UNITA. The author was told by Edmund Malone, South Africa's consul in Luanda, in May 1975, that 'unofficially we support Savimbi'.

Yet the flamboyant Savimbi was an unsatisfactory man on whom to pin South Africa's hopes. Extravagant claims during the anti-colonial war, ideological fluctuations that at one stage took in Marxism, and the personality cult of its leadership, marked out UNITA as an unreliable ally. When the author talked to Savimbi in May 1975, he showed a distinct softening of attitude towards South Africa. For eight years, he said, SWAPO had used UNITA-liberated 'areas, guns and men against the Portuguese and the Boers'. Now, when asked whether a UNITA government would allow SWAPO to continue guerrilla activities across the border into Namibia, he replied: 'We have our problems ... South Africa has the best army in Africa. Anybody who has to fight South Africa must be realistic.'

It was, however, the FNLA which made the first move in enlisting South Africa's aid. In July, after the outbreak of the civil war, the military commander in the south, Daniel Chipenda, visited the Namibia capital, Windhoek, for talks with the head of BOSS, General van den Bergh. Early in August, a platoon of South African troops crossed twelve miles into Angola to guard the dam being built at Calueque on the Cunene River. The dam was part of a R125-million hydro-electric complex on both sides of the border which would irrigate Ovamboland and provide power for the further exploitation of Namibia's mineral resources. The Portuguese government protested at this unilateral occupation of territory over which it still held sovereignty, but the troops stayed. The minor invasion was widely publicized abroad – though the South African public, subject to military censorship, was not told about it until several months later.

Early in August, Savimbi 'regretfully' declared war on the MPLA, and entered into a grudging alliance with Roberto. A month later, with the MPLA probing deep into the UNITA ethnic heartland in the south, Savimbi turned to South Africa for assistance. He was quickly furnished with military equipment and a training mission. The South Africans, who had been engaged in 'hot pursuit' operations against SWAPO guerrillas, now found it easier to come to grips with their main adversary. On 23 October, less than three weeks before independence, a convoy of the South African regular army, code-named 'Zulu', crossed the border at Oshikango.

The column, numbering some 1200 men, was equipped with armoured cars, jeeps and personnel carriers, and possessed a formidable range of gun-power. In a short time, 'Zulu' captured Pereira d'Eca, the first town of any size inside Angola; Sá da Bandeira; and the port towns of Moçâmedes, Lobito, Benguela, and Novo Redondo.

It began to look as though a South African army of occupation would be in Luanda by 11 November, to hand over the keys of the country to its UNITA and FNLA allies. Neto turned to his friend Fidel Castro for help, and on 7 November a Bristol Britannia BB-218 turboprop left Havana airport crammed full of Cuban soldiers. The operation was code-named 'Carlota', in honour of a famale slave who, according to Marquez, had 'taken machete in hand to lead a slave uprising' in 1843, and was killed in the process. As the aircraft was arriving in Luanda, three ships loaded with an artillery regiment, a mechanized battalion and recoil-less rifles, set sail from Cuba. At one stage, there were fifteen Cuban ships on the high seas, sailing with arms and men to Angola.

From Marquez's account, it appears that the MPLA were reluctant to invite Cuban troops – or any foreigners – to rescue them. Indeed, Neto had delayed his request a whole fortnight – but by early November, the situation was desperate. Marquez reports that the Cuban Communist Party leadership had only twenty-four hours to make the decision, which it took 'without flinching in a large, calm meeting on November 5'. It was an independent and sovereign act, he says, and 'only after the decision was made, not before, was the Soviet Union informed.' But even if this were so, the Russians were by then flooding Angola with weapons of war, all of which were also part of the Cuban soldier's armoury.

In the meantime, the two-pronged 'Zulu', helped by white Angolan mercenaries, Savimbi's forces and the FNLA under Daniel Chipenda, advanced 600 miles to within sixty-five miles of Luanda, and pressed up the centre of the country to Texeira de Sousa, where the Benguela railway ran into Zaire. As the front stabilized, the MPLA were left with a narrow column of territory, 300 miles at its widest, stretching from the Atlantic to Zaire. It was the tribal area of the Mbundu, from whom the MPLA drew particular support.

The campaign now depended on the attack from the north by the FNLA under Roberto himself. The pincer would cut Luanda off from the interior and leave Neto's forces an easy prey before independence day. For obvious reasons, South African troops were not to take part in the final assault on the capital. On 6 November, a South African senior army officer reached FNLA headquarters at Ambriz, 100 miles to the north of Luanda. The FNLA, helped by a large force of Zairian soldiers, attacked southwards, but the MPLA, their nerve stiffened by the Cuban troops, repulsed them. South Africa's allies had suffered their first setback.

Back in South Africa, blanket military censorship had been imposed on the invasion. All that newspaper readers and radio listeners knew was that a mystery column of black soldiers led by white officers was sweeping up southern Angola. Foreign Minister Hilgard Muller solemnly told a London audience that his country was not involved.

Then, on 14 December, Minister of Defence P. W. Botha announced that four young, white national servicemen had fallen into the hands of the MPLA. The prisoners were flown to Nigeria, which had earlier recognized the M P L A government, and pictures of them manacled to one another appeared in South African newspapers. Now all pretence that the army was merely in Angola to guard the dam or on some 'hot pursuit' mission was ended; for it required a great deal of heat to pursue the enemy 600 miles across foreign territory.

In mid December, with over 7000 Cuban troops pitted against it, the South African army (by now numbering at least 4000 men) suffered a telling defeat at the Battle of the Bloody Triangle, south-east of Luanda. The Cubans threw in a formidable weapon nicknamed 'Stalin's organ' by the South Africans, which fired a salvo of forty rockets at a time. 'We were not routed, as some of your newspapers said,' P. W. Botha told an American journalist later, though he admitted that his troops did withdraw after that. The real rout, however, came from Washington.

Over the years, the United States had voted for United Nations resolutions condemning South Africa's illegal occupation of Namibia. But, since the late 1960s, the Republican administration – and Dr Kissinger in particular – had pursued a policy, known as the 'Tar Baby option', which involved a more conciliatory attitude to the white regimes of southern Africa. Washington had imposed an embargo on arms for South Africa, but this had not stopped borderline encroachments, as with the delivery of C–130 transport planes to the South African Air Force. Suspicions that the two countries were in closer concert than was publicly realized had been encouraged by the visit to Washington of the South African defence chief, Admiral Biermann, within weeks of Caetano's overthrow.

Now, on 21 December, the Senate put a stop to all C I A aid in Angola. Dr Kissinger's strategy of keeping the Soviet Union guessing over his intentions was in ruins; the M P L A, assured of victory; and the South African army, stranded.

Ambassador Pik Botha flew home to a meeting of political and military leaders, presided over by the Prime Minister. The decision was taken to withdraw from Angola on 5 January. But the Organization of African Unity summit conference was to be held in Addis Ababa on the ninth, and Kissinger needed a bargaining chip to reassure his allies that they would not be left in the lurch. He persuaded Vorster to delay the withdrawal; so making it easier for Zambia, Zaire, Kenya and the conservative Francophone nations to deny O A U recognition to Neto's government. Africa was split down the middle, 22 to 22, and the Organization was unable to censure South Africa's intervention.

A fortnight later, the white army withdrew to a line fifty kilometres from the border, with the dual intention of guarding the pumping-station site at Calueque, and discouraging a sea of black refugees from flooding into Namibia. (The white Angolans were flown to Portugal.) The last white soldier crossed into Namibia at the end of March. By then, all but a handful of African states had recognized the M P L A.

The South African public were told of these events piecemeal, when it suited the Government to disclose them, or when there was no alternative. Strangely, the censorship had little to do with preventing the enemy from knowing about troop movements. The whole world knew of the invasion at an early stage. White South Africans who listened to the B B C or subscribed to foreign newspapers were fully informed, but they were few and far between. The main internal aim of censorship was to keep the blacks in ignorance of the war. There was good reason to doubt their approval.

It is dangerous for a country to fight a war when five sixths of the population are either neutral or rooting for the enemy. The blacks, of course, were not consulted, but public comments by even the conservative Bantustan leaders left no room for doubt. Professor Hudson Ntsanwisi, chief minister of Gazankulu, whose Shangaan tribe straddled the border with Mozambique, noted: 'Our restless youth is espousing the cause of the M P L A.' Referring to P. W. Botha's claim that an M P L A victory could lead to 'the enslavement of the whole of southern

Africa', the Professor said: 'People are saying, "The devil we don't know cannot be worse than the devil we do know."' Another chief minister, Cedric Phatudi of Lebowa, called the invasion a mistake. 'If the blacks don't have a stake in the country, they cannot give it their full loyalty.'

Sonny Leon, leader of the Labour Party, representing the moderates of the Coloured people, declared: 'I will never tell my people to fight for the perpetuation of white baasskap. It would be unfair to expect Coloured soldiers to risk their lives for their country when they are still being treated as second-class citizens.' And these were the voices of blacks working within the apartheid system. Those outside were rather more emphatic. The Black People's Convention called the MPLA 'liberators', whose victory would carry 'the greatest possibility for significant change in the sub-continent.'

The *World* newspaper asked its black readers if they 'would fight for South Africa if we are invaded from Angola'. Of the 244 replies, 203 were noes. Some of those questioned permitted themselves a little joke. 'I'm a Bantu homeland citizen, so I'd be indulging myself in foreign politics – South Africa's', said one. Another asked 'how can a black man be expected to fight with the *dompas* [pass book] in his pocket, because if he leaves it at home he will be arrested.'

These utterances prompted one senior general to warn of the dangers in failing to accommodate the rising hopes and expectations of the country's blacks. Yet when Parliament at last reassembled in late January, P. W. Botha could still declare: 'We do not want to become the slaves of Russia', and adjure fellow MPs to 'show the will to be free'. He might have been talking to the inhabitants of another planet. The unit of 190 'non-white' soldiers who did fight – and suffer losses – for South Africa in the border area, were seen as pitiful sell-outs by other blacks. They were also paid far less than whites for defending apartheid.

The need for surreptitiousness was also dictated by South Africa's pariah status in the world. No black movement could safely afford to be seen as acting in conjunction with the forces of apartheid. Once it was proven that Savimbi and Roberto were

131

in cahoots with South Africa, their support in the Afro-Asian world withered away. It could not have been otherwise. The Russo-Cuban presence might have caused shivers up the spines of neighbouring black presidents, but at least the communists didn't practise apartheid at home. So Savimbi continued to deny his collaboration with Pretoria, even as he was being carried to the gates of Luanda. All the other pro-Western parties – FNLA, Zaire, Zambia, the United States, France and Britain – did their best to distance themselves, in public, from the 'mystery column'.

The war or, more accurately, the 'non-war', exposed white South Africa to a bewildering array of emotions. Scenes at railway stations were of Second World War vintage, as tearful mums and dads and girlfriends waved goodbye to teenage national servicemen off to the 'operational area'. When calls went out for Christmas pudding for 'our boys on the border', parents could not be sure whether the celebration would take place on the Kunene River or 600 miles further north. The soldiers' radio request programme after lunch on Saturdays was punctuated with 'can't wait to see you' and '*vasbyt*' (literally, grit your teeth). Hardly a day passed without a funeral in some town or village. (Officially, twenty-nine South Africans had died in action by late February, and another fourteen in 'accidents'.) Often a burial notice would appear in the newspapers before the official announcement of death from military headquarters.

When at long last SA television made its debut in the first week of January, it was the British-made saga 'The World at War' which captured the white imagination. Many Afrikaners in particular were having their first look at the workings of Nazi racism. Get-togethers of commando (part-time) units scheduled for Tuesday night were often moved to other evenings, or few members would have turned up. The reporting of the current war, however, in which South Africans were killing and being killed, was almost totally ignored.

The news blackout served another useful purpose. It avoided embarrassing criticism from the *verkrampte* (or 'black-is-Bolshevik') wing of Afrikaner nationalism. Thus, a Transvaal doctor wrote to his newspaper to say that he had advised his son, who had fought with the South African police on the Rhodesian border, to resign if forced to serve in Angola:

In Rhodesia you defended your country and white civilization in southern Africa against the black terrorists, and if you had died there we would have been proud of you. But if you go to Angola, you will be helping one Communistic black terrorist gang against another similar gang and for that even a single drop of Afrikaner blood is too much.

The elevation of 'hot pursuit' into an everyday habit of life on the border was certainly not, as Mr Vorster claimed, an acceptable tenet of international law. The fact that 'hot pursuit', like the invasion of Angola itself, was launched from the illegally occupied Namibia made its use even more dubious. South Africa has also consistently refused to grant prisoner-of-war status under the Geneva Convention to captured guerrillas, despite S W A P O's recognition by the United Nations as the authentic representative of the Namibian people. Precious little is heard of what happens to these guerrillas, though military reports indicate that substantial numbers have been captured. S W A P O claims that many are simply shot or allowed to die from their wounds.

Under the Ovambo emergency regulations, anyone suspected of committing any offence, or intending to do so, or simply having information about an offence, can be arrested without warrant and held for questioning until the authorities are satisfied that all questions have been fully and truthfully answered. The regulation, however draconian it might be, is unnecessary. During a trial in Namibia in 1976 a former freedom fighter disclosed that he had been captured in Ovamboland in 1969 and held without charge in Pretoria for three years (he would still have been there, no doubt, had he not been 'persuaded' to give evidence for the State). No law allowed the police to do that.

South Africa's disregard for prisoners' rights included captured Cubans. The wounded were treated in Rundu in the Kavango Bantustan or in the Vootrekkerhoogte military hospital in Pretoria, and were visited by the Red Cross. But the healthy ones were handed over to what Defence Minister Piet Botha called the 'provisional government of South Angola'. Nothing seems to have been heard of them since.

The clearest illegality of all concerned the status of the men fighting the war. Under statute law, a soldier could not be made to fight outside the country's borders without his written consent. As the large bulk of the South African forces in Angola – estimated at one stage to be 4500 – were national servicemen under the legal majority age of twenty-one, it was their parents whose permission was required. In February, Parliament hurriedly amended the law to provide retrospective legality to the invasion. Since then, South African soldiers have been ordered to fight abroad whether they wish to or not.

These were all matters that could be handled in the typical cavalier manner – by imprisonment without trial, retrospective legislation or a blanket of silence. The external consequences of South Africa's invasion, however, were more difficult to stage-manage. It was, in the words of Vorster, a 'severe setback' to the policy of 'normalizing' relations with black Africa.

Mr Vorster saw the invasion as a crusade against communism in defence of the 'free world' (of which South Africa claimed membership) against Russian imperialism and to keep the Cape sea route open to Western shipping. When the United States pulled out of the war, cabinet ministers reacted with a mixture of anger and hurt disbelief. P. W. Botha referred ironically to 'what has happened in the greatest country in the Free World'. White politicians agreed they were on their own now. It was up to them to keep Africa free of communists, for the West was no longer reliable.

It is possible that the invasion was intended to be a show of strength, a warning shot that the white army was not to be trifled with. If this were so, it proved to be a grievous mistake. The black people of South Africa believed, rightly or wrongly, that their white soldiers had been given a bloody nose by the black Angolans. A small chink had appeared in the monolithic armour of the country's defence system. Coming so soon after the victory of the Frelimo 'terrorists', this had an incalculable impact on urban blacks. Small wonder that a former South African Air Force commandant described the Angolan adventure as his country's Bay of Pigs.

Now, white people devoted themselves to talking about 'change'. The heady prospect of an end to race discrimination that was heralded by Vorster's 'give us six months' plea, was soon put in perspective by the Prime Minister's explanation that he needed the time not in order to make internal changes, 'but to change South Africa's position in the world'. If the blacks were looking for meaningful improvements in their lot, they were in for a disappointment. To begin with, they had been given the scent of a 'better life'. A few days before the 'six months' was due to expire, Bantu Affairs Minister M. C. Botha announced that Africans in the urban areas would be able to obtain thirty-year leases on their houses. The white Press hailed it as a 'sweeping concession'; or just the sort of move to dampen down the restlessness of the natives.

There turned out to be one crucial catch to this new deal on housing. A full six months later (the week of the invasion of Angola), Mr Van Onselen, secretary for Bantu administration and development, disclosed that in order to qualify for the lease the householder would first have to produce a certificate of citizenship in a Bantustan. People who had never seen the Transkei or Lebowa or Kwa-Zulu would be forced to identify with one or other of these phantasmagoric 'homelands'. Only a handful of lease applications were ever made. The potentially most stable section of Soweto's population, people willing to invest their hard-earned money in a precarious dormitory city, were deeply disillusioned. It pushed resentment to breaking point and contributed to the explosion of June.

The episode throws an incidental sidelight on the impotence of the Cape Town Parliament – and on the autocratic use of government by decree. Van Onselen's devastating aside about the citizenship requirement came out casually in an address to a conference of 'non-European' administrators. No legislation was needed. Junior white officials, with absolute discretion over the lives of black people, were simply instructed to refuse a long

lease if the applicant was not prepared to give up his South
African citizenship.

Such peripheral changes as there were in the year leading up
to Soweto were aimed almost exclusively at the small middle
class. Four- and five-star hotels were granted 'international
status', which allowed them to let up to 10 per cent of the rooms
to blacks. These guests could not set foot on the hotel dance
floor (not even, it seems, partnering their wives), nor drink in the
great white South African male redoubt, the 'men's bar'. The
hotel swimming pool was reserved for 'bona fide' guests. In
addition, ordinary hotels were open to foreign blacks, who might
be asked to show a passport as proof of identity. They seldom
were. A local black with a clean suit and tie could wine and dine
with white friends in a white hotel, as long as the proprietor
believed him to be an American judge or a Zambian diplomat.

When the author travelled from Johannesburg to Cape Town
at Christmas 1975, the luxury Blue Train had become 'international'. The white coaches were fully booked, but white
passengers were not allowed to take up empty compartments in
the one coach for 'non-whites'. Three black passengers were on
board. Here was a good example of how separate development
costs money. I am sure that the passengers – American, Dutch,
British tourists, and well-to-do South Africans – would have
preferred to spend twenty-four hours next door to a black man
rather than not get a booking at all.

Blacks were allowed to eat in the dining car, but there was
one un-South African 'concession'. Whites wishing to eat meals
in their compartments had to pay a one-rand service charge.
There was no charge for blacks. One of the three travelling
blacks, a man disinterested in economy, did venture out for
lunch. He was shown to a table on his own, and no one was
permitted to join him. Hungry white passengers had to wait
for the next session.

The Johannesburg public-library reading room was desegre-
gated, but a library in Bloemfontein refused to lend playscripts
to an Indian theatre group in Pietermaritzburg.

The most publicized of all the 'concessions' was the opening
of the Nico Malan Opera House in Cape Town to mixed

136

audiences. When completed in the early seventies, many white Capetonians boycotted performances in the two fine theatres because of the 'whites only' restriction. After all, the multi-million-rand complex had been paid for with money from all the races, and there was nothing remotely resembling a plush opera house in Cape Town for Coloureds or Africans.

The Nico Malan was due to open with a performance of *Aida*, but when the Italian lead fell ill, the opera was replaced. Nobody could be found to play the dark-skinned Radames. Yet at the time, a Coloured tenor from Cape Town, Joseph Gabriels, was being acclaimed at the Metropolitan Opera House in New York.

When Dame Margot Fonteyn danced to the tune of apartheid in the Nico Malan, she was picketed by the middle-class white ladies of the Black Sash. Early in January 1975, the Nationalist administrator of the Cape Province announced that other 'population groups' would be accommodated at the opera house. It seemed as if a local boycott and international embarrassment had for once achieved a breakthrough. But then the administrator clarified his announcement. Mixed audiences would be allowed only from Tuesdays to Fridays. On Mondays and Saturdays, it was to be white only. The outcry that followed led to the intervention of the Cape leader of the National Party, Minister of Defence Piet Botha. Within three days the Nico Malan became a mixed opera-house. It was, however, as Interior Minister Connie Mulder soon pointed out, not to be regarded as a precedent for other theatres.

The concession only applied to audiences. Mixed casts are still forbidden in the theatre. In Bloemfontein, just to reassert its Voortrekker independence, the city council agreed to allow mixed casts on the stage of the Civic Centre, but insisted on segregation in the auditorium.

Nearly all the 'liberalizations', however tentative, resulted not from changes in the law, but from the granting of special permits which could be revoked at any time. When some municipalities took down 'Europeans Only' signs from park benches (the Afrikaans version is more precise – *Blankes Alleenlik*, or Whites Only), the government warned that if it led to 'friction', the signs would be restored. But the Reservation of Separate

Amenities Act and the Group Areas Act, the source of so much separation in South African life, were not repealed.

The only laws of any importance to be removed from the statute book were the nineteenth-century master and servant acts under which unskilled (i.e. black) workers were gaoled for deserting without good reason, or refusing to obey a lawful command or using abusive language towards an employer. The immediate cause of the repeal, however, was a court action in Alabama brought by the state attorney-general and the mine-workers' union to stop the importation of coal from South Africa. The U S Tariff Act prohibited the import of goods produced by indentured labour. Repeal removed the basis of the union's case.

Of real change – change that would directly involve a shift in the power structure of the country – there was not the slightest suggestion. A just redistribution of land, nationalization of the mines, a representative place in Parliament – in short, a black role in making decisions about the whole of South Africa – simply talking about these matters invited arrest and imprisonment. A Soweto African remarked to the author early in 1976: 'In Mozambique they have a black socialist republic and here we are arguing about theatre tickets.'

In a newspaper interview to mark his sixtieth birthday in December 1975, the Prime Minister was asked whether he had a message for the coming year. 'The main thing', he advised, 'is to remain cool and calm because 1976, as I see it, will be a decisive year. I think it will bring most of the answers to questions about which we are wondering now and speculating on.'

As the dimensions of South Africa's diplomatic débâcle in Angola became known, the grand debate on 'change' moved into top gear. Afrikaner leaders eagerly seized the chance to have their say on the need for a new attitude. The Chief Justice, Frans Rumpff, warned white students that if they could not accept social equality with other races, they had 'better find what they want elsewhere'. Willem de Klerk, editor of *Die Transvaler*, the official organ of the Nationalist Party in Johannesburg, called in his paper for the review of 'humiliating' laws, while the editor of *Rapport* listed 'pass laws, migratory labour, apartheid signs, wages, homeland boundaries, property and trading rights for urban Africans, job reservation, holiday resorts, education, hotels, sport, religion, etc.' as areas where changes might be necessary. A member of the cabinet, Health Minister Dr Schalk van der Merwe, entered the lists to warn that racial discrimination must be 'cast off'. Anyone who still believed South Africans could continue their traditional racial attitude was living in a fool's paradise, he said.

Mr Vorster, perhaps to prove the point, chose Dr Andries Treurnicht, head of the *Broederbond*, Afrikanerdom's legal but clandestine mafia, as Deputy Minister of Bantu Education and Development. Treurnicht represented the far-right wing of nationalism, and the promotion was seen as an attempt to still criticism of the Angolan invasion. The furthest reaches of that right wing had broken away some years before to form the HNP (Reconstituted National Party) and the Prime Minister feared another split in Afrikanerdom.

Vorster's problem was – and remains today – that his party was a prisoner of its past. For twenty years before Nationalism came to power just after the war, its only real platform was the protection of the white man. When in government, it lost no time in separating everything that moved. It did nothing to prepare the populace of Afrikanerdom for change. At not one of the previous year's five provincial congresses of the party had a single resolution been introduced, either from the floor or the executive, calling for a relaxation of 'petty apartheid'.

Despite the ominous signs of instability in many areas of the country's life, the National Party still ruled with an iron hand. The outward instrument of its power was the Cape Town Parliament, where it held 121 of the 171 seats in the (lower) House of Assembly. But Parliament was simply a rubber stamp for decisions taken by the cabinet and the party caucus. The two opposition parties were mainly representative of the English-speaking voters, and on certain issues the United Party's stance was well to the right of the Government's. All three parties were elected by white votes only, and the policy of each provided the solution for maintaining white control of the country. The real opposition was in the black townships, though this fact was scarcely reflected in the demeanour of the government and its supporters.

Nothing, however, could hide the fact that large sections of the population were unhappy with their lot. In the session before Soweto, Parliament voted two of the most arbitrary pieces of legislation on the African continent. The first of these was the Parliamentary Internal Security Commission Act, irreverently acronymed P I S C O M by its opponents. The task of the commission was to investigate matters affecting 'internal security', which simply meant any person or organization opposed to apartheid. With powers similar to those of a supreme (or high) court, it could fine and imprison anyone for refusing to appear before it or for failing to answer questions or produce documents. Its proceedings were to be held behind closed doors, and its participants were sworn to secrecy. P I S C O M was to be South Africa's version of Joe McCarthy's senate hearings into un-American activities, with the vital difference that at least in the United States there were democratic institutions capable of bringing these awesome powers to an end.

The other major security law introduced in 1976, the Promotion of State Security Bill, was immediately nicknamed the 'S S' bill, so that the embarrassed Minister of Justice, James Kruger, had its title changed to 'Internal Security'. There was no need to do so, for even the spokesman for the United Party, which had long been ambivalent about protecting the rule of law, characterized the measure as 'fascist despotism'. Previous detention-without-trial laws had at least held out the prospect of an eventual charge or release. The new law provided for detention for life of people 'engaged in activities which endanger the security of the State or the maintenance of public order'. The Government was giving itself emergency powers without having to declare a state of emergency.

And of all the factors which contributed to the Soweto explosion of 16 June, economic hardship was not the least. With military spending going up and the price of gold staying down, the white-managed economy was suffering its worst year since the Nationalists came to power. As usual, it was the lowest category of workers, the Africans, who bore the brunt of the worsening recession. If an African had managed to find a 'white' job, then he was the first out when the dismissal notices were posted. Because of the large number of under-employed in the subsistence economy of the Bantustans and the unknown hundreds of thousands living 'illegally' in the cities, the unemployment level is almost impossible to estimate. The most depressing figure was given by the University of Cape Town economist Charles Simkins, who calculated that by the end of 1976 two million would be out of a job, or between 15 and 20 per cent of the economically active population. Simkins was later banned by the Minister of Justice; perhaps an indication that he might have been closer to the truth in his figure than more conservative colleagues.

Even Africans lucky enough to have a job encountered a most depressing prospect. In the first five years of the decade, the average monthly African wage had doubled from R36 to R72. Taking inflation into account, this provided a real increase of a mere 7 per cent. The figure was still substantially lower than the poverty datum line, the level below which a family could not care for itself decently. In 1976, factory workers found their wages increasing at 9 per cent, compared with 15 per cent the year before. And the gap between white and African continued to widen. In 1970, the average white household had earned R362 a month more than its African counterpart. Five years later, the difference was R546.

A particularly glaring example of discrimination against the lowest-paid section of the community was to be found in the way that Africans were taxed. They contributed R36 million to the treasury in the year ending April 1975, compared with the R687 million of the whites. This figure did not include the vast amounts raised by indirect taxation. Furthermore, an African started to pay income tax at a salary of R360 a year, whatever his age or the size of his family. Unmarried Whites, Coloureds and Indians, on the other hand, only began their income tax contributions at a salary of R700 (and if they were over sixty years old, at R1000). An African with three children paid R65 52c on a salary of R2760, while his counterparts in the other race groups only began to pay tax at an annual income of R2800.

African widows are treated as single people without regard to the children they might have to support, while widows in other race groups are granted married status and so pay less tax. Again, unlike the other races, African householders in urban areas pay a compulsory monthly levy towards the cost of building schools for their children. And Africans are also denied deductions allowed to others as a matter of course, like abatements for children and dependants, medical and dental expenses, and life insurance premiums. In addition to income tax, every African male, be he university professor or mine worker, pays an annual flat rate 'poll' or head tax of R2 50c.

And, in company with the Indian and Coloured, whatever the African has to pay into the state coffers of Pretoria, his contribution contradicts the classic democratic principle of 'no taxation without representation'.

Four months before the outbreak of the black student rebellion, I joined a coach party of foreign visitors on a tour of Soweto. We gathered on the second floor of the West Rand Administration Board (WRAB) offices, at the corner of Delver and Albert Streets, Johannesburg, for an introductory briefing. Mrs Marlene van Heerden welcomed us with a professional smile. 'Soweto is 100 square kilometres in extent and is the biggest Bantu township in South Africa. The word "Bantu",' she reminded us, 'is favoured by the blacks because it distinguishes them from the Indians and Coloureds.' But the Bantu were themselves divided into separate nations, the Zulus, Tswanas, Xhosas and so on, 'each of which will eventually become citizens of their [lingering over the word] OWN countries. This is the policy of our Government.

'And now, ladies and gentlemen, will you please proceed to the bus for the tour of Soweto . . .'

Driver and guide was Jack Pienaar, friendly soul, ready to answer any – well, almost any – questions. We called first at a large brewery where they made Soweto's famed 'Bantu beer' – the old name of 'kaffir beer' has long been out of official favour. Above the roar of the machines a brewery supervisor recited figures about beer consumption, alcohol content and proteins.

He winked at us. 'It is very nutritious and they LOVE it.'

We drove another five miles, past eerie mine dumps, and Africans on bicycles, and the Coloured township of Noordgesig, *cordon sanitaire* between African location and white suburbia. We entered Soweto at Orlando and drove along the dual carriageway. Jack piled on the facts. 'Soweto may sound to you like some Bantu name, but it is derived from the first two letters of South Western Townships, SO-WE-TO.' Population 650,000, 14 railway stations, 252 schools, 5 millionaires, free libraries.

The February sun beat down as our air-conditioned coach nosed into Orlando Stadium, home of the fabled 'Bantu soccer team', the Orlando Pirates. Jack described a match in which several spectators had been knifed. 'Hell, man, they get carried away,' shaking his head ruefully. A Lancastrian in the party offered him Manchester United supporters in exchange. We drove on. 'Now coming up on the left is the first house to be built in Soweto. If we are lucky we might catch a glimpse of Mrs Mpetla . . .'

Lo and behold, as we crawled past, there was the old lady and her broom, just happening to be sweeping her highly polished stoep, but not without the time to give us a cheery wave. Murmur from Johannesburg housewife to visiting English mum: 'You see how friendly they are.'

For a few minutes there was silence, as the tourists observed the unending drabness of the houses. There were 100,000 'housing units' in Soweto, said Jack, and a waiting list of 1200. From the back of the coach an inquisitive American asked: 'Could we go inside, take a look maybe?' Jack kept his foot on the accelerator, peering into his rear view mirror to catch a glimpse of his passenger. 'You know, I have been asked that before, but you see Bantu women are very houseproud and if we just turn up at her front door without prior notice she will be very embarrassed if she hasn't finished her housework.' Question answered.

In the distance loomed the stark single-man hostels, each housing 5000 and more migrant workers. 'They're virile chaps, you know,' Jack observed. 'We let them do tribal dancing to use up their energy. Otherwise they might take it out on the other Bantu.'

Jack swung into a side road and announced with noticeable pride: 'Ladies and gentlemen, we are entering Dube, where the rich people live. They call it the Black Houghton, after the smart white suburb.' We drove past a few pleasant but modest homes, and the occupiers were identified – the Anglican Bishop of Johannesburg, Dean Desmond Tutu (not sweeping his stoep); the accredited representative of the Transkei government; a witchdoctor. There was even a bowling green, the only one in the country for Bantu. We criss-crossed Dube for some minutes, so that it seemed as though these nice little houses were the rule and not the exception in Soweto. Jack omitted to mention that John Dube, after whom the suburb was named – he founded the country's first vernacular newspaper *Ilanga lase Natal* in 1871 – once declared that 'justice will only be done when the African rules the country.'

'Education,' announced Jack Pienaar, speeding through dreary Jabavu; 'the central government spends R60 million a year [about £40 million] on the education of the Bantu, who only pay R36 million in taxes. We make up the difference for them. There are 274 schools, but less than one in a hundred Bantu gets through matric. I suppose it's a cultural difference, you know, because they don't lack intelligence.'

Jack decelerates. 'On my right is the Star Bioscope, which belongs to Mr Tshabalala, the richest man in Soweto. He also owns a department store, and I think it is safe to say he is a millionaire.' Jack didn't hide his pride in Mr Tshabalala's achievements.

It was mid morning and we called at the Oppenheimer Tower for tea. The tower is named after another millionaire, the late Sir Ernest Oppenheimer, who launched the first big housing scheme in Soweto. Another tourist was getting inquisitive. Why, in the heart of black Soweto, was this tea-room for whites only? Jack smiled as we clustered around to listen to his reply. 'No, man, it isn't quite so. I was actually here last week when an American negro was having tea – with a white man.' No further questions.

'Coming up on the left, Baragwanath Hospital, the largest in the southern hemisphere, and they do everything for the Bantu here. It has 3000 beds, 2500 nurses, 100 kilometres of hot water pipes, 500 doctors, but only 5 Bantu doctors. They prefer private practice.' (Again he was silent on the fact that only six of the country's most recent batch of 700 medical graduates were Africans, and that Baragwanath paid them three quarters of the white doctors' salaries.)

We rolled back along the motorway towards Johannesburg's fifty-storey skyline. As we were getting out of the coach, an elderly lady in a trouser suit whispered to me, in a Birmingham accent: 'Should I tip?' Madam, he's a white man, you know. She shook Jack Pienaar by the hand instead and thanked him for putting her right about the natives.

It was still fairly easy in those days for an outsider to enter Soweto. Whites, Indians and Coloureds had to obtain a permit for a 'Bantu township' or face a fine and even imprisonment. One could drive around for days without being asked for the permit by a policeman, but for a journalist to be found without one would mean his physical exclusion from one of the most fertile areas of reporting in the country. Foreign journalists had to be cleared by the Department of Information at Pretoria, but I put on my best South African accent and persuaded Mr Phillips at the administration offices in Johannesburg that despite seven years in England I was still a true son of the veld. There was one proviso, said Phillips, as he filled in the permit. 'No photographs. We don't want any of that dustbin stuff.'

What do you mean, Mr Phillips? 'You know, those people who come in from overseas and throw money into a dustbin in Soweto and then take pictures of the Bantu fighting for it. It looks as though they are scrounging for food. They say our Bantu suffer from malnutrition but if you look carefully at the pictures you can see they are all very healthy.'

Phillips gave me a three-week permit, a sort of multiple re-entry visa to what was, for most whites, another country. The document, issued under article 9(9) (b) of the Bantu (Urban

Areas) Consolidation Act, no. 25 of 1945 (as amended) permitted me to enter Soweto from eight to four on weekdays and from eight to noon on Saturdays for the sole purpose of 'reporting'. The permit was valid only 'if used for the purpose for which it was issued'. So if I were caught in there on Sunday or at night, even without taking photographs, I could still render myself liable to prosecution.

My immediate concern was to find out how the ordinary Soweton could survive the pressures of the 'white' city. The opportunity arose in the form of Agnes Ngwyena, who cleaned the room of my hotel in Johannesburg. After work, one Saturday, I drove Agnes back to her home in Buthelezi Street, Zola, a Zulu-speaking district of Soweto. Agnes had left her native Natal at the age of fifteen to seek work in Egoli, the city of gold. Ever since, for twenty-six years, she had been in domestic or hotel service. She was without formal schooling, and could barely sign her name.

Agnes, married in the Salvation Army Church, had six children and then divorced her husband for desertion. Though the innocent party, she had to leave home. The husband was working, but the Bantu Divorce Court made no order for maintenance. Agnes, given custody of the children, farmed them out at her own expense to give them a roof over their heads.

She remarried, and gave birth to what she hoped would be her last child, a boy called Veli. A bachelor friend of the family had taken all nine of them into his house, refusing rent and telling them to stay until they were at last allotted a council house.

The whole family was waiting for me, this strange visitor from London. The only white men who ever entered a house in Soweto were Bantu Affairs officials or policemen on a pass raid. A dark summer storm was raging so that as I entered through the kitchen I needed time to adjust to the gloomy interior. Electricity was still years away. The typical four-piece, semi-detached Soweto house had two bedrooms, living room and kitchen, no bathroom or running water, only an outside toilet and a cold water tap in the yard. The bachelor slept in one bedroom, and Agnes, her husband Josiah and little Veli in the other. Eighteen-year-old Ivy and her five brothers and sisters slept in the 9 ft by

12 ft living room, sliding the table against the wall and bedding down as best they could on the floor.

The bright hope of the family was Cynthia, who, at sixteen, was already in her second year at high school. In this room, as her brothers and sisters amused themselves, Cynthia had to find the concentration – and a candle – to do her homework. She was determined to matriculate and become a nurse. But with fifty-seven girls in her class and the high drop-out rate in Bantu schools, she would need to be conscientious to survive.

Agnes didn't see much of her children. She got up at 4.30 in the morning, lit the coal stove in the kitchen, took a communal taxi to the station, caught a train (a hybrid of a British football special and the London Northern line at its tightest) and stood for forty-five minutes, then checked into my hotel by 7 a.m. for an eight-hour day of cleaning, polishing, and making beds. Once on pay day *tsotsis* stole her month's wages in the crowded coach.

Back home at 6.30 p.m., Agnes made supper for the family, did the washing and ironing, talked tiredly to her husband in the dining room decorated only with three calendars, and retired to bed at 9.30.

Agnes worked a six-day week, with only one Sunday off a month. Then she went to church and saw her children by daylight. For all that she earned R48 (£30) a month which combined with her husband's wage of £50 and Ivy's (temporary) £18 gave the family less than £100. Each breadwinner paid £7·50 for transport to work in the white man's city, and another £5 went to the neighbour who minded Veli when his mother was working. Then there were the medical bills, which at 30p a visit to the clinic mounted up to several pounds in winter.

Mr and Mrs Ngwyena had to feed, clothe, educate and entertain their children and themselves on the remaining £70. Without electricity there was no chance of television; but that was academic because the family could not afford even a radio. They had to find £7 a year for Cynthia's school-fees and the money for most of her textbooks. The four other children at school were paying lower fees and less for books, but were still a heavy burden on the family budget.

Worst of all was the spiralling cost of food. It is one of the ironies of South Africa that prices at the corner shops in the black townships are higher than those at supermarkets in the middle-class white suburbs. It has to do with transport costs, bulk-buying and the absence of a free market in places like Soweto, where shop premises are restricted in size to a single plot.

Agnes's husband Josiah, a solemn man, also without formal education, was looking for a better job. 'I'm not afraid of hard work, and I'll do anything to find the money to feed these children,' he said. Even if in the dim and distant future a council house was offered to them, they would find it difficult to pay the rent and buy the furniture.

Driving through Soweto that day, we passed a billboard sponsored by the all-white Collective Campaign against Inflation. 'Do something, it does help', was the admonition. Agnes smiled. 'I'd like to help, but then the children will be very hungry.'

Soweto might be the largest town in Africa south of the Sahara, yet it does not merit an official existence of its own. Neither the South African Trigonometrical Survey nor the Michelin Tyre Company bothers to indicate its whereabouts on their otherwise meticulous maps of the sub-continent. The Government has been successful in creating the illusion that this town of well over a million souls is simply a temporary black spot on the veld.

While the economy becomes more dependent on black labour and skills, few employers are interested in knowing how their 'boys' and 'girls' live. Yet Soweto is an extraordinary place, a giant ant-heap, a den of iniquity, a bottomless well of joyful people who have no right to smile, a political volcano, and the most Westernized black community in all Africa.

It remains a source of profound embarrassment to Afrikaner nationalism, contradicting as it does practically every comfortable tenet of separate development. The years of money and rhetoric expended on telling the African that he is an 'ethnic' being, have been a waste of time. Twenty years ago BAD began to insist on tribal segregation in Soweto, so that today the district of Zola is almost exclusively inhabited by Zulus, while Sotho-speakers live in Jabavu or Orlando East. Primary schools and school boards, as well as the urban Bantu councils, all function on tribl lines. Yet intermarriage is increasing; English is more and more the lingua franca; and the Soweton considers himself a black South African rather than a Zulu or Tswana tribesman.

It cannot be otherwise, for the majority of people living in Soweto – and most other Johannesburg black township dwellers – were born there or have lived there long enough to 'qualify' for legal residence. As far back as 1968, a Pretoria University professor found that 58 per cent of the Soweto townsmen over sixteen were 'borners' (in Sharpeville the proportion was even higher). Over the years the high African birth-rate will have ensured that a great majority of Soweto residents know no other loyalty than that of the 'white' cities. This is not to say that people no longer consider themselves Zulu and Xhosa. They do, but in the same way as Jews, Greeks and Portuguese, even descendants of the seventeenth-century French Huguenots, still celebrate their national origins while considering themselves South Africans first. Tribal customs remain. *Lobola* (bride price) is now handed over to the bride's father in the form of money and not cattle. The old root medicines are still popular, while the *makgotla* (tribal courts) administer their own form of 'justice' in some areas of Soweto, despite the resistance of many townspeople.

The ideal of these townsmen – certainly before the June rebellion – was not of an ethnically divided South Africa, but of a society shared equally with people of other races. Those were the ideals of the African National Congress and, fifteen years after it was outlawed, substantial numbers of black men and women over the age of thirty still saw a common South African-ism as their ultimate goal.

If the black townsman refuses to be categorized according to his tribal origins, he is divided along other lines, based on the right to live and work in the 'white' city. The migrant workers live in hostels as 'single men' (whether they are married or not) for the duration of their contract, and then are 'repatriated', usually after one year. They do the most menial and uninteresting jobs and are paid accordingly.

Since the rigorous enforcement of influx control in the last decade, the number of people living and working illegally in black townships has increased enormously. They are the victims of the pass raids, and often have to accept lower wages from unscrupulous employers. They are, however, a cut above the hostel dweller, in terms of both urban sophistication and the size of their pay packet. The largest and most stable category are the residents, who have been born or are qualified to live in a black town. They alone are allowed to occupy one of Soweto's 100,000 houses, to live as a family, send their children to school and, most important, to acquire the skills to help them up the job ladder.

These residents, numbering almost a million, are by no means free. But at least if a policeman asks them for their pass book they will have one to show him. Most of them are ordinary working people with four to eight years' schooling, the children or grandchildren of migrants. They are poor, but they have steady jobs in commerce and industry or in domestic service. They call themselves the 'middle people'. Above them socially and economically are the 'better-off' – semi-skilled factory workers, policemen, drivers, teachers, clerks, sales representatives. These may have an old car parked in the street outside their house, and a lounge and bedroom suite being paid off on the never-never (and with South Africa's hire purchase rules, it very often is never-never) to a white furniture dealer. At the summit of Soweto life are the 'top people' of Dube, that small but active bourgeoisie which has the same interest in evolutionary change as the white capitalists in Houghton. They, however, also have to show their passes on demand.

Most African townships were once administered by a local authority – for Soweto, it was the Johannesburg city council. The Government was understandably suspicious of the 'liberal' government of the English-controlled cities of Johannesburg, Cape Town, Port Elizabeth and East London. In the years 1972 and 1973, township administration was handed over to twenty-two all-white Bantu Affairs administration boards, appointed by the Minister of Bantu Affairs and responsible to him. As each board's writ covered a wider area than that of the several local authorities which it took over, it did give an African a wider area in which to seek work. But this was a small advantage compared with the rapid deterioration which the new system introduced into the life of the black man. The change-over took place too quickly, with little time to train inexperienced staff for some very responsible jobs. The relative efficiency of the city hall was infinitely preferable to the tightly controlled central-government civil servants.

The West Rand Administration Board took over Soweto, Alexandra and four other townships to the west of the city in July 1973. Its chairman, appointed by Minister Botha, was Manie Mulder, brother of the Interior Minister, Dr Connie Mulder. The vice-chairman was the leader of the Nationalist Party on the Johannesburg city council. One of the government appointees is from the company which sells R1-million worth of malt a year to the Board. He recuses himself when the contract is discussed.

Malt, or the beer made from it, plays a crucial role in the life of the community. Soweto is supposed to be self-financing, with its income drawn from beer sales, liquor outlets and rents. The only way that W R A B could find the money to build houses, provide sporting and recreational facilities, and install electricity was through raising house rents and encouraging even greater consumption of alcohol. Three years after the Board had taken over, not a single house was electrified and not a single new housing scheme was initiated. In early 1976, Board departmental heads wanted R100 million for capital development. They got R10 million. Manie Mulder and his yes-men were not prepared to fight with Pretoria for the extra money.

As for the residents of Soweto themselves, they were given an Urban Bantu Council (U B C), known locally as the 'Useless Boys Club'. Its members were elected on tribal lines from among residents of the townships. In the 1974 elections the poll was 14 per cent. In theory, the white Board should consult the U B C, but it rarely does. When rents – a testy area of Soweto life – went up by R2, the black councillors were not even told, let alone consulted. The main political party, *Sofasonke*, was despised as an instrument of apartheid. Its name is taken from an episode in the 1940s when squatters in Orlando shantytown refused to be moved, singing 'We shall all die here' – in Zulu: *Sofasonke.**

Despite the impression of stability in the small middle-class pocket of Dube, an average of fourteen people lived in the normal two-bedroomed township house and more than 17,000 families were on the housing list. The Board director, J. C. de Villiers, did not entirely agree with these figures, suggesting instead that there were 7891 families on the waiting list, 'and about 9000 families waiting to get on the waiting list'.

However the hairs are split, 80,000 people, all of whom have satisfied the rigorous qualifications required to live in the city, were crammed into the homes of friends, or simply lived in tin and cardboard shacks while they waited for their houses to be built. Most of them would wait a lifetime. A mere 575 new houses went up in the year before Soweto, while 2500 couples were married in the same period.

These were the 'legal' residents of Soweto. The official population figure was 650,000, but a more realistic estimate by opposition politicians, academics, and the residents themselves is closer to 1,400,000. A knowledgeable Johannesburg city councillor put the figure at one and a half million. More than half the population of Soweto are, therefore, non-persons: the targets of the nightly pass-law raids and the rounding-up of Africans at railway stations and in the white suburbs. It needs endless guile to avoid being sent to prison and at the same time keep alive. Africans can expect to be prosecuted at least once in their lives under the influx control laws. Not surprisingly, many city youths turn to crime. These petty gangsters, the *tsotsis*, live off their fellow non-persons, as well as the legal inhabitants. They trade in forged and stolen pass books, pick the pockets of black wage-earners in the overcrowded trains, and contribute to the situation that makes Soweto one of the most lawless cities in the world.

*The U B C was later replaced by another piece of Pretoria's puppetry: community councils.

152

In the year before 'Soweto', there were 468 reported cases of murder in the township, 1300 rapes, and more than 8000 assaults 'with intent to do grievous bodily harm'. Fewer than half of the murders resulted in trials. By comparison, in England and Wales, with a population of almost 50 million, 451 homicides were recorded in 1975. The Soweto murder rate was far worse even than that of Northern Ireland, in the midst of a near civil war, where a population only slightly larger than Soweto's produced 296 murders in 1976.

Many of the crimes of violence in Soweto were committed with theft as the aim, but drunken brawls contributed heavily to the carnage as well. Eminent criminologists viewed crime among blacks as a backlash against the apartheid society and its discriminatory laws. Black welfare workers also warned of the 'immutable relationship between unemployment and crime'. In Soweto, and other black townships where official statistics ignored the 'illegal' residents, the out-of-work could number as many as 25 per cent.

Soweto commuters spend much of their day and a giant slice of their pay packets on the overcrowded trains. The matter is especially touchy because Africans have not asked to be driven out of the white cities far from their places of work. Train transport is partly subsidized by employers and Government, but both stations and coaches are hopelessly inadequate. And the trains are a rich hunting ground for the *tsotsis*, who turn Friday into a nightmare for workers with wages in their pockets.

In March 1976, the PUTCO bus company (which operates in Soweto as well) raised its fares from KwaThema township to the nearby town of Springs from 10c to 15c each way. When PUTCO took over the service in 1975 the fare had been 6c each way. The commuters refused to accept the rise, and for many weeks walked the six miles to and from work. The boycott was only broken up by strict police action against non-licensed taxi drivers. The episode did, however, indicate the desperate economic plight of the average Witwatersrand black worker.

Throughout those months black leaders warned that matters were coming to a head. The Zulu leader Chief Gatsha Buthelezi told a mass rally of his followers at the Jabulani stadium in Soweto one Sunday afternoon in March that he was 'offering a black hand of friendship to the whites of South Africa, probably for the last time'. Speaking as 'a kaffir who has forgotten his place', Buthelezi warned that it was 'entirely up to white South Africa whether the revolution that is unfolding will be peaceful or bloody'. Early in May, the black Anglican dean of Johannesburg, Desmond Tutu, wrote a front page article in the *Rand Daily Mail*. 'We are going to be free,' he said, 'genuinely free, all of us white and black together in a genuinely free South Africa. Nothing, and I repeat nothing, will eventually stop us becoming free.' Later that month, Mrs Winnie Mandela, wife of the gaoled A N C leader Nelson Mandela, said the general black view was that 'time has run out for the white man and that he no longer has any role to play in the black struggle ...'

All the while, the struggle over the use of Afrikaans in Bantu schools was growing fiercer. In 1974 the Bantustan leaders themselves had asked Vorster that the medium used at schools in the reserves – invariably, this was English – should be adopted at schools in the white areas. Instead, the Government hardened its attitude. It ordered that in the first years of secondary school, general science and practical subjects be taught in English, and '*wiskunde, rekenkunde en sosiale studie*' (maths, arithmetic and social studies) in Afrikaans. A circular explained how a principal of a Bantu school could apply for exemption from this ruling, but many applications were simply dismissed.

The minutes of the Tswana school board in Meadowlands (Soweto) of 20 January 1976 provide an insight into the official way of handling the matter:

The [white] circuit inspector told the school board that the Secretary for Bantu Education has stated that all direct taxes paid by the Black population of South Africa are being sent to the various homelands for educational purposes there. In urban areas the education of a Black child is being paid for by the White population, that is English- and Afrikaans-speaking groups. Therefore the Secretary for Bantu Education has the responsibility towards satisfying the English- and Afrikaans-speaking people.

The black school-board was told that if teachers taught through a medium not prescribed by the Department for a particular subject, 'examination question papers will only be set in the prescribed medium with no option of the other language.' Despite this threat, the board voted unanimously that the medium of instruction in its schools should be English only.

This defiance led to the dismissal early in February of the chairman and a member of the board. No reason was given, but fellow board members knew that it was the language issue. The whole board resigned in protest, and was backed by the parents, who threatened to remove their 14,000 children from school in support. Questioned in Parliament, Deputy Minister Treurnicht quoted a regulation which empowered him to sack a member of a school board if his membership was, 'for whatever reason, not in the interest of the Bantu community or the education of Bantu . . .'

Asked in Parliament how many applications for exemption from Afrikaans had been received from school principals, Dr Treurnicht replied haughtily that he did not 'deem the requested information of such importance to instruct my Department to undertake this time-consuming task to obtain the required information'. Pupils were angered to find that the only text-books available for social studies and mathematics were in Afrikaans. At the end of February, the principal of the Thomas Mofolo secondary school in Soweto called in the police when his pupils refused to be taught in Afrikaans.

While Soweto schools simmered over the language issue, white inspectors did the rounds to 'test' whether a teacher was proficient in Afrikaans. A principal has described the 'test' as follows:

Inspector: '*Gooie more meneer Mapetla hoe gaan dit*? (Good morning Mr Mapetla, how are you?)

Teacher: (hesitantly, remembering his job is at stake) '*Gooie more. Goed dankie.*' (Well, thank you.)

Inspector: '*Maar jy kan goed Afrikaans praat*' (But you speak good Afrikaans.)

And the teacher, stretched to the limit of his vocabulary by the simple exchange, is ordered to teach mathematics at high school level in Afrikaans.

On 17 May Orlando West junior secondary school went on strike over the use of Afrikaans. The pupils, aged between twelve and fourteen, told circuit inspector Thys de Beer in a memorandum that they had a right to choose what language they wanted to be taught in. The inspector, they said, 'has proved he is afraid of us by not meeting us to hear our grievances'. There was no official response to their appeal. The strikes spread. By the end of the month another six schools in de Beer's patch were 'out'.

Soweto was building up for a mighty explosion. When a woman teacher was molested by two men near her school, hundreds of pupils poured out of their classrooms and kicked and punched the assailants to death. A white policeman came to the school assembly the next morning. He asked who had been responsible for the killing. '*Sonke*', they shouted in unison. 'O.K., Sonke, come out then,' he ordered. The schoolchildren howled with laughter. *Sonke* meant 'all of us'.

Police and special branch visits to schools became more frequent. On 8 June, pupils at Naledi high school stoned security policemen and burnt out their car. Yet when Minister M. C. Botha was questioned about it in Parliament on 11 June, only five days before the rebellion, he professed 'no knowledge of this incident'. At Morris Isaacson high school, one of the most politically active institutions in Soweto, a placard proclaimed 'No S.B.s allowed. Enter at the risk of your skin.' Pupils at several schools refused to write their mid-year exams in Afrikaans.

Earlier in the month, the chairman of the 'dummy' Urban Bantu Council had met Mr M. C. Ackerman, director of Bantu Education in the Southern Transvaal, to discuss the strikes. Nothing, he was told, could be done about them. On 14 June, the Monday before the explosion, Urban Bantu Councillor Leonard Mosala warned that enforcing Afrikaans in Bantu schools could result in another Sharpeville. The next day, leaders of the South African Students' Movement began preparations for a peaceful protest march through the streets of Soweto ...

6. The Year of the Schoolchildren

An icy wind drove through Soweto that first week-end of the uprising. The people withdrew to lick their wounds and count their dead. It was by now obvious that there was more to 'Soweto' than a mere objection to the enforced use of Afrikaans. 'To say that the uprising was over Afrikaans language instruction,' one black remarked, '. . . is like saying that the American revolution was over King George III's stamp tax.'

By Sunday night, the rebellion was launched on its nation-wide spread; first to Pretoria and other Transvaal towns, then to the 'homelands', and eventually to the Coloured communities of the Cape. In practically every township where the youth organized protests in solidarity with Soweto, the police – all peas out of the same Transvaal pod – reacted by opening fire. In each black and Coloured township, the parents, workers, and in the end, after some false starts, the migrant workers, reacted by joining in the rebellion as well.

The defiance of black people was much more sustained than the protests which followed the shootings at Sharpeville. This was largely attributable to the vastly improved network of communications that stretched across black urban South Africa. There were black newspapers now, and there were also blacks working on white newspapers, even Afrikaans ones. The day after the first shootings, any black virtually anywhere in the whole vast country could read an eye-witness account of how a Soweto girl had been shot in the back while going to the corner shop to buy margarine for her mother. The report was by-lined in the un-mistakable syntax of an African, and the picture was attributed to Peter Magubane or Willie Nkosi. If the radio maintained its blindfold version of the events, the television cameras were unable to obliterate the open rebellion. Few blacks owned sets, but many worked in houses which had them. A skilful 'houseboy' might catch a glimpse of Soweto in flames on the nine o'clock news, as he poured the coffee for madam and master.

Parliament entered the last week of its annual sitting with debates on Kruger's three ministries: police, justice and prisons. Back-bench MPs and ministers, loyal to their belief that they knew what was best for the Bantu, blamed the uprising on 'agitators'. They found their scapegoats in the small Progressive-Reform Party, which, as its links with Harry Oppenheimer of Anglo-American indicated, was the party of big capital in the House of Assembly. Now, however, they were dubbed 'communist', 'travelling ambassadors of Moscow' and 'political tsotsis' for daring to suggest that the real 'agitator' was apartheid itself. The deeply conservative Johannesburg *Sunday Times* also received the 'communist' label.

That Monday in Parliament eloquently illustrated how tragically out of touch the white rulers were with the majority of South Africans. An Afrikaner Nationalist barrister from Pretoria, Thomas Langley, waxed loud and impassioned on the 'maltreatment of children . . . one of the most abhorrent and serious crimes which can be committed, because the object of the maltreatment is usually a helpless child who is assaulted by the person to whom he should actually look up to for his protection and care.' Langley's sympathy for the needs of white children did not extend to blacks. The purpose behind the 'riots', he said, was to damage the Prime Minister's discussions with Kissinger. Another MP thought that 'this diabolical element . . . was only waiting for our beloved Prime Minister to go to Europe to hold talks with American and other heads of state.' A third contribution from the back-benches suggested that the demonstrations were 'arranged to coincide with the independence of the Transkei'.

When an opposition speaker listed the grievances which might have been the real reason for the uprising, a Government MP chided him for 'prescribing to the blacks what grievances they ought to have'. But an editorial that morning in the government-supporting *Beeld* newspaper declared: 'Only people with just grievances are amenable to agitation on such a scale.' The editorial added: 'Can we honestly say that the hundreds of thousands of people in Soweto, placed next to the pomp and circumstance of a rich city, have no reason for dissatisfaction over many aspects of their life?'

With the police facing growing criticism, Kruger went out of his way to 'pay tribute' to the nineteen white policemen who had died while on duty during the previous year. Reminded that sixteen 'non-white' policemen had also died, sympathy was duly extended to their families as well. His words set the tone. One MP praised the 'superhuman self-control' of the police in Soweto; a colleague declared that 'any South African – white citizen, immigrant, black, Coloured or yellow – who does not want to associate himself with the action of the police outside [Parliament] does not belong in South Africa.'

The public relations offensive included a statement that morning by the Commissioner of Police that only forty-two of the 130 blacks killed had died at the hands of the police. Later Kruger was to say that ·22 bullets were found in twenty-two of the bodies, and as the police did not use this calibre ammunition they could not have been responsible. The implication was that Africans had shot Africans. The fact that no policeman hed been shot by ·22 bullets, however, pointed a finger at white free-lancers from among one of the world's most heavily armed communities.

Kruger's colourful turn of phrase was brought into play to answer opposition queries over why bullets and not water-cannon had been used on the students, and why the police had not worn face guards. He rightly pointed out that face guards were unnecessary because policemen were not 'injured on a large scale' and he added: 'Therefore to have our policemen running around like knights of the Middle Ages, heavily armed with coats-of-mail and visors and goodness knows what else – policemen in such a garb pursuing fleet-footed little Bantu all over the veld – is something I can hardly imagine.'

If Parliament had intended to inform an anxious public of the reasons for the previous week's momentous events, it proved incapable of doing so. It was left to Mr Langley to lament:

'Where do those riots come from all of a sudden, now that we should be reaping the fruits of the years of positive work to establish a model state in South Africa?'

There was one white man who had taken the call for change seriously. Just as the students were beginning their protest, the stationmaster at the Transvaal country town of Standerton had removed the 'whites only' signs from the lavatories, waiting rooms and even the pedestrian bridge. There was no reaction for a few days, then a white resident complained. Out came the white paint and the signs were restored. 'Nobody meant him to go that far,' said a railway official.

At Atteridgeville, near Pretoria, posters went up proclaiming 'Don't pray – fight' and 'Support Soweto'. On the Monday the township of Duduza, near Nigel (which Mr Vorster represents in Parliament), was astir. Ten more people died that day in townships near the capital, while bottle stores, municipal buses and government buildings went up in smoke.

Though the security forces had ringed off the townships there were isolated reminders to whites that their lives were in danger as well. Blacks from the township of Mabopane invaded the nearest white farming district, Rietgat. In days reminiscent of the 'kaffir wars', women and children were evacuated to Pretoria while patrols of armed white vigilantes guarded their farms. One optimistic farmer thought that the trouble would soon pass, 'like the drought or the measles'.

And though the black workers of Johannesburg remained outwardly calm, their despair was getting out of control. In the middle of the city, in the gardens of the city hall, a black man wielding an axe and demanding 'revenge for the children of Soweto' injured four whites, before he was shot by the police. He was taken to police headquarters at the near-by John Vorster Square, but within minutes he had 'fallen out of a fourth-floor window'. Nothing has been heard of him since.

The rebellion spread rapidly to several Bantustans. In Bophutatswana – which had townships within commuting distance of Pretoria, and tribal areas in the Cape Province and the Orange Free State – schools and training colleges were stoned and burned down by angry students. The Tswana chief minister, Lucas Mangope, was particularly unpopular for his enthusiastic conversion to 'separate development' and his declaration that the Bantustan would follow the Transkei to 'independence'. Two opposition MPs in Lebowa, a Bantustan in the eastern Transvaal, issued a statement declaring that 'the situation has unearthed the innermost frustrations of the black people, which were hidden from the outside world.' The determination of the students and their contempt for separate development was going to make it more difficult for Mr Vorster to sell independence to other tribal leaders.

The uprising also exposed the chasm that separated the mental attitudes of teenagers from those of their parents. In traditional tribal society children were meant to be seen and not heard. Now, in many urban families, the reverse was true. Parents had lost status in the eyes of their children. 'We cannot take it any longer,' one student lamented. 'It is our parents who have let things go on far too long without doing anything. They have failed. We have been forced to fight to the bitter end.' One parent, in the language that reflected the anguish of the times, said, 'they will spit on our graves when we are dead.' When parents complained that 'we can't talk to our children any more', it sounded like an echo from the West.

But the rift in Soweto was not the traditional 'generation gap'. Both generations understood only too well the nature of their common grievances. The parents, however, were so bound down by long hours of work and travel, by rising prices and the insecurity of their jobs and homes, and the need to find the money to educate their children, that it was very hard for them to step out of line.

A Johannesburg psychiatrist has suggested that children in black areas resorted to violence as a result of the breakdown of home life and the indignities to which their parents were subjected. Better educated, without the responsibility of supporting a family, and with time on their hands, schoolchildren were the obvious spearhead of demands for political action. Now, the barricades, the running battles with the police, the sleepless nights on the run, the deaths and injuries of schoolfriends, had raised their defiance into a truly revolutionary mood.

A week after the beginning of the uprising, a group of respected leaders in Soweto founded the Black Parents' Association (BPA) with a primary aim of bringing children, parents and teachers together. It's leader was the Lutheran churchman Manas Buthelezi, a cousin of the Zulu chief minister, and a man once banned under the Suppression of Communism Act until world-wide protests persuaded the Government to revoke the order. Another prominent BPA member was Winnie Mandela, herself a long-time victim of bannings and imprisonment without trial.

The BPA did attempt to talk to the Government on behalf of the students. Its leaders took pains to make the point that they were simply acting as a conduit for grievances. However, there was no positive response from any cabinet minister.

The Government, having destroyed every representative black political organization, had nobody to negotiate with but the discredited Urban Councillors. Minister Botha, who had treated them with contempt for years, now attempted to bolster their standing. On 21 June he announced that in future there would be 'continuous consultation' between black urban leaders and white authorities, and that these discussions would not be limited to the language issue. The black 'leaders' were grouped into a Government-backed 'Committee of Thirty'.

On 6 July, M. C. Botha, following discussions with these 'leaders', announced the first major concession: school principals would be able to choose the medium of instruction. Appearing on television that night, Botha tried to cover up the retreat by claiming that principals had always had a choice but that there had been 'confusion' over the matter.

No such platform was allowed to the secretary-general of the Black Teachers' Association, Mr H. H. Dlamlense, when he referred to departmental circulars which stated categorically that social studies and arithmetic *must* be taught in Afrikaans. Principals had been able to apply for an exemption, said Mr Dlamlense, but these applications had been refused.

The teachers' union had other demands: among them, the removal of six senior white Bantu Education officials and the reinstatement of the dismissed school board. A fortnight later,

Joseph Peele and Abner Letlapa were reappointed to the Meadowlands Tswana school board by the Department of Bantu Education, while Mr W. C. Ackerman, regional director of Bantu
Education, and the circuit inspector Thys de Beer were told
to expect to be transferred. Never before in twenty-eight years of
Nationalist rule had blacks persuaded their masters that some
aspect of apartheid might be unacceptable. Now they had done it
by the use of force. The lesson was not lost on the protesters.

One other task of the Black Parents' Association was to
arrange for the burial of the dead. But the chief magistrate of
Johannesburg refused permission for a mass funeral. Dr Aaron
Matlhare, one of a handful of black doctors practising in
Soweto, was told that 'if a mass funeral were to be allowed, the
police would have to be there and that could spark off more
trouble.'

By the end of June, two state mortuaries – at Hillbrow and
Fordsburg – were full to overflowing, despite the fact that the
piles of black bodies were being ceaselessly carted away. The
dead were also stored in Soweto police stations. These inadequate
facilities provided scope for commercial enterprise. A man looking for the body of his brother-in-law was confronted by a
group of black men in camouflage uniforms sitting around a fire
in the grounds of Moroka police station. 'One approached me
and said I would have to pay R200 if my brother-in-law had
been killed by a bullet, because the Government needed the
money to rebuild Soweto.'

The exact, or even approximate, number of dead was a
matter for widely diverging estimates. But rumours abounded
of mass burials in the grounds of police stations and of mysteri-
ous 'undertakers' who buried bodies at night. For some time
police patrolled all cemeteries, day and night. One grave-
digger reported having dug a number of new graves each day
and finding them filled in the next morning.

On one matter there was little doubt. The police reacted to
demonstrations by blacks with bullets only. Chief Gatsha Buthelezi reflected the opinion of most blacks and many whites when
he lamented that South Africa had learned nothing since

163

Sharpeville. 'We should be able to disperse mobs with the minimum of violence by using chemicals or rubber bullets.'

James Kruger disagreed: 'As you will appreciate,' he told foreign pressmen, 'in the open air tear-gas does not have a very good effect.' Rubber bullets, he added, made people think the police were soft, while water-cannons were not used because of their 'ineffectiveness'.

The disturbances could not have come at a more embarrassing time for the Government. Apart from Mr Vorster's meeting with Dr Kissinger, the annual conference of the Organization of African Unity began at the end of June. Mauritius, the host country, suspended its lucrative trade in South African tourists for a week, and local hotels removed the labels on Cape wines. Zambia declared a national day of mourning for the dead of Soweto.

South African journalists on the inside of the Vorster-Kissinger talks yet again forecast that a 'new and positive direction to policy in southern Africa may be in the process of being forged'. Justice Minister Kruger, however, did not think that the disturbances would 'blacken the name of South Africa'. There were social problems all over the world, he said. 'I've just been to places in England, just to give one example, that I think compare with Soweto. I am not trying to whitewash our situation. I think in all fairness to my Government ... we are definitely trying our best to better the standard of living of black and brown people. There's no doubt about it.'

Doubt or not, Kruger might have been at least partly correct in his assessment of foreign and, in particular, Western reaction. The world had had a surfeit of bloody shootings and rioting students on their colour-television screens in the decade and a half since Sharpeville. The sight of white policemen – or maybe even a black policeman, which somehow made it more acceptable – shooting black students was not so upsetting after the Vietnam War. Anti-apartheid groups across the world attempted to explain the significance of the uprising, but for the most part those who listened were already converted. The world had become numbed and confused by a succession of African disasters: from the Congo, through innumerable coups and counter-coups, to the person of President Idi Amin of Uganda. (The Israeli raid on Entebbe and the humiliation of Amin provided a heaven-sent opportunity for the S A B C to take the minds of its listeners away from the townships.)

Unlike the days after Sharpeville, there was now no 'state of emergency'. It did not matter that South Africa, thanks to half a dozen detention-without-trial measures, was living under a permanent but undeclared state of emergency. This time, the only whites to be arrested were students from the universities of Cape Town and the Witwatersrand.

Mr Vorster conveyed the impression of stolid realism, which for the Western world meant that the man would protect its investments. The blocked rand prevented an outflow of foreign capital. In the first week of July the *Financial Mail* surveyed the country's top executives. Its conclusion: 'Caution – yes. Pessimism – no. The [average businessman] has noted the muted reaction overseas and has drawn comfort from it; he is confident the wrath of the world is not about to descend on South Africa and snap his foreign trade and investment links.' This view would have to be revised in the months to come.

After a week, Soweto was reasonably quiet, its inhabitants sullen and tense. The road blocks had been removed, including the sewerage pipe with the words 'Kruger, we want to see you' painted across it. Hundreds of boys and girls, some only eight years old, were in prison. The police at first denied that any children were in custody. But when reporters claimed to have seen them in prison they were told: 'What do you think would happen if we let them run around the streets? Do you think that we would ever find them again?'

In places where rebellion had not yet broken out, police were preparing for the worst. The author flew from Johannesburg to Kimberley a week after the first protests in order to see the banished Pan-African Congress leader, Robert Sobukwe, who was normally allowed to hold discreet meetings with foreign correspondents. His arrival was known to the local security police, who immediately sealed off Sobukwe from outside contacts.

If the security police were highly embarrassed at not having had prior warning of the Soweto march, their unpreparedness was shared by the two liberation movements, the African National Congress and the Pan-Africanists. Yet the Government, in the shape of Bantu Affairs Minister M. C. Botha, still insisted that the uprising was planned in advance. On 24 June, the day before the end of the parliamentary session, he claimed that there was 'a great deal of premeditation and preparation', not just by blacks but by 'certain white people as well. I wish I could know who they all were. I admit that I do not know who was involved.' He would accept anything except the explanation that blacks had a just grievance, or were capable of organizing home-grown resistance.

Mr Botha's memory was put to the test soon afterwards when a Durban newspaper revealed that in 1943 the young Botha had employed almost identical tactics against the introduction of English as a medium of instruction in some subjects at Afrikaans schools. Botha, then secretary of the *Afrikaanse Kultuurraad* (cultural council), a *Broederbond* front organization, had secretly distributed a document exhorting Afrikaans parents and children to boycott school. 'The strike', he had written, 'must last long enough to bring the government (of General Smuts) to its senses', and he had added that the time for peaceful negotiations was over. The document had been intercepted – and stifled – by Smuts's wartime security network. Questioned on the episode, Botha denied all knowledge of the document. 'How can I be expected to remember what happened in 1943?' he asked.

The lull that followed the events of June was merely a pause in the external manifestation of black anger. Behind the scenes, parents were being told by their children what was now expected of them, as the students planned their next moves. The schools were on holiday until 22 July, but four days before they were due to reopen, James Kruger announced that they would remain closed until 'agitation' ceased. Nobody seemed surprised that the Minister of Justice, Police and Prisons should open and close schools while the man in charge of Bantu Education, M. C. Botha, was still very much at his post.

Soon afterwards, Kruger met the Committee of Thirty as part

of the operation to boost the standing of Government-supported 'leaders'. Then, though the 'agitation' had by no means ceased, he allowed the schools to reopen on 22 July. Few pupils turned up. Heavy police-patrols drove other students off the streets. Soweto's 400 school principals, anxious to get classes back to normal, called for the removal of the 'hippos' from the vicinity of schools. Colonel Jan Visser of the C I D explained that the police were there 'to protect the public in cases of intimidation'.

Demonstrations began again with stones thrown at police and schools being fired. Kruger received the favoured Urban Bantu Councillors and promised that the police would stay away from school premises during lesson times. The concession made no difference, though the student leader Tsietsi Mashinini lent his weight by urging a return to school and an end to arson. The police, for their part, were incapable of leaving matters alone. They entered a number of schools in a search for partisans of black consciousness. The unwelcome visitors were taunted, and clenched fists were thrust in their faces, even though, the week before, two blacks had been sentenced to three years' imprisonment for giving the black power salute in Alexandra. The police opened fire.

The following day, Wednesday 4 August, marked a significant point in the Soweto struggle. The Students' Representative Council (S R C) had used the time to develop a basic strategy. They understood that the bravery, perhaps even the foolhardiness, of their colleagues in the face of police bullets was admirable, but it hardly seemed to dent the complacency of the white suburbs and city, cosily sealed off from the explosion a few miles away. Now parents were told to stay away from work as a show of solidarity in the campaign for the release of detained student leaders. To encourage the strike, the traffic control mechanism of the Soweto railway line was sabotaged, and passenger coaches were stoned. It was a three-cornered battle, as parents resisted their children, and the police stepped in to resotre order in their own way. At times it was vicious: a black woman broke her neck jumping out of a bus under attack by students.

The reasons for the parental resistance might have been found in the latest poverty-datum-line figures for Soweto, published the week before by the Johannesburg Chamber of Commerce. In the previous six months the cost of living had risen 5·5 per cent – including a 7 per cent increase in the price of food, which accounted for over half of the average Soweto's family budget. At the end of the day, Mashinini declared his disappointment at 'the number of parents who went to work this morning when we pleaded with them that they should not do so until our brothers are released'.

Mashinini had underestimated the success of the stay-away. The streets of Johannesburg were empty; some factories and stores were without half to three quarters of their black work-force; and often those workers who did arrive came from Alexandra or the edges of Soweto. One industrialist received a deputation of black workers asking him to tell newspaper inquirers that nobody had turned up for work that day. Who worked where was common knowledge in Soweto.

Whites had to take over black jobs: they sold newspapers on street corners and carried messages about the city; white office workers waited hungrily at undermanned lunch counters. It was a taste of the event long feared by white employers – the general strike.

Inside Soweto, the police were again shooting students in an effort to counter that other white South African fear – an invasion of their suburbs by a black mob. Students and their supporters, estimated by the police at 15,000, began a march which they hoped would reach police headquarters at John Vorster Square. Here they would demand the release of their colleagues and ask for an interview with Justice Minister Kruger.

They marched in school uniform, some carrying the optimistic banner: 'We are not fighting, don't shoot.' Near the New Canada railway station, the main junction into the city, the police were waiting. But, anxious to avoid bloodshed, the police sank their pride momentarily and chose the only people they knew who might have some influence with the marchers – the Black Parents' Association. Dr Buthelezi and Mrs Mandela pleaded with the students not to proceed, but they were angrily dismissed. Battle recommenced.

By now, the students had acquired some amateur antidotes to the weapons of the enemy. Women had brought along bottles of water, and after each tear-gas attack, they washed out the eyes of friends who had come close to the exploding canisters. Some marchers fled up near-by mine dumps and regrouped, trying again to break the police cordon. The police opened fire and three more died.

With Soweto ringed off once again, armed police reserves manned road blocks, pulling homeward-bound blacks out of cars, searching and insulting them. One reservist, an immigrant, was heard to tell a passing African motorist: 'We will call in the Army and shoot all you kaffirs down.' A young government official told a group of Coloureds: 'You hotnots [a perjorative term derived from Hottentots] should also be shot.' In that atmosphere a white traffic cop on point duty at the road block was run down and killed by a black truck driver. He was the third white to die in the month and a half of disturbances.

The students did not break through the cordon. They went on the rampage in Soweto burning down the one beer hall that had survived, and razing the homes of black members of the special branch. That night, too, petrol bombs were thrown through the windows of the houses of Winnie Mandela and Dr Aaron Mathlare. Mrs Mandela was not at home, which was fortunate as she invariably barricaded herself in at night and would have had some difficulty escaping. The police tried to blame the arson on students who, it was suggested, might have been annoyed at the Black Parents' Association's efforts to stop the march on Johannesburg. In Soweto, however, it was widely believed that the culprits were the police themselves. Said Mrs Mandela: 'No black man throws a bomb at the home of Nelson Mandela.'

By the end of the week, eight more blacks had died. The police were now on stand-by throughout the country. Soweto was closed once again to whites. The stock exchange was knocked flatter than ever. Mashinini had gone into hiding, vowing that 'we won't rest until our objectives have been achieved.' He later fled to Botswana and then to England, having appointed his successor. Nobody collected the price of R500 that the police had put on his capture, dead or alive.

On the Saturday, M. C. Botha broke a long silence, in which he had appeared to avoid all responsibility for the events, to announce Government plans to give blacks greater opportunities to control their own affairs in their own residential areas. He did not go into details but, again, the concession followed hard on the violence earlier in the week. The Prime Minister, who had displayed unaccustomed reticence on his favourite subject, law and order, assured the magazine *To the Point*, that the Government was coping and would not be 'railroaded into panic'.

The Government was attempting to 'cope' by the simple device of putting the leadership of the black consciousness movement behind bars. In mid July, Kenneth Rachidi and Mxolisi Mvovo, respectively president and vice-president of the Black People's Convention, as well as Zweli Sizani, secretary of the South African Students' Movement, were held under the security laws. When debating the Internal Security Bill in May, Kruger had expressed the hope that he would never have to resort to the measure. 'I do not like this kind of legislation,' he declared, 'and the Government does not like it either.' In mid July, however, Kruger had overcome his dislike sufficiently to impose the preventative detention clause of the Act in the Transvaal. Other black consciousness leaders and students were picked up. Then, on 11 August, it was given force throughout the whole country.

'Indefinite preventative detention' was necessary, he explained, to wipe out the 'Black Power movement, which is the main cause of unrest in the townships'. He added that the ideology was completely negative and destructive, and did not hold any possibility for discussion, 'and it is a very difficult thing to try and contain'. Kruger was later to call black consciousness 'black nazism'.

Within days, some fifty black leaders – members of the Black Parents' Association, the Christian Institute, the S A Council of Churches, women's community groups as well as students, doctors and journalists – were in special detention centres

(Modderbee, outside Johannesburg, for men; with the women at the Fort, in the suburb of Hillbrow). Lekgau Mathabathe, headmaster of Morris Isaacson school, the most radical in Soweto – where Mashinini had studied – was detained. Nor was Mrs Mandela, who only the week before had intervened with the students at the behest of the police, spared. Major-General Geldenhuys, the country's security chief, refused to confirm her detention to inquiring newspapermen. 'The right people, such as the next of kin, know about the arrests,' he explained curtly. Mrs Mandela's next of kin was serving a life sentence on Robben Island.

Later in the month, Kruger threatened to introduce legislation to prevent the publication of the names of people detained without trial under the security laws. People held for questioning under section ten of the Internal Security Act were not neces-sarily guilty, he explained, '. . . and to go and give his name is to stick a stigma on him, which may be unfair to him.' He also felt that publication of the names might 'actually stimulate the very trouble you are trying to stop . . . by indiscriminately giving names you make the members annoyed.'

The only black consciousness leader of any standing to avoid arrest was the BPA chairman, Dr Manas Buthelezi. He was taken by the police from his office in Braamfontein, but on arrival at John Vorster Square police headquarters, was told that it was a 'mistake' and he was free to go. The likeliest explanation for this curious incident was that Dr Buthelezi, with his American theological degree, had too many friends in the United States for the Government's liking.

The voluble Kruger, who had told the BPA that he would only talk to them if they restored peace in Soweto, could now justly complain: 'There is no one to see. They are all behind bars.' But he added, comfortingly, that 'We have the whole thing in hand and we will be able to contain it altogether.' After that he assured fellow Nationalists at Heidelberg that the black man 'knows his place, and if not, I'll tell him. The blacks always say "We shall overcome" but I say we shall overcome.' Kruger did not realize that an experienced *Rand Daily Mail* reporter, John Mattison, was in the audience. When the speech appeared in the papers the next morning to be picked up by the foreign Press, the Minister issued a denial.

So nervous were the authorities that they even arrested Steve Biko, the 29-year-old father-figure of black consciousness, despite the fact that he was already banned under the anti-communism laws. Several other black leaders in the King-williamstown area of the old British Kaffraria were detained. The police there were particularly sensitive to the possibility of repercussions following the death in a local prison of Mapetla Mohapi, one of the most promising black consciousness leaders. Mohapi, aged twenty-five, a social science graduate, was at the time of his death administrator of the Zimele trust fund, which cared for released political prisoners and their families. He was a level-headed man, and during his detention had smuggled letters to his wife, which had not indicated 'any desperation or frustration'. Yet on 5 August the police claimed that he had committed suicide in his cell by hanging himself with his jeans. When she identified her husband's body, Mrs Mohapi said she had seen no evidence of suicide. The two African doctors who attended the post-mortem examination were themselves detained, thus making it dangerous for them to communicate with the family solicitor.

The chairman of the Zimele trust fund, Mr M. Tembeni, commented that black people were 'highly suspicious of the frequent alleged suicide incidents among people detained under the Terrorism Act'. He, too, was detained. Perhaps the best clue to the circumstances of the 'suicide' came from an African woman journalist, Tenjiwe Mthintso, who was detained by the same security police squad. On one occasion they put a wet towel round her neck, telling her: 'Now you know how Mapetla died.'

All the while, black people in ever increasing numbers were going out into the streets to express their hatred of 'the system'. At Fort Hare in the eastern Cape, students met to discuss a day of prayer for Soweto. The meeting got out of hand, the university was closed down, and its students were sent home. The near-by Lovedale teachers' training college was extensively damaged by fire. In Zululand the university would remain closed till the end of the year. Students marched through a

township near Mafeking, in the Cape section of the Bophutha-
tswana Bantustan, and a black 'Guy Fawkes' burnt down
Chief Mangope's parliament building. The disaffection reached
Mdantsane, the giant Ciskei township which supplied labour to
East London; and then Cape Town, the legislative capital,
where the fighting was even fiercer than in Soweto.

M. C. Botha chose the moment to make another important
concession. On 14 August he announced that the leasehold for
Africans wanting to acquire their own homes in a 'white' town
would no longer be dependent on producing a certificate of
citizenship in a Bantustan. Furthermore, the lease would be for
an unlimited period, not just for thirty years; though Botha
later reverted to type by reminding blacks that they were
present in white areas 'to sell their labour and for nothing else'.

Within days of the 'concession', Port Elizabeth, the country's
fifth largest city, was the scene of a two-day flare-up in which
thirty-three blacks died at the hands of the police. The men who
marked the incidents on the map of South Africa at police
headquarters in Pretoria were having to work overtime.

Later, the senior state pathologist at the Johannesburg
mortuary, Professor Joshua Taljaard, disclosed that, up to the
end of August, the majority of blacks killed by police bullets in
the townships around the city had been shot in the back.
Giving details of post-mortem investigations, Taljaard said that
eighty people had been shot from behind, forty-two from the
front and twenty-eight from the side.

By the end of August, 800 people, including seventy-seven
black consciousness leaders, were in detention without trial.
Students were arrested at a meeting in Daveytown, near
Germiston, and brought before the local magistrate. There were
no defence lawyers. They were quickly convicted and most of
them, including nine children under the age of sixteen, were
given cuts (strokes of the cane).

A senior riot squad policeman prophesied that the violence
which had disrupted South Africa for two months was in its
'final throes'. The assessment was hopelessly wide of the mark,
for, by then, rebellion had erupted in the Cape Peninsula. What
should have worried both white police officers and theoreticians

of separate development was the cross-racial nature of the protest.

Students at the Coloured university of the Western Cape in Bellville South (Belville proper is the centre of the peninsula's largest Afrikaner population) and other black consciousness supporters at high schools and training colleges demonstrated with the Africans of Soweto. The police held off and there was no bloodshed. Early in August, the students began a week-long boycott of lectures. Their Coloured rector, Dr Richard van der Ross, suspended lectures altogether; to the fury of his students, who regarded this as a betrayal of their cause. The whites-only staff association (only a handful of lecturers were blacks) dissociated itself from the student protest. The students set up road blocks outside the university. The police were called, and their vehicles were stoned. Soon enough, the administration building was in flames and other educational institutions were set on fire. The process of action and reaction between Coloured students and police was heading for bloodshed. But when this came, on 11 August, it took place not in the Coloured areas but in the three African townships of Langa, Guguletu and Nyanga.

It was surprising that the rebellion had taken so long to reach Cape Town. The city's 200,000 Africans were the worst-off of all the country's urban blacks. The thirty-year leasehold concession was never available to them, because white politicians still cherished the hope of one day expelling every single African, whether migrant worker or 'borner', from the western Cape. Langa had the highest proportion of 'single-men' hostel dwellers of any township in the country. Many had seen their wives and children driven out to the Bantustans under the influx control laws. Their sense of insecurity was heightened by the prospect of being forced to become Transkeians (they were nearly all Xhosa) when the first Bantustan became independent in October.

The trouble began with a Soweto sympathy march by Langa high school pupils, stones thrown at a bottle store, a police order to disperse in five minutes, tear-gas and more stones, clashes in the two other townships, government buildings ablaze and, finally, police roaming the streets taking pot shots at the young protesters. By morning sixteen blacks were dead.

The confrontations continued into the next day. In Langa, students paraded placards proclaiming 'We are not fighting'; but they were gassed and shot all the same. White students marched from their ivy-leafed campus on the slopes of Devil's Peak. The show of solidarity led, as the townships began to burn, to seventy-six arrests. One hundred and thirty riot police were airlifted from the Reef under the direction of the veteran of Soweto, Brigadier Visser. He had been sent down to stop the rioting, he said 'and that is just what I am going to do.' By the next morning another seventeen Africans were dead.

The success of the August stay-at-home had demonstrated to the students of Soweto that the one really weak point in the fortress of apartheid was the white man's almost total dependence on black labour. Increasingly, this was to become a major factor in their planning. Now the S R C prepared for a three-day general strike starting on 23 August. Blacks with access to photocopying machines at their places of work produced pamphlets; posters went up at street corners; and in the homes of Moroka, Dube and other Soweto suburbs, fathers were told by their twelve-year-old children: 'On Monday, Tuesday and Wednesday you are staying away from work. Just to ensure that you do, will you please see to it that your car stays in the yard.'

Over the week-end the students delivered leaflets to houses, to emphasize their point.

The racists, in our last demonstration – called by the cynics a riot – lost millions of rands as a result of the people not going to work. Thus they thought of immediately breaking the student–worker alliance, [and] called on workers to carry knobkerries and swords to murder their own children who are protesting for a right cause. Parent-workers, you should take note of the fact that, if you go to work, you will be inviting Vorster to slaughter us your children ... We want to avoid further shootings. Parent-workers, heed our call and stay away from work.

The anonymous leaflet recalled that: 'Vorster is already talking of home ownership for blacks in Soweto. This is a victory achieved because we, the students, your children, decided to shed their blood.' The clandestine African National Congress lent its weight to the strike, printing and distributing leaflets in its own name.

The '*Azikhwelwa*' call – the word, 'we won't ride', had its origins in earlier bus boycotts – resulted in an absentee rate of up to 80 per cent in Johannesburg, with the supposedly apolitical manual labourers especially solid. And the alarming fact for white employers this time was the relative absence of intimidation by students. No barricades went up in Soweto to prevent workers from travelling into the city. Students did picket railway stations, but they were heavily outnumbered by police. The taxi drivers, who were affiliated to the parents' association, took the day off, while the municipal buses had not dared enter Soweto for several weeks.

The only substantial group to ignore the strike call were the hostel dwellers, who had been given a free hand by the police to arm themselves (with knobkerries or wooden clubs) against the students without fear of prosecution.

At Orlando station, police fired on students, killing a by-stander on his way to work. By mid morning strike-breaking workers were trickling back to Soweto, either because they and their employers feared reprisals or because there weren't enough men and women to keep the production lines moving. Two student picketers were beaten to death by returning hostel dwellers. That night, rooms in the Mzimphlope hostel in Orlando West 11 were burnt out. It was the pretext for a police-encouraged backlash that led to forty officially-admitted deaths in the next week.

The stay-away held firm on the Tuesday. In the old days, strikes had been broken by the simple device of sending policemen to round up or assault every adult who was not at work. This time, perhaps fearing that such methods would have the opposite effect, the police contrived to set black against black. The hostel dwellers were used for this purpose.

The hostellers, as we have seen, are the premeditated result of the policy by which Africans are uprooted from their homes in white cities, dumped in the tribal areas, and allowed to return to Johannesburg, or wherever they are needed, in the guise of 'bachelors'. In Soweto they included one-year contract workers, but also a fairly large number of people, especially Zulus, doomed to live there for much of their working lives.

Often, twenty men are housed in a bleak dormitory, devoid of privacy, family warmth and lasting friendships – a prey to all manner of social and psychological evils that were uncommon in traditional society – broken marriages, homosexuality, prostitution, venereal disease, alcoholism. To Soweto residents, hostel dwellers were country bumpkins, and contact between these two well-defined sections of township life was scant. Now, boys and girls still in school uniform had the impertinence to order the hostellers not to go out and earn their keep. Nobody bothered to tell them what the strike was about. The fires in the hostel had destroyed not only their worldly possessions, but also their earnings, stored in boxes under their beds for dispatch to destitute families in the Bantustans.

The 'backlash' had been prepared in advance of the strike. On the preceding Sunday, security chief Mike Geldenhuys had warned that 'agitators who attempt to enforce a work stay-away will experience a backlash from law-abiding citizens in the townships.' On the Tuesday, the *World*, the African newspaper, quoted Colonel Visser, head of the Soweto CID, as telling people to go to work 'and just thrash the children stopping them'.

On Tuesday evening, a thousand frenzied Mzimphlope Zulus, armed with knobkerries, pangas, assegais, rampaged through the streets and into the private houses of Orlando and Meadowlands, robbing, raping, killing. The 'Zulu warriors' banded together into '*impis*' and scoured the streets for cheeky children, terrifying the residents. They were led by police 'hippos' which fired on groups of youths who were blocking their way in an effort to defend the houses. Having cleared a path, the police then stood aside, sometimes shouting the two Zulu words that they had lately acquired – '*Bulala zonke*' (kill them all) – before leaving it to the *impis* to impose law and order. Panic-stricken housewives seeking help at the Orlando police station were reminded that 'you did not want protection to go to work, so why do you want it now?'.

Confirmation of the central role played by the police in inciting the 'backlash' came from a black reporter on the *Rand Daily Mail*, Nat Serache. Finding it necessary to escape from the mob – while on the look-out for a good story – he hid all night in a coal box near one of the hostels. At 2.15 a.m. he heard a policeman with a loudhailer tell the hostel dwellers not to raid and damage houses, which after all belonged to the government. 'We didn't order you to destroy West Rand [Administration Board] property,' the police voice said in Zulu. 'You were asked to fight people only, so you are asked to withdraw immediately.' And peace was immediately restored in Orlando West.

Another black journalist, this time from the *Star*, got into the Mzimphlope hostel, where he heard a white policeman, dressed in a camouflage uniform, tell the hostellers through an interpreter: 'If you damage houses you will force us to take action against you to prevent this. You have been ordered to kill only these troublemakers.' Two hostel dwellers were later shot while disobeying instructions.

The Wednesday stay-away figures were as high as ever. The police swept through Soweto in convoy, shooting and rounding-up students. Minister Kruger commented: 'The situation will calm itself once people realize there is a strong backlash.' On the Thursday, the three-day strike having achieved its aims, the workers of Soweto returned to their jobs. The 'backlash' had nothing to do with it.

It was known in Soweto that the police had used the Zulu cultural movement *Inkatha* to orchestrate the hostel violence. Chief Gatsha Buthelezi, as founder of *Inkatha*, made an early call on his members to stop fighting. When he flew into Johannesburg from Durban he was warned by Kruger not to interfere. But Buthelezi's representative in Soweto, Gibson Thula, also warned him that if he did not intervene he would never gain the support of the people of Soweto. On the Friday, Buthelezi met the hostellers and afterwards told reporters that the Zulus had been given *dagga* (marijuana) by the police, who had encouraged them to kill and even driven them to areas where crowds were gathering. The hostel dwellers, he said, had been joined by heavily-armed black groups, whose black boots 'looked similar to those worn by the police'.

Now, for the first time, the migrants were told what the strike was about. Buthelezi apologized to the people of Soweto on their behalf. The students rushed out pamphlets to the hostellers telling them that they too were victims of oppression. A reconciliation of sorts was effected. The 'backlash' had backlashed on the Government. When the next stay-away was called, many hostellers were among its most active supporters.

Leaders of commerce and industry had decided not to pay absentees, irrespective of whether or not they thought that their workers had been intimidated. The president of the Transvall Chamber of Commerce, Ernest Housmann, declared that employers had 'every sympathy with law-abiding workers who are intimidated, [but] they simply cannot afford to pay absentees'. And Hausmann added that some employers 'may decide to dismiss employees who have given trouble in the past'. During the first strike a black woman earning R50 a month as a chambermaid in a posh Johannesburg hotel was so determined to get to work that she took two taxis into town and two back to Soweto in the afternoon. That cost her R2 – more than her day's wages. The proprietor of the hotel refused to reimburse her. 'Why don't you bring your children up properly?' he asked. On the Tuesday night of the strike, as if to compound their hardship, the people of Soweto heard that the price of bread, which was more of a staple food in the townships than in white suburbs, was going up by a quarter.

The Prime Minister, preparing for another meeting with Dr Kissinger, admitted that South Africa had problems, but declared that there was 'no crisis'. His energetic Justice, Police and Prisons Minister, in the meantime, expressed a willingness for another round of talks with black 'leaders'. Progressive MP Helen Suzman replied that by detaining almost every African regarded as a representative by the black community he was making 'a mockery of the prospective talks'.

Unabashed, Mr Kruger found just the 'leaders' he was looking for: the bush lawyers of the Makgotla, the dispensers of tribal justice. These vigilance groups had been operating in

Soweto and other Witwatersrand townships for some years. Indeed, several Urban Bantu Councillors were Makgotla men, though the only qualification necessary for sitting on the 'bench' was an annual subscription of R1. The vigilantes had unofficial powers to arrest, try and punish. In June two Makgotla men were gaoled after a youth had been thrashed so severely on his genitals that he died. Victims of floggings had included people carrying dangerous weapons, schoolgirls sleeping away from home, and children who defied the authority of their parents.

The day before the June rebellion, the *World* newspaper reported that five youths and a woman were given hospital treatment after being flogged by Makgotla members for breaking school windows. Indeed, Captain G. J. Viljoen of the Jabulani police station in Soweto had himself interrupted a flogging session to tell the Makgotla people that 'the days of the law of the jungle are gone. Bring the criminals to the police and please don't dump them here half-dead from savage floggings.'

It was, however, one area where Kruger publicly disagreed with his police force. He told Parliament in June that Makgotla 'is a good system, provided they do not go to extremes with the penalties'. He mused on the possibility of asking 'these people to deal with their own people and to give them certain statutory rights'.

The attractions of Makgotla had suddenly become irresistible. It reinforced the tribalism so long nurtured by the Government while at the same time removing urban Africans from the ambit of Western judicial procedures. With the responsibility for the punishment of their upstart young people safely in the hands of black people, white courts and policemen could wash their hands of the disturbances. There was a heaven-sent opportunity to set black against black once again.

After a meeting with unnamed 'leaders' of Soweto early in September, Mr Kruger was asked whether Makgotla members had attended. 'It is difficult to say,' he replied, 'because I am not the fellow who knows who is here. I got a lot of names of leaders of Soweto.' The Minister knew well enough that all but two of the 'leaders' were tribal vigilantes, including Mr Siegfried Manthata, whose Naledi Makgotla had been involved in several brutal punishments. The system which the *World* called 'backyard tribal justice' was about to become the law of the land.

Throughout this period, the shootings, arrests and police brutalities were taking place in Cape Town's 'non-white' areas, down wind, beyond the *cordon sanitaire* that separated white from black. On 1 September, the African children took their protest into the streets of the city itself. Several hundred aged from twelve to eighteen marched in solemn and orderly procession along Adderley Street, the country's most historic thoroughfare. 'How much longer must we suffer?' asked their banners. The white Capetonians, who pride themselves on their 'liberal' racial attitude, gaped in amazement. Traffic policemen on motorcycles followed watchfully, but did not intervene. The marchers then returned to the main railway station, passing through the 'whites-only' concourse, where blacks are only allowed as cleaners, on to the third-class section of the platform, where they caught their trains back to the townships. There was no shooting, no baton charging, no tear-gas. The riot squad had been elsewhere in the Peninsula, restoring law and order.

Impressed by the manoeuvre, the Coloured schoolchildren tried the same thing the next day. They too took trains into the city and marched down Adderley Street. But this time the riot squad, with Coloured policemen conspicuous among them, was waiting. The procession was smashed by batons and tear-gas. The students retreated, regrouped, were dispersed once more, only to coalesce again. They were joined by Coloured clerks and delivery boys who had been driven out of offices and shops by the tear-gas seeping through the air-conditioning system.

The Coloureds are South Africa's cockneys. They can joke when they are most serious, and know just how far to go with a white 'konstabel'. On that day they played 'tease a copper' to the limit, taunting, side-stepping the flailing batons of the riot squad, tripping the clumsy policeman on the beat. '*Hulle kan ons nie skiet nie*,' they shouted gleefully, '*want die wit men sal hulle sien*' (They can't shoot us in front of the whites). The students, the serious core of Coloured defiance, brought their message direct to the whites: 'Down with apartheid. Release all detainees, equal rights and freedom for all ...'

White pedestrians refused to disperse, leaning back against the walls of banks and insurance companies as a solid phalanx of police fired bird-shot at weaving groups of Coloureds. The police were themselves stoned, and the windows of Stuttaford's department store, Cape Town's Harrods, were broken. Bryan Williams, the half Samoan wing-three-quarter of the visiting All Blacks rugby team, was overcome by fumes in a bookshop and only escaped after a bout of vomiting. The Prime Minister's wife, Tienie Vorster, was also reported to have got a whiff of gas and had to be hurried out of range.

This time, however, it was not so easy to get back to the railway station. Vans loaded with masked riot police roamed the streets of the city, lobbing tear-gas canisters at anyone who was Coloured. By mid afternoon the business centre of Cape Town had closed up shop for the day. The riot police had imposed law and order.

The ordinary white Capetonian had firmly believed that the police brutality seen in newsreels of South American revolutions 'could not happen here'. Now, if they wanted to, they would listen with different ears to their black employees when police behaviour in the townships was described to them. Cape Town's newspapers received scores of phone calls and letters from angry white readers, complaining about the police. The students, determined as ever, came into the city again on the Friday (3 September), and the police reacted yet more violently. The riot squad invaded schools, tear-gassing classrooms and then entering with masks to beat up children and teachers. A policeman threw a boy in school uniform into a van containing an alsatian dog with the words: '*Laat die hond die kind opvreet*' (Let dog eat child).

All hell broke loose in the townships. Police used words like 'civil war' and '*slagveld*' (battlefield) to describe the pitched battles. The unarmed Coloureds needed all their skill at improvisation to confront the police. Rudimentary political organization had for some time existed in the form of street committees. Now they tried the tactic of armed ambushes under 'regional commanders'. But the results were poor. On one occasion an armed patrol was ambushed and a petrol bomb chucked into their vehicle. The soldiers jumped clear and put out the blaze with sand ...

Police violence united the Coloured community, from the squatter camps to the prosperous area of Athlone. Anyone who was Coloured and happened to be walking in the wrong place at the wrong time – on the one side of the street which the police had made out of bounds – or who paused to help a wounded friend, was liable to be tear-gassed, arrested and even shot. Sometimes the victims of police violence were people who had themselves been censured for collaborating with apartheid. The security police detained Lydia Johnstone, who had upset both women's liberation and black consciousness movements by representing her country as the black Miss Africa South at the Miss World contest in London the previous year. She had been seen waving her arms and shouting 'black power'. John Noble, who had played on the wing for the mixed South African invitation rugby team against the touring All Blacks earlier that winter, was arrested and charged with public violence.

It was a symbolic moment when white motorists were stoned outside the township of Ocean View. Here were housed the Coloured who had been expelled from near-by Simonstown when the naval base became pure white. Ocean View is twenty-five miles south of Cape Town. Beyond it there is a nature reserve, a promontory which Sir Francis Drake called 'the fairest Cape in the whole circumference of the globe', and the imaginary line where the Atlantic and the Indian oceans meet. You could go no further. Now, Africa's black revolution, launched in Algeria a quarter of a century before, had finally crossed the continent and reached the southern seas.

While Africans remained reasonably quiet, Coloured people in separated group areas in nearly every town and village in the Cape Province were joining in the widening rebellion. The violence was spilling over into white areas. At Stellenbosch, where South Africa's prime ministers receive their university education, students armed with revolvers, chains, knobkerries and hockey sticks mounted all-night vigils. Farmers met hurriedly to organize vigilante groups.

When the Cape Coloured joined in the Soweto mid-September strike, almost 80 per cent of the workforce stayed away. David Currie, deputy leader of the Coloured Labour Party, commented: 'The myth that the Coloured people will stand with the white man against the African has been finally destroyed.'

Only time would prove the correctness of Currie's assessment. What was indisputable, however, was that the Coloureds were undergoing a profound psychological metamorphosis. In recent years, the South African political arena had been dominated by 'Bantu' and 'Boer', with Briton safely on the sidelines, but Coloured often caught up in the cross-fire. A generation of prolific law-making had seen the Coloureds humiliated time and time again, seemingly incapable of hitting back in the smallest way. And the feelings of rejection harboured by these two and a half million '*bruin mense*' (brown people) had been made the more bitter by the knowledge that they shared the same forefathers as the Afrikaners.

There is an old saying in Cape Town that the first white settlers arrived from Holland on 6 April 1652 and nine months later the 'colour problem' was born. The early Dutch had few inhibitions about sexual mixing with the Hottentots and Malay slaves. Genealogies of the early Cape show many of today's well-known Afrikaner family names beneath those of mothers listed as 'van der Kaap', meaning a Hottentot or Indonesian Malay slave 'of the Cape'. Two of the early governors, Willem and Simon van der Stel, were Coloured. The naval port of Simonstown and the Afrikaans university town of Stellenbosch, cradle of intellectual racism, are named after them.

By the mid nineteenth century the blood of Hottentot, Bushman, Malay and Boer had been fused into what are today called the 'Coloured people'. One of South Africa's most distinguished historians, Professor J. S. Marais, said of the result of this uninhibited miscegenation: 'Thus did the Boers keep their own race pure and bring into existence a nation of half-breeds.' Despite legal equality with the white man, the Coloured suffered from two problems which survive to this day – landlessness and the demoralizing effect of the wine and brandy introduced by the French Huguenot settlers. Farmers still soften up their Coloured farm labourers with a large 'tot' of cheap wine, which blurs their minds and keeps them docile.

When the British took over the Cape in the early nineteenth century, they soon incurred the wrath of the Dutch by their 'liberal' attitude to the Coloured people. Two measures in particular were unpopular – the emancipation of the slaves and the 'liberation' of the Hottentots (who were not slaves). The Boers (Dutch farmers), who never forgave the British for these acts of philanthropy, left the colony soon afterwards and trekked north. The English colonial government at the Cape chipped away mercilessly at the theoretical equality of the Hottentots, so that by the turn of the century they had become in fact, if not in law, second-class citizens.

After the Boer War (1899–1902) the victors, the British, were content to assume control of the diamond and gold mines, while handing over political power to the vanquished Boers. The Union of South Africa did not grant voting rights to blacks in the former Boer republics, but in the ex-British colonies of the Cape and Natal many Coloureds and some Africans retained their franchise rights, though without being able to stand for election to Parliament.

The victory of the Afrikaner Nationalists in 1948 meant the full turn of the circle for the old Voortrekker revanchist tradition. They immediately set about disfranchising the Coloureds and relegating them from second- to third-class citizens (Africans having been removed from the common voters' roll before the Second World War). Whereas the English-backed government of Generals Botha and Smuts had handled race relations with a medley of legislation and social convention, now a doctrinaire programme of tough racial statutes was voted through Parliament.

For the Coloureds, the basis of these apartheid laws was the Population Registration Act, which classified every man, woman and child, on reaching the age of sixteen, into a racial group. The Coloured group was subdivided into seven categories – Cape Coloured, Malay, Griqua, Chinese, Indian, 'Other

Coloured' and 'Other Asian'. In the Cape Town area, where more than half the population was Coloured, many thousands were borderline cases, with children from the same family sometimes sent to separate white and Coloured schools. Government officials would stick a pencil into a boy's hair: if it fell to the ground he was white, but if it stuck, his short curls indicated that he was Coloured. Such was the science of apartheid. Once issued with a population registration card, the 'K' (for Kleurling or Coloured) or 'A' (for Asian) in the top right-hand corner determined a person's existence from cradle to cemetery.

Of all the apartheid laws it is the Group Areas Act which has caused the most direct suffering to the Coloureds (and the 750,000 Asians). The whole land mass has been divided up into a patchwork quilt of white, Coloured, Indian, Chinese and even Malay residential areas. (Africans have no property rights outside the Bantustans.) The Coloured people were expelled from the city and suburbs, from pleasant homes nestling up against Table Mountain, or from District Six, Cape Town's casbah, and dumped on the windswept sand flats miles from their factories and workshops.

In all, over half a million Coloureds and Indians were uprooted from 'white group areas', yet no more than 10,000 whites suffered in this way. Joyce Waring, wife of a Nationalist cabinet minister, went into the business of converting these vacated Coloured houses into trendy cottages, and today even whites of the most liberal hue live in them. Coloured people are tried in the courts for living in a 'white' area. The magistrate usually postpones sentence for six months, after which the guilty party has to show proof that he has moved into Coloured lodgings.

The historic irony of the Coloured race laws were the two post-war measures prohibiting marriage and sexual intercourse between white and Coloured. (For some years these activities had been illegal between white and African.) Now the Boers were attempting to deny the origins of the Coloured people. The Immorality Act actually provides for a maximum of seven years' imprisonment, with hard labour and up to ten lashes, for intercourse across the colour line. Its aim, in the words of a Cape Town magistrate, is to 'prevent the mongrelization of the races'. Yet the practice has continued without break, despite the harsh punishment involved. The white private secretary of a previous prime minister, a dominee (pastor) of the separatist Dutch Reformed Church, town councillors in small Afrikaner towns: the list of Afrikaners who vote for racialist laws and still take pleasure in black bodies is never ending.

Mixed marriages are illegal, even when contracted abroad by South Africans of different races who then return to settle. Only white and Coloured spouses who married a quarter of a century ago, before the law was enacted, may now live together legally. Their children, on the reasoning that 'colour drags down', become members of the Coloured group. As part of the 'four stream' policy to provide separate facilities for the four main race-groups, Coloureds were kicked out of the 'open' universities; lost their right to become Cape Town city councillors (there were once half a dozen, elected by Coloured and white ratepayers); had to travel in separate coaches in trains, and upstairs in buses; had to swim from their own beaches – though a Coloured nursemaid was permitted to enter the sea up to her knees if helping a white toddler in the breakers.

The Senate was packed with Government supporters in order to obtain the two-thirds majority needed to take away the 'entrenched' Coloured common roll votes. The Coloureds were given, instead, a brown 'parliament', with powers rather fewer than those of an old English county council. The great majority of Coloureds boycotted the 'parliament' – known officially as the Coloured People's Representative Council – either by not voting or, at the risk of prison, by refusing even to register as a voter. Those who did vote in the first elections supported the Labour Party, which, though ambivalent over its methods, was outspokenly opposed to the separate Coloured system. The Government cynically nominated twenty people from the pro-apartheid opposition party, appointing as chairman of the Council a man who had been beaten into third place in the elections. Labour was left a minority party.

To cries of 'sell-out', Labour stood for the second Coloured elections in March 1975, and this time won a yet more convincing victory. But the inexperienced leaders, instead of carrying out their election promise to resign once they had shown their strength, changed their minds. Sonny Leon, who had fought in the Coloured battalion of the South African army in the Second World War, became the 'brown prime minister'. In the end he refused to sign the Council's budget (drawn up in the white Ministry of Coloured Affairs) on the grounds that it discriminated against Coloureds, and was sacked by the Prime Minister. The Government's Coloured policy was in ruins.

Two days after the Soweto uprising, the Government published a report on the Coloured people from a commission that it had put in the hands of dependable Afrikaner academics and politicians, with a handful of safe Coloureds to give it a representative appearance. The commission of inquiry under Professor Erika Theron, a Stellenbosch University sociologist, had worked for three years to produce a devastating record of the feelings and aspirations of the Coloured people. Its recommendations were hardly radical, but the Government immediately rejected a call for the direct representation of Coloureds in the central Parliament, and for the repeal of the mixed-marriage and immorality laws.

The Coloured policy of Mr Vorster's Government tells more about the mind of the Afrikaner than it does about the Coloureds themselves. There can be no rationalization here that the Coloured – unlike the Bantu – have a culture and way of life alien to that of the West. They have acquired the language, the religion, the customs of the South African white. The only thing that separates them from the white is the olive complexion of their skin. The way in which they are singled out for special attention by the architects of apartheid shows that the aim is subjugation on the grounds of colour rather than on any grounds of culture.

Indeed, the most intense antagonism to Coloured integration comes from the white worker who fears that it would lead to a recurrence of the 'poor white' class. It was by dint of the 'civilized labour policy' between the World Wars that landless peasant Afrikaners were rescued from the poverty that Coloureds experience to this day. If that protection were withdrawn, many whites, despite their superior education, would be relegated to

the ranks of the unskilled working class or even of the unemployed.

Certainly, the Coloureds do have a few rights that distinguish
them from the blacks. They are, after all, despite political
deprivation, second in the economic and social pecking-order,
treading a twilight world of racial prejudice. They don't have
to carry a pass, and if ever a white cannot be found to fill a
job, the 'brown' man will get it. Ten thousand Coloured and
Asian furniture workers resigned from the multi-racial Trade
Union Council of South Africa, which favoured opening up the
industry to blacks. The Indian general secretary, echoing the
words of his white colleagues, explained: 'We are not racialist
but we believe we are acting in the best interests of our members.'

There are signs, however, that the young, the radical and
even the middle class have moved far towards an alliance with
the blacks. Many, instead of 'trying for white', are now identify-
ing 'downwards' with the Africans in the near-by townships.
They have, after all, seen the writing on the wall elsewhere in
Africa, where *metisse* and *mestico* were left with little choice but
to make peace with black governments in the former colonies.

Back in Soweto it was apparent that not all the hostels had
been won over. Four more people died early in September as
residents attacked Mzimphlope. Once again, the barometer of
violence rose a few points. High school pupils clashed with
police in the diamond capital, Kimberley. Mr Kruger entered
the fray once more. As there were not enough police to go round,
he hinted that businessmen might arm themselves to protect
their premises against rioters. They needed little prompting.
Soon the newspapers were carrying pictures of jaunty whites
outside factories and second-hand car marts pointing revolvers
at the unseen foe. Management militia would become another
ox wagon in the laager that the white man was feverishly
constructing.

But the real threat to business was the work stoppage, and
13 September saw the start of another three-day stay-away.
The week before, leaflets in Zulu, Sotho and English had
appeared in Soweto under the name of the S R C. The printing

and distribution of these leaflets were in themselves a mark of student success. A combination of *samizdat*, Chinese wall-poster and – thanks to the muscle of the students – virtual decree, the leaflets played a vital role in the success of the strike. It is not illegal for a black to have a duplicating machine in his house, but it would quickly arouse the suspicion of the special branch. If the leaflets were advertising a church bazaar or an inter-tribal soccer match, they might pass muster. But a call for strike action from an address in Meadowlands would mean immediate confiscation of the machine and arrest of the owner, with expulsion from his house thrown in for good measure. So how did the tens of thousands of leaflets escape detection until they were in the hands of the people at whom they were aimed? The answer was simple – they were printed in white territory.

Drake Koka, the black consciousness trade unionist, and adviser to the students until he fled into exile, turned leaflet-making into a minor industry. He found a friendly African who worked at a white-owned printing firm and here, after hours – and without the owner's knowledge – rolled off thousands of leaflets. Koka, though house-arrested, stole out of Soweto late on the Saturday before the September strike, but it was light before the 40,000 leaflets were printed. On his way back through central Johannesburg, he stopped at a confectioner's to buy some cakes for his daughter's birthday party. He put the cakes on the passenger seat, with the leaflets in cardboard boxes on the back seat. Near Soweto he was stopped by a police road block. He pulled up obediently, hopped out and coolly opened the boot. The young policeman, not recognizing the familiar face, caught sight of the cakes. 'You work for a bakery, heh?' he asked. Koka told him about the birthday party. 'Do you want to come?' he joked in Afrikaans, but the policeman had already moved on to the next car. That night, the 40,000 circulars were distributed throughout Soweto.

The leaflets advised workers to keep off the streets. They chronicled the now-familiar grievances – police shootings, detention without trial, Bantu Education, and the docking of the wages of those who had stayed away three weeks before.

Half a million blacks obeyed the strike call. Trains (with their white drivers) and buses (when their black drivers turned up) ran almost empty into the city. Again, intimidation was hard to find. The students had discussed the aims of the strike with the hostel dwellers and felt reasonably confident of their support. They were, for the most part, justified.

Two men from the Nancefield hostel who did go to work were killed by their fellow inmates on their return. The only other violence came from the police. At Alexandra, hundreds of blacks were arrested in what Major Kriel of the riot squad called a 'clean-up operation' with the aims of protecting those who wished to work, and rounding up 'agitators'. Colonel Swanepoel, the interrogator, assured the public that innocent people would be released after 'screening'.

By now it was clear to white business and industry that the stay-away was meeting with the approval of the vast mass of Soweto's million inhabitants. When there was talk of a three-week strike, Marius de Jager, director of the Johannesburg Chamber of Commerce, admitted that his members were 'very worried; they don't see an end of it'. Mr de Jager had learnt a lesson as well. He refused to comment on the effect that the strike was having on business, because his pessimistic remarks about the previous stay-away had been quoted in the latest pamphlets.

Businessmen were hardening their attitudes on wages. Many took their cue from the firm considered to lead the field in liberal race relations, Harry Oppenheimer's Anglo-American Corporation. Although its mines were not affected by the strike, the company did have a fair-sized black staff in its Johannesburg head-office. 'Anglo' refused to pay absentees 'unless the employee's absence is supported by an acceptable reason.' Others, including British firms like Premier Milling and Metal Box, followed suit with enthusiasm.

The Government seemed deaf to the message that although the entire black consciousness leadership was in prison the strikes were becoming more effective each time. As the strike week proceeded, fire-bomb attacks were made on buses in white areas of Johannesburg, on the *Star* building in Sauer Street, and inside the Eloff Street branch of O.K. Bazaars in the heart of the city. Could this be the beginnings of urban terrorism, so long feared by the whites? *Die Transvaler*, the official Government organ in Johannesburg, ran a story on the Friday predicting that 'a black organization will today kidnap six white children.' Two would be murdered and the other four would be held as hostages to force concessions from the state. For the moment, at any rate, the prediction proved false.

In the countryside, however, there seemed to be more veld fires than normal in the dry winter months. While the usual cause was lightning or accident, now there was a nervous hint of arson in the air. Minister of Agriculture Hendrik Schoeman suffered R100,000 of damage on one of his Transvaal estates. Down in the Orange Free State, Mr Vorster's son-in-law, Andre Kolver, lost 2000 sheep, a large expanse of grazing land and several buildings in another blaze. In the timberlands of the eastern Transvaal, at least seven sawmills and much surrounding forest were burnt out. A cache of dynamite exploded in a fire at Modderfontein in late September, hoisting a mushroom cloud over much of north-east Johannesburg. There was no confirmation of sabotage, but the police reported shooting five Africans who tried to hinder firemen fighting the blaze.

Back in the world of white politics, Government ministers were doing the rounds to reassure the faithful with a confusing array of promises about 'change'. The limitation of their horizons was illustrated by the warning from a watchful Government back-bench MP, Mr Hennie van der Walt, who thought that 'every agent of change must be viewed with suspicion because he would be furthering the aims of communism without realizing it.' At the Natal National Party provincial congress in Durban, three senior ministers had their say. '*Verligte*' (literally, enlightened) Sports Minister Piet Koornhof warned that 'dramatic adjustments' would have to be made if the battle for survival were to be won. Connie Mulder, taking a '*verkrampte*' line before the faithful, promised 'no deviation from the policy for which the Government received a mandate from the electorate at the last general elections'. Jimmy Kruger bisected the viewpoints with a call for a new dispensation for blacks: 'Not a change of policy but a change of gear.' In mid September, Minister M. C. Botha, the man with a special knack for saying the wrong thing at the wrong time, reiterated that blacks were in 'white' areas in a secondary capacity. This was not discrimination, he pointed out, because whites were in black 'homelands' in a secondary capacity as well.

The week before the Prime Minister set out for Zurich to meet Kissinger again, he assured the country that there was no crisis. He had looked over the history of South Africa's achievements, and there was no reason to feel guilty about anything. In Churchillian vein, he claimed that 'nowhere in the world have four million done so much for eighteen million as in this despised South Africa.' Back from Switzerland, Vorster assured the Orange Free State congress of the party that the Government was always prepared to talk about anything which would improve conditions for blacks, 'but not on the question of one man one vote'. He then flew to Pretoria for an unprecedented briefing of Nationalist MPs and senators – though refusing opposition pleas to recall Parliament and keep the country informed of the gathering crisis.

As Henry Kissinger was preparing his visit to South Africa, the Postmaster General came up with a 'concession': apartheid signs at post offices throughout the country would gradually be scrapped. The 'basic pattern of separate service for the different race groups would be preserved', but he could see no objection to a limited number of blacks being served at counters 'traditionally used' by whites, as long as the service flow – presumably for whites – was not disrupted.

Henry Kissinger flew into Waterkloof military airfield, Pretoria, on Friday, 17 September, amidst a welter of security cover that must have impressed the members of the welcoming committee, prominent among whom was General van den Bergh of BOSS. The Secretary of State had come to discuss Rhodesia, but the students of Soweto thought that he should also turn his attention to their problems. At first they considered making the 35-mile train journey to the capital to demonstrate in person. Cautionary counsels prevailed, and instead they held protests at their schools. One banner, nailed to a churchyard fence, told

Kissinger to 'get out of Azania – don't bring your disguised American oppression into Azania.'* Another, rather more pithy, declared: 'Kissinger, your existence in Azania is bullshit. Even animals are hungry.'

The students remained inside the school grounds, singing freedom songs. Undeterred, the police shot off the padlocks on the gates and fired at the retreating students. Six died that day. Khotso Seatlholo, the new S R C president, commented: 'The so-called American peacemaker never uttered a word of protest at this atrocity and bloodshed.'

The next afternoon, Dr Kissinger did find time to meet white opposition leaders, Bantustan chief ministers, newspaper editors, and several blacks associated with separate development. The man who could have told him about the previous day's shootings, Manas Buthelezi, was relegated to a meeting with William Schaufele, Assistant Secretary of State. The suggestion by the Indian National Congress that Kissinger meet the gaoled Nelson Mandela was ignored.

Soweto was at boiling point again, with school attendance virtually nil. On 23 September more than 3000 black school-children infiltrated central Johannesburg and set off on two marches – to the central post office and the railway station. The freedom songs, the banners proclaiming 'This is our country', and the black power salute gave the city's whites their first close-up view of the rebellion. They were not as sympathetic as the white Capetonians. The police, informed of the march in advance by the S R C, and urged on by white bystanders, set about the students with their batons. In the clashes six whites were reportedly taken to hospital with stab wounds and an

*Black students shouting 'Viva Azania' may be insulting their country, according to Mr M. D. P. Molofo, an exiled history teacher living in London. The name, he says, was first evolved by Pan-Africanist refugees in Ghana at the time of Tanzanian independence. 'They found the Sea of Azania on a map, thought it sounded nice and so named their country Azania.' Now Molofo finds that Azania is derived from '*zenj*', a word used by the early Persians for black slaves. 'Azania' is also wrong, geographically. Molofo has an eighteenth-century map which shows that Barbaria vel Azania ran down the coast from present-day Somalia only as far as the island of Zanzibar, the island of slaves – and no further. Molofo has written a pamphlet suggesting that the future South Africa be called Maluti, a Sotho word for the country's greatest mountain range; or its Zulu counterpart, Ulundi; or even a combination of the two – Malundi.

elderly lady dislocated her shoulder in the panic that followed the arrival of the police. Nearly 1000 students were arrested.

Other students, white Afrikaners at Pretoria University, heard Minister Kruger declare that there was no choice but to implement separate development on a just basis and as rapidly as possible. A black middle class would have to be created, he said, and a black proletariat, with its accompanying danger, avoided.

In the meantime, Soweto's roads, dangerous enough at the best of times, had been temporarily deprived of their traffic cops, thanks to the students. Khotso Seatlholo and five colleagues had collected a pile of circulars from a house in Dube. Instead of seeing to their distribution, they first called at Orlando high school. An African traffic policeman on point duty recognized them and radioed the information to headquarters. Within minutes the school grounds were surrounded. Carrier bags full of the circulars were unceremoniously jettisoned, but the youths managed to slip through the police net. After this the SRC ordered all traffic cops off the streets (there are no white traffic cops in Soweto). 'They are interfering with the "state cars" carrying our MPs,' the SRC complained.

By then, Soweto's driving habits had taken a further turn for the worse, with children barely out of their teens driving about in hijacked cars then dumping them when the cars would go no farther. With the prospect of death by run-away car becoming greater than death by police bullet, the traffic cops and the students got together for a palaver. There was just one condition: no students in cars were to be arrested. The traffic cops agreed and Soweto's roads soon returned to 'normal'.

The confusing element in the story of the end-of-year examinations in late October was the students themselves. Khotso Seatlholo, by then on the run, wrote in the church magazine *Pro Veritate*: 'Twenty years ago, when Bantu Education was introduced, our fathers said: "Half a loaf is better than no loaf." But we say: "Half a gram of poison is just as killing as the whole gram!"' The magazine was immediately banned. Despite this tough condemnation of Bantu Education, the *Weekend World*, which was in the closest contact with student leaders, carried an official SRC statement in mid October calling on pupils to return to school. In fact, the leaders only wanted them back for organizational purposes, chief among which was the planning of future strikes. The SRC's ability to influence events was undoubtedly growing, but it was a series of extraneous factors that raised tensions and ensured the failure of the exams.

After the resurgence of the police violence that marked the anti-Kissinger demonstrations, school attendance on the Reef dropped to 20 per cent. It was much the same in Cape Town: 'Not one child at school.' Parents were not prepared to allow their children out of the house while police opened fire in playgrounds and lobbed tear-gas canisters through classroom windows.

Tension soared again following the funeral of a sixteen-year-old schoolboy, Dumisani Mbatha. With gatherings banned under the Riotous Assemblies Act, funerals had become a prime opportunity for public protest. Mbatha had been arrested during the previous month's march in Johannesburg. The anxious parents had not known his whereabouts until a Prisons Department spokesman disclosed that the boy had become ill in prison and later died in hospital.

The body was handed over to the family a fortnight later, without the cause of death being made public. Nor was it known whether there had been a post mortem examination. Thousands of schoolchildren were among the 15,000 mourners at the funeral. The emotionally charged ceremony was punctuated by shouts of '*Amandla*' (power), the clenched-fist salute, many speeches, each followed by a freedom song. Seatlholo began his address with the words: 'Mothers and fathers, brothers and sisters, policemen and sell-outs, I greet you all in the name of Africa ...' As the grave was being filled with soil, groups of students ran off to attack government property, as well as the home of an African policeman who had been seen shooting and killing blacks. The next day the schools were once again empty.

Minister M. C. Botha threatened to withdraw state subsidies from teachers made idle by the boycott and to transfer them to other areas. If he was serious in his desire to get classes going again, his Cabinet colleague Police Minister Kruger had other ideas. A week before the matriculation exams, the police surrounded Morris Isaacson school and arrested fifteen teachers and sixty-two children, to add to the headmaster, who was already in detention. School attendance plummeted once again.

The SRC still denied that it was calling for an exam boycott, and appealed to students to 'come to school and to teachers to start doing their work'. On Saturday, 24 October, a thousand people gathered for a funeral procession outside the house of a Naledi high school girl who had died of natural causes. The riot squad arrived in force and ordered the coffin to be opened 'to see if you are hiding a petrol bomb inside'. In the ensuing uproar, the police shot one man dead, and arrested 115 people.

The next day, the riot police turned up at Doornkop cemetery for the funeral of Jackie Mashabane, a Zululand university student who had 'committed suicide' in a police cell. When the mourners gave the black power salute, the police opened fire, killing six, including a local undertaker. General Kriel, Deputy Commissioner of Police, explained that if there was subversion at funerals, his men would not hesitate to intervene. Political speeches, slogans and song, he said, all constituted subversion.

In the next few days, dozens of children in Soweto and neighbouring townships were arrested. When the matriculation exams began on 29 October, the stay-away was almost complete. By the end of the week, Soweto's 500 schools – and those in Cape Town, too – were empty. Wherever students did present themselves, as in Tembisa, hundreds of their colleagues intervened forcibly to stop them. So, with police guarding exam halls, even willing candidates thought it prudent to stay at home.

For African high school pupils, 1976 was an academic write-off. They calculated that the sacrifice was worth while. For the Government, however, it was a setback of serious proportions, as bad in a way as the rebellion itself. As with the Portuguese and their 'civilizing mission', so with the Afrikaner: black educational statistics were important ammunition in showing the world that 'we are doing more for them than any country in Africa.'

Les de Villiers, a senior Ministry of Information official,

recounts in his book *A Skunk among Nations* how, when South Africa was being expelled from the Commonwealth, Verwoerd said to the Indian Premier, Nehru: 'Within ten years we will stamp out illiteracy on the part of our blacks, but you won't do so in fifty years.' His forecast was unhappily very far out. But the relish with which the episode is still recounted does show the importance of education as a smokescreen for hiding the nastier side of apartheid. Thus, students in detention were promised the chance of sitting exams, though it is not known whether any did so. The Transvaal Bantu Education chief, Jaap Strydom, offered supplementary exams in March for those who were 'unable' to write them in November.

One other reason for the decline in high school attendance was the growing numbers of young people fleeing across the border into black states. With the police seizing school registers and then calling at homes to find out why a boy or girl was absent, the exodus had grown into a flood. It is known that Bantu Education officials were annoyed with the police for causing panic just as the exams were approaching. By mid November over 600 children had fled into the former protectorates, with huge numbers in hiding within the country. The figure was almost certainly higher, as many had moved on to Mozambique without registering in Swaziland.

The situation had become serious enough for Minister Kruger to go on television with an offer not to prosecute students for leaving the country without travel documents if they returned within a week – though the exemption would not apply for other charges. The students were sceptical, and very few took up the offer. On the contrary, with continuing police harassment, and the arrest of students who had not written their exams, the exodus continued unabated.

Four of the five senior white officials considered in Soweto to have been the cause of the rigid Afrikaans-language ruling, were still in their posts in September. It showed that the Government had still not admitted the error of its ways. A new regional director of Bantu Education was reported to be investigating the unpopularity of the system. There were hints that a new national education body would be set up, with the word

'Bantu' excluded from its title! The overseas propaganda service had already renamed it 'black education' – confusingly, because 'black' did not include Coloureds and Indians. Otherwise, the relabelling was on a par with Connie Mulder's stroke of genius in getting separate development retitled 'plural democracy'.

It is surprising that the students, and particularly their representative council, remained so moderate. There was violence, certainly, but it was directed against Government installations, and not against private houses, unless these belonged to particularly hated policemen or to informers. If a man was suspected of working for B O S S he was ostracized, or sugar was poured into the petrol tank of his car, or slogans were spray-painted on his house, or at worst the house itself might be burnt down and the victim beaten up. The arson and looting was mostly the work of non-students, of *tsotsis*, and even, as the external wing of the P A C claimed, of their members on the spot settling accounts with police spies.

Certainly the S R C used threats of violence to close down the shebeens (illicit drinking dens), but this was part of the war against alcohol. Government beer halls and bottle stores had been prime targets because they helped finance the apartheid townships. But the students had other reasons for detesting liquor. They considered the tot system (for Coloured farm labourers) and the heavy drinking in legal beer halls and in shebeens to be part of a white campaign of pacification.

The campaign began in Cape Town's African townships, where students scattered the contents of liquor vans, set fire to the shebeens and even forced pedestrians with bottles to pour the contents into the gutter. The drinkers, usually lonely hostellers with few other pleasures in the world, defended themselves, and one incident, when the police intervened, proved fatal. The police were put in a difficult position because they had been trying for years to stamp out illicit liquor stills. On the Reef, the students called for the closing of shebeens as a mark of respect for the dead of the townships. Fearful of getting the Cape Town treatment, the Soweto shebeeners complied. Even if the resourceful shebeeners were soon to find ways of getting back into business, the students had achieved a major victory.

These avowedly non-violent and puritanical exercises did not spare student leaders from constant police harassment. Dimakatso Phakathi, a nineteen-year-old studying science by correspondence, was arrested at his home in Mamelodi at 3 a.m. At Compol, the police headquarters in Pretoria, he was paraded in front of a man covered with a blanket, who viewed him through two eye-holes. Identified by the anonymous informer as a member of the Mamelodi S R C, Dimakatso was detained under the Internal Security Act. Hundreds of ordinary schoolchildren were arrested and held in prison without charge. A number of schoolgirls, some as young as fourteen, were put into cells with long-term male prisoners and were pregnant when they were released.

By the end of October, almost 3000 cases relating to the disturbances had been brought to trial. Only rarely did the accused have the benefit of defence solicitors. Magistrates seldom delayed the cuts (cane) to allow the children an appeal, and even if the parents had been told about the trial beforehand, they were not informed of the right to appeal. By the end of October, a known 667 people had been sentenced to corporal punishment. Of these, 528 were adolescents under eighteen years of age. The eight-year-old African boy who was given five cuts for attending an 'illegal gathering' in New Brighton location, Port Elizabeth, must have been the world's youngest political prisoner.

By early November, 135 black leaders were being held under the Internal Security Act. They were not all Africans. Ms Fatima Meer, Natal University sociology lecturer and president of the Black Women's Federation, and Rev. Alan Hendrickse, chairman of the Coloured Labour Party and one-time head of the United Congregational Church, were also in detention without trial. The fifteen black journalists arrested were a tribute to the brave reporting from inside the townships. Foremost among them was Joe Thloeloe of *Drum Magazine*, president of the Union of Black Journalists, which represented most of the country's 150 black journalists. The U B J's close ties with black consciousness led to the banning of its journal. Most of the detainees came from the *World* and the *Rand Daily Mail*. There was clearly never any intention of actually charging them with a breach of the law. It was their reporting which was being silenced.

The *World* had once concentrated on a diet of sex, crime and sport. But when its editor, Percy Qoboza, returned from a year's study in the United States, he set it on a brave path of questioning white rule. In June he wrote that 'Whites must realize that they either share with us what they have or lose everything.' He called for a national convention attended by black consciousness and congress leaders, including Nelson Mandela.

While the police were clocking up overtime arresting the youth and their leaders, Soweto's murder rate reached unparalleled heights. Police reported 145 murders in the township in September. On some days there were 18 murders. Brigadier Tiny Visser, the C I D chief, complained that 'since the June riots the disregard for human life has increased drastically. We have investigated cases where a man was killed because he accidentally stood on another man's foot or because he spilt his drink on someone else in a crowded place.'

Visser, a studious man of the law, was preparing a Master's thesis on 'the influence of ethnicity on the political aspirations of the urban black'. It did not seem to cross the policeman's mind that the frustrations of township life, enforced bachelorhood, overcrowded housing, and the sight of blacks being mown down remorselessly by police bullets, might have had something to do with it. The police were too busy encircling school playgrounds to be able to maintain law and order.

On 26 October, separate development gave birth to its first child – an 'independent' Transkei. The occasion was snubbed by the outside world, ignored by the vast majority of South Africans, scorned by the black students, celebrated only by Afrikaner nationalism, and capitalized upon by Kaiser Matanzima and his handful of Xhosa followers.

If 'independence' was overshadowed by the events of the winter, it had also contributed to the tensions that led to the student rebellion. Of particular significance was the way in which all the other Bantustan leaders except one had turned against the idea of separate nationhoods. Two months earlier, at the height of the unrest, they had issued a statement blaming the Government for not heeding their warnings. Matanzima, needless to say, was not there. With the exception of Chief Lucas Mangope of Bophutatswana, all eight chief ministers rejected independence as a solution to the country's problems.

There was, however, no special reason to take their statement seriously. Once before, Matanzima himself had sworn allegiance to black unity, only to break cover and ask Vorster for independence, without consulting his fellow chief ministers. Mangope was to follow suit a year and a half later, while Dr Cedric Phatudi admitted he might be open to persuasion if his Bantustan, Lebowa, were granted more land.

Now, however, the township dwellers were vicidly underlining the huge gap that separated their political aspirations from those of the tribal leaders; Buthelezi and his colleagues fell over each other in their rush to expose the iniquities of apartheid. Caswell Koekoe (pronounced Kwekwe), interior minister of the smallest Bantustan, Basotho Qwaqwa, announced that 'we are against the policy of separate development, but we are using it as a platform to say things which could otherwise put us on Robben Island.' Mr Koekoe, a successful businessman whose political ideology would hardly attract the sympathy of the Soweto students, none the less put his case in sophisticated conspiratorial terms. 'We don't have the means at our disposal to overthrow the mighty South African Government, so we infiltrate the system with the aim of bringing about a multiracial government from within.'

Early in October, the Bantustan leaders had a seven-hour meeting with Vorster, their first in almost two years. They got precious little satisfaction. The Prime Minister declined to discuss the unrest on the grounds that it was the subject of a judicial commission of inquiry. Nor did he see any merit in the idea of a multiracial national convention, a proposal then popular amongst opposition opinion. Nor would the detained leaders be freed to take part in discussions, because Vorster said he could not and would not interfere with the law. Vorster was simply reminding his puppets that their sole political role in white South Africa was to negotiate the independence of their tribal territories.

An angry Buthelezi then called a secret meeting of 'black leaders' in a white Johannesburg hotel to discuss a strategy for the future. High on the list of priorities was the bridging of the 'dangerous and increasingly widening gap' between rural and urban blacks. The meeting issued a statement announcing the formation of a Black Unity Front. While Buthelezi's undoubted charisma made him popular among large sections of the Zulu tribe, his opportunism was distasteful to the leaders of black consciousness. The students were in no mood to be led by blacks walking a tightrope which was tied at one end to Pretoria.

All the while, as independence drew near, Kaiser Matanzima wheeled and dealed, squeezing what he could out of the white Government. The most controversial issue was a legalistic argument over the status of the 1,300,000 Xhosas living permanently outside the confines of the Transkei. Would they, as is normal under international law, be allowed to remain citizens of South Africa, or were they to be forced into becoming citizens of the Bantustan against their will? The point involved the very *raison d'être* of separate development. There could be no point in setting up a string of independent states if 'white' South Africa was still left with a majority of black South Africans.

Years before, Dr Verwoerd had expressed the view that 'the mere fact that foreigners are employed in a community or in another country does not constitute integration.' To him, and to successive Afrikaner leaders, it did not matter that many of these blacks were born in the 'white' cities, had never even seen the rolling hills of their 'motherland' nor had any intention of living there. In the course of time, when the last of the Bantustans had acceded to independence, there would be no black South Africans any more.

The plan was devastating in its simplicity. Even if Bantu physically outnumbered whites in 'white' South Africa after the attainment of the apartheid millennium, it would not matter, for they would have no claim to civil and political rights. The citizenship clause was absolutely crucial, for it reconciled the apparently contradictory notions of white economic prosperity based on cheap labour with a black proletariat which somehow belonged somewhere else. In the meantime, South Africa would become the only country in the world with a majority of foreigners living permanently within its borders.

The all-embracing definition of Transkeian citizenship had been enshrined in statute since the Self Government of Transkei Act in 1963 – thanks to the collaboration of Kaiser Matanzima himself. The reasoning behind it was similar to that of the Nazi decree of 1941 which deprived the Jews of German citizenship according to criteria of ethnic and racial origin.

Matanzima certainly did not wish to foist himself on a million strangers in the white cities, for there was the likelihood that at least some of them might soon enough be dumped in his already overcrowded Bantustan. They could become a focus of internal opposition. But without these external Transkeians, there could be no independence. So he indulged in an elaborate game of bluff. The Transkei 'recess committee' – comprising representatives of Matanzima's own party and a few members of the opposition Democratic Party – spent much of early 1976 discussing the draft constitution. The committee agreed unanimously that external Xhosa should not be forced into becoming Transkeians against their will. The objection was presumably conveyed to Vorster when he met Matanzima to discuss the constitution. Yet when the Status of the Transkei Bill was published in the Cape Parliament it was clear that the white Government had got its way entirely. The Transkei's own version of the constitution provided the same definition. Yet despite the unequivocal language of the draft laws, Matanzima and his brother, Justice Minister George, insisted that Xhosa in the 'common area' would have the right to choose their country.

A public slanging match ensued between Matanzima and Bantu Affairs Minister Botha, who warned that 'if the Transkei refuses to grant citizenship to people outside the territory, they will become stateless by an act of the Transkeian government and not by South Africa.' The agreement on the citizenship clause, he assured Parliament, had been reached at Cabinet level between the Transkei and the Republic.

Then, in mid May, the Transkei parliament, by unanimous vote, amended its own version of the draft constitution so that no external blacks would be forced to become Transkeians on independence. On closer examination, however, the amendment turned out to have nothing at all to do with the external Xhosa. All it did was to set up a sort of ethnic classification board to adjudicate in borderline cases where an African was an offspring of Xhosa and non-Xhosa parents. These were relatively few in number.

Kaiser Matanzima, a solicitor of skill and intelligence, must have appreciated the plain language of the bills. At the same time he was concerned that the racist overtones of the citizenship clause were making Transkei independence even more difficult to sell abroad. Now, when he and several Transkei ministers toured Africa, Europe and America in a desperate mission to canvass recognition for their country, they could claim – falsely – that the citizenship issue had been settled to their satisfaction.

It may have been a coincidence that soon after the two governments finalized the drafts of the constitution, the Matanzimas moved into two farms recently bought from whites by the South African-controlled Bantu Trust. The farms, worth a total of R400,000 (£275,000), were meant for a state-run beef and dairy project.

The independence of the Transkei completed the first stage of Afrikaner nationalism's final solution to the 'colour problem'. For this very reason there was little chance that it would win international support. Equally important, however, was the palpable lack of enthusiasm on the part of the Transkeians themselves. Both Pretoria and Umtata governments were justifiably wary of calls for a referendum to test the attitude of the people towards independence. In 1963, after the first general election, Matanzima was supported by only twelve of the forty-five candidates in the voting for chief minister. The remainder were opposed to the policy of divide and rule. His majority was obtained through the non-elected chiefs. In later elections he did achieve a clear majority of elected members, but by then the percentage poll had dropped markedly. There were also other factors which made free elections impossible.

By the time of independence, the Transkei had been living under a state of emergency for sixteen years. It should be recalled that the emergency was proclaimed as a means of putting down the Pondoland peasant revolt against the tribal authorities. It was through these authorities that the chiefs operated as direct agents of the Government in imposing Bantustan rule. Without the chiefs' cooperation, there could be no separate development. Those chiefs who refused to go along with the new system were simply sacked and others appointed in their place. It led to the largest uprising of African peasantry since the Second World War. The emergency regulations were thus a constant reminder of the Transkei's troubled political past.

With the rule of law suspended, white Bantu commissioners and police officers could (and still can) detain suspects until they answered 'fully and truthfully all questions'. An offence meant anything from murder to the most trivial and technical of misdemeanours. Meetings were to be held only with the written consent of a Bantu commissioner, and then at a time and place stipulated by him. He could ban a person from attending a meeting, even if it was authorized, and order an illegal meeting to be broken up. Conversely, it was an offence to organize any boycott of a meeting convened by government officials, who included chiefs and headmen. These chiefs and headmen, civil servants on the payroll of Pretoria, were turned into ancient satraps, their powers greatly in excess of those once exercised under tribal law. It was now an offence to treat a chief with disrespect. While hundreds of people were detained for their real or imagined role in the revolt, in later years the regulations were used to neutralize the real political opposition to Matanzima.

Coupled with the powerful influence of these 'emergency' laws was the flagrant misuse of the secret ballot. It has been estimated that well over half the Transkeians of voting age can neither read nor write (excluding, of course, external Xhosa, who scarcely participated in the elections anyway). At the polling station the illiterate voter revealed his choice to an electoral officer in the presence of two witnesses, and the 'X' was then inscribed for him. The ballot could not by any stretch of the imagination be called secret and, besides, the chief would invariably have made his choice of candidate known to his tribesmen. Pretoria wanted 'independence'. The National Independence Party (TNIP) was its chosen party. The chiefs and headmen were appointed and paid by the Government. It was an irresistible combination.

As we have seen, Matanzima's initial lack of electoral support was converted into a parliamentary victory with the help of the non-elected chiefs. In the independent Transkei, half the parliament consists of chiefs, an arrangement without parallel in Africa. In the first three elections the chiefs actually outnumbered elected members by sixty to forty-five. This built-in majority for the TNIP took the spice out of elections and interest fell away. It was easier not to vote at all than to express support for Mr Vorster's candidate.*

Matanzima was wont, in public, to regret the fact that his country was ending up 'an unwilling one-party state'. Admittedly, the opposition Democratic Party had helped by its ineptitude, and by the political ambivalence of its leader, Knowledge Guzana, an honest if naïve solicitor from Umtata.

Some months before independence, the party was taken over by a black consciousness sympathizer, Hector Ncokazi, outspokenly opposed to a separate Transkei. He promised to reject independence if he won the general elections in September, but there was never the slightest chance of that happening. At the end of July, brother George Matanzima's security police rounded up Ncokazi, two opposition MPs, party officials

*Matanzima, himself paramount chief of the Emigrant Tembus, justified the parity of chiefs to the author some months before independence. 'They are the traditional leaders of the African people. They are not appointed ... they are merely recognized because the people bring them forward to the Government and say he is our leader. They are by birth given the position. It is a blood tie, like that of the royal family of Great Britain. I stem back many generations, we were never elected, never appointed. And the people look to these chiefs to guard their interests. In the absence of chiefs from the legislature, the people will ask, 'who made these laws in their absence?' and there will be chaos, bloodshed and revolution. If we did not have this system probably we should have had trouble, which is what you find everywhere where people arrogate to themselves leadership.'

and others intending to stand in the coming elections. The pretext was that a 'leftist, revolutionary group' was planning to create disturbances on independence day. Matanzima's 'party of liberation' could not even wait for independence to lock up the opposition.

Perhaps the most cynical aspect of the arrests was that they were ordered just before the debate in the Umtata parliament to discuss the draft constitution. The two M Ps had been delegated to introduce an amendment on the citizenship clause, which would have categorically excluded Xhosa living outside the territory. When the matter came up for discussion in the house, there were no speakers. The elections at the end of September returned seventy-one Matanzima candidates (out of seventy-five) to add to the seventy-one chiefs who supported him.

There were other detentions. The two Port Elizabeth actors, John Kani and Winston Ntshona, who had collaborated in Britain and America in plays by Athol Fugard, were held after performing *Sizwe Banzi is Dead* before a packed house in Butterworth. The play provided scope for improvisation, which the actors used to the full to ridicule independence. The arrest created an international storm, with actors holding widely publicized demonstrations in London and New York. The embarrassed South African authorities told Justice Minister George Matanzima to release the men. The Umtata government later made it a capital offence 'to cast reflection on the sovereignty of Transkei and against office bearers of state' – and the planned legislation would be made retrospective to the day of independence.

Inevitably, the Government's policy of tribal identification encouraged all kinds of rivalries and resentments. Two leaders of the Sotho-speaking minority were detained for demanding that the part of the Transkei where they predominated be handed over to the neighbouring Basotho Qwaqwa Bantustan. The 40,000 Sothos had signed a petition urging Mr Vorster to intercede on their behalf. The Qwaqwa education minister, James Ngaka, accused the Transkei government of sacking Sotho-speaking school principals and forcing Sotho children to learn through the medium of Xhosa. The bill of rights to protect minority groups, which many white liberals and black Transkeians were calling for unavailingly, seemed more necessary than ever.

In terms of the constitution, apartheid laws would remain on the Transkei statute book until such time as they were repealed. 'We shall repeal the laws of South Africa progressively,' Matanzima said before independence, 'but we cannot do it in a day, a year or even five years ...' He was in no hurry to abolish the immorality and mixed-marriages legislation, nor to get rid of the Terrorism Act. The 10,000 whites, whom Matanzima called the 'thirteenth tribe', would still be allowed separate hospital wards and country clubs. White schools would carry on as if nothing had changed: still run by the Cape Province department of education, with the occasional token blacks to suggest the idea of a non-racial society. (Among the first blacks to enrol at Umtata high school were the children of a Transkeian diplomat; they had grown up in the United States and could not speak Xhosa.) The much-needed white, and particularly Afrikaner, middle managers of new factories in the territory would not be wooed unless their children went to 'traditional' white schools.

The Bank of the Transkei was launched, with the majority holding going to *Volkskas*, the original *Broederbond* financial institution. Kaiser Matanzima became a shareholder. There were other bargains for the Xhosa nationalists. Kaiser was a shareholder in companies which bought four hotels – and their lucrative liquor trades – formerly owned by whites. The hotels had been acquired by the Bantu Trust, a South African Government agency, which then made them available to the chief minister's companies at knock-down prices. Thus, one company paid R8000 for the Cofimvaba Hotel, when it had cost the Bantu Trust R31,000.

In much the same way, the Matanzimas bought a series of 'white' farms at prices considerably below what the Bantu Trust had paid for them. The chief minister's vanity was pandered to by naming the Umtata landing strip the 'K. D. Matanzima Airport', while the American Holiday Inn chain, which has been doing good business in South Africa, made the 'K. D. Matanzima Suite' the most expensive at its new hotel in the capital. South Africa poured money into prestige projects, mainly in Umtata: R30 million for a hospital, R6 million for a stadium, R12 million for the airport, R13 million for a midtown 'Whitehall' building, R15 million for a base for the embryo army ('to defend our borders', Matanzima explained), and R2 million for a presidential palace. A start had also been made on a R70-million university campus. Yet, at the time of independence, the Transkei was able to generate less than R30 million a year from its own agriculture and industry.

Transkei's solvency rested on the twin pillars of handouts from Pretoria and the remittances of migrant workers. That dependency could only increase. The dimension of the problem facing the new 'state' was graphically illustrated in the agricultural sector, which employed four out of five of the economically active population within the territory. Government officials estimated that 100,000 people would have to be taken off the land in order to carry out vital reforms. Where would these people find work? In ten years, the industrial 'growth point' programme had provided barely 12,000 jobs for blacks – and there were 15,000 males coming on to the job market every year. The number of Transkeian migrant workers jumped from 175,000 in 1969 to over 300,000 six years later. They were mostly gold miners recruited after Malawi withdrew its workers from South Africa.

It was surprising that so few foreign and South African firms were attracted by the 'growth point' incentives offered by the Pretoria-controlled Xhosa Development Corporation (XDC). These included tax-free profits 'for a number of years', loan capital, cash grants, rail rebates and special facilities for the construction of factories.

In addition, South African legislation guaranteeing a minimum wage to blacks was suspended in the Bantustans. Low wages would become a permanent way of life, for Matanzima had decided views on trade unions. 'My government', he told Rand industrialists in April 1975, 'has consistently taken the stand that trade unions, with all their potential for disruption, are undesirable and even harmful in a developing country like the Transkei where continuing peak productivity is essential.'

Some thought might be given to unions 'at a later stage', he said, but if they were ever allowed, 'their powers will be carefully circumscribed'.

One reason for the failure of the 'growth points' is to be found in the slightly more successful 'border industry' programme. Given the choice, foreign companies clearly thought that 'white' South Africa offered a more stable future than the unknown quantities of Kaiser Matanzima. Once again, it all worked nicely for the whites. Border industrialists paid taxes to Pretoria, and their black employees, though resident in the Bantustans, spent much of their money in the 'white' areas. Even if some of the taxes were remitted to the Transkei, it meant that seven eighths of its general tax was being collected by the Republican Receiver of Revenue and the Department of Bantu Administration. It was, as Matanzima admitted, 'a sobering thought'. South Africa's murderous grip on this scrawny pullet of an economy was institutionalized through the X D C (later the Transkei Development Corporation), which controlled two thirds of total industrial investment.

The day before 'independence', the United Nations general assembly, by 134 votes to none, declared the state invalid. The Organization of African Unity and the E E C had already decided to ignore the new state. Kaiser Matanzima was particularly angry at the British, accusing the former colonial power in the Transkei of 'denying its own baby'. (The snub wasn't absolute – the United Kingdom state-owned British Petroleum placed an advertisement in the Johannesburg *Financial Mail* in the week before 'independence' which said: 'congratulations to the Transkei. B P is proud to play its part in the development of agriculture, industry and commerce'.)

There were two grains of truth in Matanzima's complaint. The British Government had handed over control of the new Union of South Africa in 1909 to a white-dominated parliament, ignoring objections by blacks and by white liberals. And, if the Swazis, Basothos and Tswanas could gain their own countries, how different were the Xhosas? The several tribes which made up what today corresponds to the Transkei and the Ciskei were scattered by British Victorian armies. The former protectorates were annexed directly by Britain, whereas the Transkei became part of the Cape Colony, only indirectly the responsibility of Westminster. It was a cruel mishap of history. 'We cannot be blamed for the situation in which we find ourselves,' Matanzima complained to the author. 'Great Britain should assist us to get recognition from the rest of the world and admit that we are her responsibility.'

Only South Africa and the unborn state of Bophutatswana recognized the Transkei. Basotho Qwaqwa proclaimed a day of mourning. Some 15,000 Xhosas voted with their feet and fled to the near-by Ciskei. Taiwan expressed its willingness to cooperate with the Transkei in matters 'practical', while Israel was expected to send experts. The 'B L S' countries (Botswana, Lesotho, Swaziland) stood out by their absence – they had even refused to extend the customs agreement with South Africa to include the Transkei. Even Rhodesia shied away from sending a representative. Likewise, Mr Vorster's friends from the military juntas of Latin America were loath to give public acceptance to the new state.

The author travelled on the 'uhuru train' from East London to Umtata. The most celebrated official guests were the vice-president of the Paraguayan senate and General B. Montou, of the Uruguayan military junta. Pinochet's Chile and the Argentine were represented in a semi-official manner. Faced with these neo-fascist honoured guests, it was not surprising that the Press were not given the 'distinguished visitors' list.

The journalists flown out from North and South America, Britain and Europe at Pretoria's expense far outnumbered the foreign dignitaries. Vorster did not turn up for the celebrations, leaving it to State President Diederichs, Foreign Minister Muller and Bantu Affairs Minister M. C. Botha to do the honours in the Independence Stadium (formerly the town's cricket field, where the scoreboard still showed last man 'nought'). The bands played '*Die Stem*', South Africa's national anthem, followed by '*Nkosi Sikelele Afrika*' (God Bless Africa), the hymn which the Transkei would share with Zambia and the banned African National Congress. Matanzima made a suitably defiant criticism of apartheid, and gave the black power salute as he drove away. But it was not enough to make his country the fiftieth state of the continent.

While the solemn ceremonial of the still-birth of a new state was being acted out in Umtata, the youth of Soweto continued quite justifiably to behave as if nothing had changed. The SRC issued a detailed appeal calling on all workers, except nurses and doctors, to stay at home for the whole of the first week of November. Black grocers, butchers and dairies would be open in the morning, and there was to be 'no purchase from white shops'. *Tsotsis* were asked, 'Please do not rob people', while shebeeners were told rather more forcibly to close down. 'No Christmas shopping of any kind, no Christmas cards and decorations, no Christmas parties ... Blacks are going into mourning for their dead.' Students in the Vaal Triangle locations, south of Johannesburg, issued a blunt statement: 'We are warning the Vaal people in advance that this should be their last week of boozing.'

This time, the strike call was not followed. Few blacks stayed away – a reminder that student–worker collaboration was still a far-off dream. By now, however, the nervous business world was telling Vorster to institute 'changes'. It had happened once before, after Sharpeville, but no sooner had law and order been reimposed and business begun to pick up than the reformist voices had died away altogether. Now the threat of recurring strikes and a boycott of white shops came in the midst of the worst recession that the country had known in forty years. If there was action now to reform the system, Harry Oppenheimer said, there would be 'a good chance to get change without revolution'.

Sometimes the reaction was more quaint than resourceful, as when the Transvaal Chamber of Industries issued a pamphlet attempting to explain to workers the consequences of a stay-away. Ian Murray, the Chamber's director, said: 'We feel many black workers don't understand the free enterprise system. We want to explain to them that employers simply cannot afford to pay workers if production is lost.'

These worries of the business world were understandable in

the face of the students' acknowledgement that the November strike was also designed as a reprisal against companies which had docked wages or dismissed workers 'because they obeyed our call to stay away from work'. A month after the rebellion began, the Transvaal Chamber of Industries had sent a memorandum to the Prime Minister. Pointing to the 'simmering discontent of the urbanized blacks', the Chamber recommended a host of improvements, covering transport, housing, an urgent review of discriminatory legislation, the phasing of free and compulsory education, better job opportunities.

There was the usual self-interested call for a black middle class. 'Only by having this most responsible section of the urban black on our side', the memo suggested, 'can the whites of South Africa be assured of containing on a long-term basis the irresponsible economic and political ambitions of those blacks who are influenced against their own real interests from within and without our borders.' All this would, at a pinch, have fitted into future Government plans, but what Mr Vorster must surely have objected to was the call to recognize town blacks as 'permanent urban dwellers'. That would have destroyed separate development. Months later the Chamber had still not received the courtesy of an acknowledgement for its memorandum.

If industry feared the strike weapon, commerce could justly be worried by talk of boycott. Though the November strike had failed, the students were still serious about a boycott of white shops. They planned a campaign to stop and question people carrying parcels into Soweto from Johannesburg. An early target were the hire-purchase furniture dealers, whose notorious swiftness in repossessing, the moment a payment was overdue, was matched only by their tardiness in actually delivering the wireless or bedroom suite to the black householder. Black delivery – or repossession – teams were, like black policemen, threatened and sometimes assaulted for being willing agents of their white masters.

When organized commerce plucked up the courage to suggest moderate changes in the life of the urban black, Vorster rounded on them with a thinly veiled warning to mind their own business and stay out of politics. The two chambers were dominated by English-speaking businessmen, and so could be safely ignored. But Afrikaner academics and editors joined the chorus for an improved quality of life for urban blacks, while Piet Cillie, veteran editor of *Die Burger*, Afrikanerdom's *Pravda*, even questioned the basis of apartheid ideology, arguing that Africans outside the Bantustans must be given political rights in the 'common area'. And a liberal churchman, Professor Tjaart van der Walt of the *Afrikaanse Calvinistiese Beweging* (Calvinist Movement), warned that unless the Government introduced fundamental social change, increasing numbers of Afrikaners would be unable, as Christians, to support it much longer.

The mass of whites, however, and the Afrikaners in particular, responded in a less spiritual manner. An Afrikaner salesgirl told the author at the time: 'Let's face it, Vorster does rule well. But he has been a bit asleep about Soweto. He has waited too long. They won't stop till we fire on them and they get frightened. We shouldn't worry about the wrath of the rest of the world. Everybody I meet thinks he should act. Most of my friends are Afrikaners. The riots are caused by Black Power, which comes from overseas. Otherwise all would be calm. They don't have justifiable grievances. The whites will fight for the future and what they've got, that's for sure. Black and white cannot live together in South Africa.'

Dr Connie Mulder, not put out by any such mild criticism of his Prime Minister, recommended that he be awarded the Nobel peace prize (and so follow in the steps of the late African nationalist, Chief Albert Luthuli). 'Even if it is not awarded to him officially,' Mulder told (white) nationalists in Vereeniging, 'his supporters across colour and party lines award it to him in their hearts.'

The predictable white reaction to the restlessness of the natives was to arm themselves. Even before June the number of licensed fire-arms exceeded the number of white households. (Blacks, if they bothered to apply for a licence, were allowed to carry guns only on the rarest occasions.) In 1975, there had been 108,142 licence applications, of which 106,646 were approved – so that only 1 per cent were considered unsuitable. In the second half of 1976, selling guns became one of the few boom sectors in the economy. In the midst of the six weeks of disturbances in Cape Town, a local dealer sold out his entire stock of handguns. A Durban armourer commented that whites were 'buying anything that goes bang. We'll be selling catties [catapults] soon.' Guns were fetching twice or more their new price on the second-hand market. Dealers offered a course of instruction on their shooting ranges, and security firms, fencing manufacturers and purveyors of fire-fighting equipment were unable to keep up with demand.

On the East Rand, a R20,000 fund was created to enable Bantu Affairs officials to buy revolvers or pistols as personal protection while carrying out their duties. At Turfloop University, white staff set up a vigilante service to warn the police of impending trouble on the campus. The assistant registrar, Mr L. T. Rautenbach, would receive reports of 'unauthorized student movements and unusual behaviour' in his 'control room'. If 'it gets too big for us', he explained, 'we call in the police.'

Not everyone could stand the changed atmosphere. The post of 'pest control officer' in Soweto, once the sinecure of a white man, was handed over to an African. Johannesburg city health department, which was responsible for the health of the township, explained that it was 'unlikely that circumstances will ever permit the resumption of a rodent control service by white personnel'. There was no indication that the new incumbent would earn the same salary as his predecessor.

It was the little man whom Vorster listened to, not the *verligtes* in the ivory tower. Any talking about political rights was over, he said. His hot-and-cold Police-Justice-Prisons Minister Kruger was more blunt in refusing blacks rights in 'white' areas. 'There is no other option as a solution to our problem but separate development,' he declared. 'We will learn to love this policy – all South Africans, black and white – and love it warts and all.'

The people of Soweto and other townships were getting their full share of 'warts and all'. In mid November, the (white) University of Port Elizabeth economics department released its half-yearly breadline report on black living-standards. Average African earnings in practically every industry were below the Household Subsistence Level (H S L), which included only expenditure on the basic essentials of food, clothing, fuel, lighting, cleaning, rent and transport. Spending on 'non-essentials' like education, entertainment or replacement of furniture was not accounted for. With the H S L at its highest in Johannesburg, at R134 a month, average earnings included R109 in manufacturing and construction, R91 in the motor trade, R84 in the wholesale trade, R78 in local government and R51 in hotels.

The West Rand Board, which had to run the township by its own revenue-raising schemes, had lost a large slice of its income when the beer halls were burnt down. The number of new houses that went up in the year dwindled to a mere 441 – and that with 20,000 families waiting to be housed. (This compared with 761 new houses the previous year and 1009 in 1974.) The figures infuriated big business, for a stable home was the linchpin of the plan to promote an African middle class.

At the end of November a multiracial congress, which included the private sector's top decision-makers, public officials, urban planners and black leaders, met at the Carlton Hotel in Johannesburg to discuss the problems of the black communities. Dr Anton Rupert, the Afrikaner boss of the giant Rothmans cigarette empire, launched an Urban Foundation, which would help the African in the massive task of improving his housing. It was essential, Rupert urged, to avoid 'any semblance of philanthropy'. Fellow multi-national tycoon, Harry Oppenheimer, nodded in agreement, as Rupert explained that 'a prerequisite for achieving our overall objectives should be the adoption of free enterprise values by urban blacks.' But black speakers thought that any sort of community scheme carried out within the framework of separate development would be seen merely as 'making apartheid more comfortable'. The assembled capitalists also pledged, almost as an afterthought, to remove colour discrimination in industry.

In the shadow of these grandiose plans was the annoying problem of insurance. Some weeks before the first beer halls were burnt down, the West Rand Board changed its insurers, handing the lucrative contract to S A N T A M, the Kohinoor in the crown of the *Broederbond*. By December, S A N T A M's bill was over R21 million (because of reinsurance, other companies were sharing some of the burden of damage, by then climbing to the R200-million mark). But the companies were loath to pay out until it was established whether the damage had been caused for political reasons or by simple vandalism. If a beer hall had been burnt down with the intention of overthrowing the state then riot cover would be waived and S A N T A M saved. If, as the police often said, it was the work of *tsotsis* with purely criminal motives, then S A N T A M would have to pay. So, often in the meantime increasing their non-political riot premiums by 140 per cent, insurance companies waited for the report of the Cillie commission on the causes of the unrest.

The Cillie commission of inquiry got down to work at the end of July. The choice of the Judge President of the Transvaal, Piet Cillie, to conduct the inquiry on his own, hardly helped to overcome black suspicions that the commission would be a whitewash. Cillie, in the words of a former colleague at the Johannesburg Bar, had never been known to disbelieve the word of a senior police officer. His elevation from pedestrian advocate to senior counsel (equivalent to Queen's Counsel) to judge had taken place in the course of a week, inspiring suggestions of a political appointment.

He had presided at several political trials, including that of the editor of the *Rand Daily Mail*, Lawrence Gandar, and reporter, Benjamin Pogrund, whom he convicted under the Prisons Act. His controversial conviction of the former Anglican Dean of Johannesburg, the Very Reverend Gonville ffrench-Beytagh, under the Terrorism Act, was reversed by the Bloemfontein Appellate Division.

Now, this latest appointment prompted Sydney Kentridge, defence counsel in many political trials, to take the unprecedented step of writing to the *Star* to question the wisdom of the judge's sitting alone. It would inevitably be regarded by many, 'especially blacks, as being somehow connected with "the Establishment"'. Kentridge suggested that a Bantustan leader sit with Cillie in order to obtain the full cooperation of the black community. Later, a black court interpreter who had recently obtained a law diploma was appointed to assist the commission.

Cillie and his entourage called in at the troubled township before the hearings got under way. In Soweto, the Bantu Council chairman, T. J. Makhaya, gave the judge an idea of the problems he faced. The Bantu Councillors were labelled 'stooges and sell-outs', Makhaya told him, 'and if you only talk to us you will not get to the bottom of this matter.' Using dramatic language, Soweto's 'mayor' warned: 'You are facing the last generation of blacks who are willing to negotiate. The younger generation are calling us stupid fools because we achieve nothing. They say if we can't achieve our rights through dialogue, we must take up spears and shields and meet in the field to sort out answers for this country.' Cillie promised that he would listen to everybody who wanted to talk, even those in detention.

In the event, very few blacks appeared before the commission. The reasons were obvious enough. No one wanted to be called a collaborator or, worse, an informer. Two days after the Soweto witchdoctor Credo Mutwa had told the commission that the army should have been sent in to quell the unrest his house was burnt down.

There was also the fear that a witness might be arrested if his evidence incriminated authority. Students at the University of the North refused to cooperate after the experience of several of their number, who had given evidence to an earlier commission of inquiry into campus unrest and had then been refused re-entry to the university.

Of the dozens of 'witnesses' who appeared before Cillie at the Old Synagogue in Pretoria, only a handful represented the radical youth. And they could not be said to have gone into the box willingly. One high school pupil from Pretoria was awaiting trial on sabotage. Had he been offered a lesser sentence if he appeared? Certainly Cillie assured him that his evidence would not be held against him at his trial, but as his name was withheld and he had no solicitor, who could be sure? The boy cheekily raised his hand in a black power salute as he took the oath, explaining that it was a tribute to Nelson Mandela, 'our leader who is on Robben Island because of his love for us'.

The hearings were not entirely without relevance. They revealed that the extent of the disturbances was wider than the public had believed. Police officers in out-of-the-way dorps described 'riots' which had not previously been reported in the newspapers.

Conflicting evidence on how the first victim, Hector Petersen, had died, showed up the police as unreliable witnesses. The policeman in charge, Colonel Johannes Kleingeld, said that he had fired warning shots 'in front and above the crowd'. Four black journalists contradicted him. The first shots, they said, were fired directly into the crowd. They were not warning shots. This was not damning evidence in itself, for the word of a white policeman would normally outweigh that of four blacks. But then the commission heard from the man who conducted the autopsy on Petersen, Dr Hans Bukhofzer, Johannesburg's district surgeon. Considering the position of entry and exit wounds in Petersen's body, said the doctor, the boy had been killed by a direct shot and not a ricochet.

It was inevitable that the police and Government officials should attempt to cast the blame everywhere except on the policy of apartheid: on 'Black Power', *tsotsis*, agitators and, not to neglect that old, tired whipping horse, the English-language Press. This, according to a Bantu Affairs official, had played an important if not decisive role in sparking off the disturbances. 'An extreme form of censorship' was necessary to prevent 'negative or inciting reporting'. He also said that church leaders who opposed Government policy on race matters should be ordered to remain silent.

A policeman from Benoni conjured up the 'long-standing friction between the Indian and African communities'. The commission heard the Cape Town riot squad chief, Colonel Andries van Zyl, latch on to alcohol as playing 'an intensive role' in the disturbances. On 11 August, the day that the rebellion spread to Cape Town, twenty-seven people had died, of whom, said the Colonel, twenty-six had been shot in the process of looting bottle stores.

The other recurring police theme, resorted to from the early days of the shootings, was that blacks were largely responsible for the deaths. The district commandant of the East Rand police, Brigadier J. Wiese, told Judge Cillie that twenty people had been killed by police bullets in his area and another twenty by 'township residents in various incidents'.

Police imaginings appeared to be contradicted by medical evidence. A state pathologist, Dr G. J. Knobel, reported on ninety-six post mortems performed in Cape Town between 11 August and the end of October. All but two had died from shootings: fifty-one from rifle fire, thirty-nine from shotguns, and four from both. These were instruments possessed only by police or white vigilantes.

The most surprising 'contempt' of commission came from the man who was actually leading the evidence, Dr Percy Yutar. When the hearings were being held in Cape Town, Dr Yutar told local Rotarians that car-loads of agitators had toured the country instigating the 'riots'. His conclusions, he said, were based on 'evidence heard so far'. Well before all the evidence had been heard the commission appeared to have made up its mind.

Dr Yutar, though not an Afrikaner (he is a leading member of the Jewish community) had played a vital role in eliminating political activists in South Africa, particularly as prosecutor in the Rivonia trial a decade before: now his role was to protect the police and Government officials. When a witness criticized Bantu Education inspectors for their handling of the Afrikaans language issue, Dr Yutar intervened: 'I must draw your attention to the fact that they were only doing their duty.' On another occasion, when a priest thought that ninety-two deaths at the hands of the police was 'very high, in this civilized world, so called', Dr Yutar came back quickly with, 'Many more than ninety-two have been killed in rioting in Ireland, surely...?'

The most dangerous aspect of the Cillie commission 'evidence' was that it was not contested. There was nobody in

court to cross-examine witnesses, because the Black Parents'
Association refused, after some soul-searching, to take part in
the inquiry. Many witnesses, particularly black policemen,
gave their testimony anonymously, some even behind closed
doors. On one occasion a letter from an 'anonymous black
student' to the Cape Peninsula Bantu Board accusing other
named students of making petrol bombs was accepted as
evidence by the inquiry.

Nervous Government officials indulged freely in passing the
buck. Mr J. C. de Villiers, chief director of W R A B, made
a scathing attack on the Bantu Education system, calling it
'cumbersome, frustrating and unfair'. Bantu Education
inspectors were 'making fires alongside the Soweto haystack'.
Mr de Villiers, perhaps not wishing to be categorized as a
'liberal', also attacked the police for not using stronger action.
The policy of the police, Mr Kruger hastened to assure the
nation, was to treat uprisings with a minimum of violence.

When Cillie began his hearings at the H. F. Verwoerd
Building in central Cape Town, the police suddenly found
themselves on the defensive. Whereas in other centres it was the
Africans who had been involved in the disturbances, now it was
the Coloured community as well, and they had close links with
the city's whites. Ordinary whites had been genuinely shocked
by the police viciousness in Adderley Street, in September. Now,
though black students boycotted the hearings, much valuable
eye-witness testimony was heard. Thanks to detailed reports in
the English newspapers, whites could learn what Africans and
Coloureds had known all along – that the police, and especially
the riot squad, far from restoring calm and protecting the
innocent, had often incited rioting. It was not without justification that the Coloureds called them '*die terroriste*' (the terrorists).
A coloured Second-World-War veteran heard members of the
riot squad 'boasting among themselves how many people they
had shot and in what ways they had shot them'.

If Judge Cillie was looking for proof of police callousness
he heard it in the story of Sandra Peters, an eleven-year-old
girl living in the Cape Town Coloured-group area of Athlone.

Early in September, during a break in the unrest, Sandra's mother sent her on an errand to the corner shop. Minutes later she heard that Sandra had been shot in the head by riot police and been taken to hospital. Mrs Peters and another daughter went to the Athlone police station but were not allowed into the building. The women remonstrated, there was an 'exchange of abuse' with the police, and soon enough, mother and daughter were locked up for the night.

Not until the next afternoon did Mrs Peters appear before a magistrate. All this time a social worker had been trying to contact her so that she could give permission, as the next of kin, for Sandra to be operated on. At 4 p.m. – a full twenty-four hours after the shooting – she was able to give that permission. But Sandra died at 7.45 p.m.

With the police now being publicly assailed for their brutality and callousness, Colonel A. P. van Zyl, chief of the riot squad in Cape Town, explained that without 'drastic measures' they would not have effectively been able to bring the disturbances under control. In 'extreme circumstances, he said, when fire-arms had to be used by the police, the ringleaders were singled out to be shot at and thereafter firing was for 'deterrent effect'. In some cases, he admitted, 'people who got in the way have also been hit by the bullets fired at ringleaders.'

However, a Cape Town University sociology professor, Dr H. W. van der Merwe, disagreed with the deterrent effect of the riot police's actions and accused them of 'unbridled savagery'. Often in the disturbances, Dr van der Merwe said, violence had broken out *after* the appearance of the riot police. Their camouflage dress, designed for operations in the bush, was out of place in a city environment. It was associated with soldiers chasing the enemy, whose task was to shoot – and to kill. The fact that they did not carry identification numbers made it difficult to bring to book any riot policeman who behaved improperly. The actions of the riot police, van der Merwe said, appeared to be in conflict with the universally held view that the role of the police was to maintain order with a minimum of force. There were many indications of young recruits coming from 'racist' homes, or from areas where racial prejudice ran high. 'They regard non-white people as inferior and un-civilized – and possibly believe for this reason that these people must be subjected to hard-handed treatment.'

So horrific were some of the allegations made against the police – both of shooting peaceful people and of the disregard of bereaved parents searching for their dead children – that Cillie was constrained to take action. The result was an 'inquiry' by a police officer, which not surprisingly came up with explanations unrecognizable to the complainants. After some jarring moments in Cape Town, Judge Cillie moved into the Cape Boland (hinterland) before returning to the safer northern pastures. He knew enough to identify the real causes of the 1976 rebellion – but would he have the nerve to write them into his report?*

The extensive official cover-up of the nature and extent of the black casualties was sometimes hinted at but only occasionally confirmed. Hospitals, which are controlled by the provincial administrations, were loath to supply information. Dr P. J. Beukes, superintendent of Baragwanath, which was the most important hospital for treating casualties, was accused of a hush-up by the English Press after offering a 'no comment' on whether black children had been blinded by police birdshot.

Cape Town University students ran a Riot Information Services which reported that the city's main hospitals were under heavy armed guard. The students quoted doctors and nurses, many of them Coloureds, at Victoria and Groote Schuur hospitals as having counted seventy-three dead on the night of 8 September alone. That was far in excess of the official figure.

The ubiquitous activities of the police were naturally extended to the mortuaries. Though the mortuary in Cape Town was controlled by the municipality, the city's chief engineer was refused permission to enter the building even with the written permission of his council. A Cillie commission witness said that next-of-kin were not given the body of a person from the township unless they first signed a form admitting that the dead person had taken part in the 'riots'. Bodies were sometimes sent

*At the time of writing, Judge Cillie has still not presented his report.

to distant mortuaries for burial. The authorities were helped in the identification of African dead by the register of documents in Pretoria, which has the fingerprints of all Africans aged sixteen and over in possession of a pass. But thousands of Africans, especially in Cape Town, survived without their papers being in order, so that the police did not have to worry about reporting all the deaths.

In South Africa, newspapers must be wary of making allegations against the police unless the sources are absolutely reliable. So the carefully documented list of identified victims which appeared in the *Rand Daily Mail* at the end of December is of great importance. The newspaper counted 499, which is greatly in excess of the 386 officially accepted as having been killed as a result of police action. How many hundreds more of unidentified blacks lie buried will never be known.

As the year drew to a close, all the 123 black leaders were released from their Internal Security Act detention. Some, like Winnie Mandela, Oshadi (Jane) Phakathi of the Christian Institute, and the East London *Daily Dispatch* woman reporter, Tenjiwe Mthintso, were banned and restricted under the Internal Security Act and prohibited from continuing in their old jobs.

For the most part, the detainees were not ill-treated, if only because they escaped interrogation by the security police. Two of them, William Tshwane, who died on the first day of his detention from 'natural causes', and Edward Mzolo, did not come out alive. Another eleven political prisoners died during the year from a variety of euphemistic causes, which appeared on the death certificates as 'suicide' or 'accidental'.

Police 'interrogation' methods came under special scrutiny following the death in March, by 'natural causes', of Joseph Mdluli, an old-guard member of the African National Congress. His four security police 'interrogators', two white and two Africans, were charged with culpable homicide. The men did not appear in the witness box, but their counsel outlined their story. Mdluli had attempted to escape while being interrogated and had been forcibly overcome by the four accused. Later that day, after interrogation had been resumed, Mdluli had stood up, holding his head and complaining of dizziness, staggered and fell, hitting the back of a chair with his neck or chest. He died an hour later.

The judge later listed the injuries:

— three areas of bruising on the neck;
— abrasions over both cheeks, left elbow, right upper thigh, both shins, ankles and right foot;
— extensive deep bruising of the scalp and abdominal muscles;
— deep bruising and haemorrhage over the left lower rib cage;
— three fractured ribs;
— extreme congestion of the brain and many small haemorrhages;
— bloodstaining of the fluid of the brain;
— fractured Adam's apple; and
— blood-congested, water-logged lungs.

The three main prosecution witnesses were all forensic experts. One of them at first thought that 'strangulation' had been the cause of death, but later changed it to 'the application of force to the neck'. Two other pathologists expressed strong doubts that the fatal injuries had been caused by a fall. Judge James himself considered that the police version was open to 'very considerable doubt' and further investigation was required to establish how Mdluli met his death. This important matter, said the judge, should not be left in its 'highly unsatisfactory condition'. The Natal Attorney-General announced that no further action would be taken over Mdluli's death, as there was 'not even a *prima facie* case for doing so'.

Throughout this time 'black consciousness' was on trial in Pretoria. In late December, all the nine accused were duly convicted and sent to Robben Island for five or six years. The judge, admitting that they were sincere in believing themselves victims of an oppressive system, did not expect prison to reform their views. The sentences were a deterrent to stop like-minded people from indulging in similar acts. It was no victory for the regime – and now black consciousness, like S W A P O and the South African liberation movements, could claim to have martyrs on the island gaol.*

By the year's end, over 4000 people had appeared in court on charges of public violence and riotous assembly; nearly 1800 blacks had been fined or given strokes of the cane or imprisoned for up to three years. Many, however, had gone free, usually after weeks or months in prison. The high acquittal-rate reflected the indiscriminate manner of police arrests. A thirteen-year-old Tembisa boy spent seventy-seven days in prison before the charge of public violence was withdrawn. He was luckier than other 'rioters'. In a case at Bellville, near Cape Town, a policeman described how he ordered his men 'to fire at the rioters because it would be easier to arrest them if they were wounded'.

· The riot police were persistent to the last in attempting to set black against black. On Boxing Day, at least thirty African residents in Nyanga, in the grim sand flats outside Cape Town, died at the hands of migrant workers. It was the old story of the hostel dwellers – frustrated, bored, dehumanized by their existence – being used as the instrument of white domination, so that the police could happily refer to 'faction fights'. Fortunately, the local priests, white and black, recorded the residents' version of the events. Mrs B. reported:

I was washing dishes in the kitchen and my husband was reading his newspaper in the sitting room, when we suddenly heard a knock at the door. My husband opened the door, and saw the riot police, who then allowed a group of migrants to come in, and they beat my husband until he was half dead. One riot policeman remarked, 'You are lucky that he is not stone dead.' Minutes later my husband died of head injuries.

When this and other accounts were published, Minister Kruger refused to hold an inquiry. Instead, security policemen questioned the clergymen, one of whom was sent to prison for refusing to disclose the names of his informants.

By the end of the year there were signs that resistance was entering a more violent phase. In November, two policemen were seriously wounded by a hand-grenade thrown by a group

*Prisons Minister Kruger intends to close down Robben Island prison and move the inmates to a maximum security gaol near Johannesburg.

of Africans near the border with Swaziland. A few days later a bomb exploded in a white Johannesburg restaurant, blowing off the hand of the African who was carrying it.

In his New Year message to the nation, Mr Vorster forecast a grim time ahead for South Africa. Nobody could accuse the Prime Minister of overstatement. The year of the schoolchildren had brought about incalculable changes in the climate of South Africa. Where they would lead was anybody's guess. But they had to be taken seriously. As Khotso Seatlholo, the Soweto student leader, wrote before fleeing into exile: 'I smelled the smoke of a gun. I felt the sting of a bullet. I tasted blood. I suffered wounds. I saw death snarling into my face. I became a fugitive in the country of my birth. I cannot forget. I cannot forgive the white man . . .'

7. The Forming of the Laager

There was a time when white South Africans, John Vorster among them, would say: 'Ah yes, we do have a problem with the blacks, but there's no hurry.' After the 16 June 1976, only the most ostrich-like whites, and there are many, can still say that time is on their side. For the nationwide uprising, coming so soon after the appearance of a Marxist government in Mozambique and the ill-judged intervention in Angola, constituted the first step on the long haul to black rule. With the benefit of hindsight it is possible to discern how much has been changed since the black youth took South Africa into the era of Soweto.

For the whites, the most alarming new factor introduced has been psychological – a new-found black confidence; a determination not to accept society as unchanging and unchangeable; a readiness on the part of a growing number of blacks to die for their cause. At Sharpeville, blacks were shot in the back while running away from the police. At Soweto, many were shot in the chest, advancing.

White rule depends on force, but it must be the right amount, or it will become counter-productive. Thus, the violence is normally turned inward, with the whites leaving the blacks to kill themselves. Life is worth little in the townships, thanks to migratory labour, uprooting from the 'white' areas, unemployment, drink, seemingly deliberate under-policing. You cannot grow very old in Soweto without seeing a corpse lying face down in a gutter, or a friend or relative stabbed by a frustrated hostel 'bachelor'. Whites also killed blacks, but more selectively: a policeman felling a prisoner 'attempting to escape', the hangman with his yearly bag of fifty or seventy-five, the farmer 'punishing' his servant for disobedience. Just enough, as the popular expression has it, to keep '*die kaffer op sy plek*' (in his place).

Then in June 1976, as the police turned to tougher measures to contain black discontent, the violence spiralled. It is vividly illustrated in the figures for prison deaths, an accurate barometer of official nervousness. No political prisoners had died in the hands of the security police for several years before 1976. Joseph Mdluli, a few months before Soweto, broke the spell. With the townships out of control, the police cast aside the thin veil of restraint. Cell deaths soared. It is easy to understand the resentment at Steve Biko, the man who inspired the events of that year. He was killed by a gratuitous blow from a special branch officer who was unable to comprehend that a dead black man could become a martyr to his people and a spur to yet greater violence.

The resulting protests led to the proscription in October 1977 of all the black consciousness organizations; the detention of most of the Committee of Ten, the first body of black leaders to have won the support of the people of Soweto; and the closing-down of the Johannesburg black daily the *World*, with the imprisonment of its editor, Percy Qoboza.

The banning of black consciousness cleared the field for the Zulu-based organization *Inkatha* (literally, 'mystical coil'), brain-child of the dissenting Bantustan leader, Gatsha Buthelezi. All-powerful in Zululand, and not without followers in Soweto, *Inkatha* hopes to cross tribal lines and win general African support. In March 1978 Buthelezi announced the formation of a South African Black Alliance (S A B A), encompassing the Coloured Labour Party, the small Indian Reform Party, and the tiny ruling party in the Sotho Bantustan of Qwaqwa. The Alliance's primary aim was to prepare for a national convention at which all South Africans would map out a non-racial con-stitution for the country.

The Alliance leans heavily on the charisma of its founder, and as long as he keeps within the framework of separate develop-ment, the Government will hesitate to ban him. The three other members of S A B A also claim to be using the system in order to destroy it. But their willingness to go along with apartheid will not endear them to the radical youth, nor to the older banned movements, despite Buthelezi's public acceptance that ANC, PAC, black consciousness and *Inkatha* must work together for change.

It is the altered mood of the Coloureds which makes the Alliance so dangerous. Sonny Leon's Labour Party is, by any standards, moderate, even right-wing. The dominating factor in the lives of Coloured people had long been the reassurance of a second place in the South African order of priorities: comfortably distanced from Africans, decently in the shadow of whites. Then came the generation of rejection and, in 1976, the Government's refusal to accept the main recommendations of the Theron commission report, followed by the shootings of Coloureds in the townships.

Pretoria relies heavily on the $2\frac{1}{2}$ million Coloureds (and 750,000 Indians) for the success of its numbers game. Together with the whites, these 'non-Africans' make up almost 8 million people, which just about balances the African population in the 'white' areas. And well over half the people of Cape Town are Coloured. So any desertion in the ranks endangers security and makes apartheid harder to sell abroad. Even if, at this late hour, the Nationalists suddenly opened their arms to their half-brothers, many would willingly come over. Then, the bulk of the Coloureds would simply melt into the ranks of the Afrikaner working class, while a few thousand moved into Cape Town's posh white suburbs and the business centre on the city's foreshore. But even this modest liberalization – which would be acclaimed by the English-speakers – is beyond the imagination of Afrikaner ideologues.

The proscribing of black consciousness has benefited the radical wing of black resistance. Indeed, one of the ironies of recent events is that the African National Congress, which has little time for the students' ideology, stands to gain enormously from the Soweto uprising.* In 1975, Oliver Tambo, external leader of the ANC, was asked when the armed struggle would

*Though its gratitude was not always apparent. When the British National Union of Students organized a march in London to mark the first anniversary of the uprising, they were persuaded by the ANC to withdraw their invitation to Tsietsi Mashinini, the lad who had done more than anybody to put the name of Soweto on the map of the world.

begin in earnest. 'We are waiting for South Africa to rise up,' he explained.

Certainly, the appearance of sympathetic regimes in Mozambique and Angola had been a considerable shot in the arm, but the ANC always maintained that without internal resistance, little could be achieved. In the decade from the mid sixties, black nationalism had no answer to the rule of General van den Bergh's security police. It was these doldrum years which gave rise to black consciousness. The black youth did not despise the old leaders, they simply considered them to be out of touch with developments inside South Africa.

Then the Black People's Convention and the South African Students' Movement were banned, putting them in the same boat as the ANC and the Pan-Africanists. Black consciousness had gone a long way towards achieving its first objective – psychological preparation for the liberation struggle. It was this dynamic force which drove the youth into the streets. Their success took them quickly into the next stage – the elaboration of a strategy of liberation. But now, with so many of its members banned, detained, in exile or dead, black consciousness appears to have run its course. Significantly, during a German television interview, in one of the last public statements that Biko made before his death, he expressed the hope that his own followers would get together with the illegal movements to carry on the struggle.

When the students fled into Botswana, they entered a Persian market, with ANC and PAC agents bidding aggressively for their favours. Several hundred were recruited by the ANC, but many others accepted offers of education in 'neutral' countries. A large group found school places in Nigeria, and there were reports that the Lagos government was encouraging the formation of a 'third force' liberation movement under Tsietsi Mashinini. Little has been heard of it since.

Those recruited by the ANC, on the other hand, were fed into a well-oiled machine: military instruction from the resident Cubans and political education from exiled stalwarts.* But

---

*On their visits to Luanda, the comrades, including the Communist Party strongman Joe Slovo, stayed at the former South African official residence.

this is still a long way from the moment when the freedom fighters can expect to march triumphantly along Church Street, Pretoria.

The ANC has problems of ideological orientation which appear to be endemic, and may hamper its effectiveness. Since before the First World War it had avoided the blandishments of white, Indian and Coloured communists. It was over this issue that Robert Sobukwe marched out in 1959 to form his all-African Pan-Africanist Congress. Ten years later, at a meeting in Tanzania, the exiled ANC opened its ranks to non-Africans. Almost immediately, communists moved into influential positions in the ANC, ensuring the growing radicalization of this branch of African nationalism – and direct access to the Kremlin. In 1975, a group of nationalist purists, among them expelled members of the central committee, gathered in London, the most important external mission outside Africa, complaining of 'the undue influence' of the South African Communist Party. Their half-hearted attempt at a *coup* came to nought, but it certainly reflected the suspicions of the faithful inside South Africa that an alien solution was being foisted on them.

And since Soweto, the bond between African nationalism and communism has been solidly sealed, at the top at least. The Pan-Africanist Congress has problems of a different kind. As with black consciousness a decade and a half later, it went into exile too soon after its formation to think out a viable political plan. With its founder, Robert Sobukwe, in prison, PAC-in-exile was soon rent asunder by ruinous personality clashes, and never really recovered. It did obtain arms and training, notably from Peking, but today it has no fraternal country to give it access to the enemy, as does the ANC in Mozambique and Angola. The Pan-Africanists' strength is the extent of their following in parts of South Africa, particularly in the Cape Province.

There were unmistakable signs before Soweto that the great fund of allegiance to both nationalist movements was beginning to shake itself into open resistance once again. Since then, several Supreme Court trials, arms and explosive caches found in raids in Soweto, and attacks on whites by blacks wielding Russian-made weapons, leave little doubt that urban terror has come to stay – and that it will grow on a scale never seen in southern Africa before. Soweto refugees trained in Angola have already returned home – and, in one case, been sentenced to death for killing a white.

Urban terror will be facilitated by the heightened political awareness of the township parents. Their stay-aways and attempts to boycott white business reveal an appreciation of the techniques of economic warfare. Few families in the townships of Johannesburg or Cape Town do not have a son or brother who suffered in the uprising. And all of this means that more people are prepared to risk giving refuge.

Since Soweto, Pretoria has attempted to speed up the timetable of Bantustan independence. One motive is that the Bantustans trace a giant horseshoe round South Africa, from Mafeking to Grahamstown, and, bolstered by white-trained armies, would become a defensive cushion for the white core within.

But independence could have the opposite effect. South Africa shares more than 4000 miles of frontier with her five black neighbours and cannot hope to seal them hermetically from every passing warrior. Some tribes straddle national frontiers, so that a Shangaan-speaking guerrilla could cross from the home of cousins in Mozambique to his parents in the Transvaal without attracting attention. Encouraged by poverty, unemployment and rough treatment at the hands of white soldiers, these tribal areas could just as easily provide fertile soil for revolt. The Pondoland peasant rebellion against Verwoerd's imposition of Bantu authorities revealed a tradition of rural militancy which is liable to reappear at any time. Once independent, the fragmented Bantustans would provide South Africa with 9000 miles of border to guard – more than Canada's, the earth's second largest country.

The infiltration of guerrillas and their communist-made weapons has taken place mostly across the Mozambique frontier into the eastern Transvaal. For the foreseeable future, however, President Machel, though in sympathy with its aims, is unlikely to allow the ANC more than 'bird of passage' status. Apart from the heavy dependence on economic ties with South

Africa, his country is wide open to 'hot pursuit' reprisals, which the white army is now perfecting across the Angolan border from Namibia. Much depends on the political colour of the successor regimes in Zimbabwe and Namibia. If radical, they would combine with a bolder Mozambique in the more active encouragement of guerrilla warfare across hundreds of miles of border.

The expansion of the war in Ovamboland is directly traceable to South Africa's miscalculation over Angola. Had she kept scrupulously to the side lines, the M P L A would still have prevailed – and given sanctuary to S W A P O guerrillas – but the Cubans would not be there in anything like the numbers they are now. S W A P O, for its part, is steadily winning support right across the territory. As it is easier to fight S W A P O on the battlefield, rather than at the hustings, the war will continue in the north. But the longer it goes on, the more radical S W A P O becomes, with the prospect that some day South African soldiers will be fighting 600 miles to the south, on the borders of the Cape Province itself.

It has not gone unnoticed by the blacks of South Africa that whatever progress there has been in recent times is due to 'war, war', and not to 'jaw, jaw'. Force brought down the Portuguese empire. And in Zimbabwe and Namibia, where a mountain of words, promises, court cases, U N resolutions, had shifted colonial rule not an inch, black guns broke the deadlock of white intransigence. The turn of events in south-western Africa has converted the whole sub-continent into an area of superpower conflict. Before then, Pretoria could look after itself adequately with the help of the middle-strength European powers and Japan. But now, with the Cubans spreading their wings, only the United States can provide a heavy enough counter-weight.

Cynical blacks do not believe that President Carter would have pleaded for human rights in southern Africa had the Cubans stayed at home to cut sugar-cane. And they see the belated Western efforts to find a peaceful settlement in Namibia as not unrelated to their vast economic interests in the territory. If the Soviet Union now appears to be taking risks, it is a calculation based on the unwillingness of the United States, still chastened by the Vietnam experience, to get involved away from home. The real test of the Soviet Union is still to come. Will it be prepared to furnish the liberation movements with the gigantic amount of arms necessary for an effective assault on South Africa? And will it keep its nerve if the United States chooses to respond?

There have been important changes in American policy towards southern Africa since 1976. The first outward sign of a new direction was Dr Henry Kissinger's bludgeoning but not ineffective journeys through the continent. The out-going Secretary of State had belatedly discovered the crises of Africa and was now hoping to devote another paragraph to himself in the history books – and perhaps get President Ford re-elected as well. When he arrived at Pretoria in September 1976, the townships were clearly out of police control. The wily Secretary of State was able to exploit this weakness, so that Vorster would leave his Rhodesian ally in no doubt that the game was up. Smith flew back to Salisbury to declare on television that blacks would be taking over within three years.

At the time, Jimmy Carter was musing aloud, with an eye on the black vote, that he might abandon his campaign for the presidency to 'start a crusade for black majority rule in South Africa'. That summer and autumn black Americans were shocked to see on their television screens how their brothers and sisters were treated in South Africa. Once elected, Carter put blacks in important roles. Andrew Young, ambassador to the United Nations, with a seat in the Cabinet, became roving envoy in Africa; while Don McHenry later became Chief United States negotiator on Namibia. Senator Dick Clark, as chairman of the Black Caucus, had visited South Africa and influenced his country's thinking.

Washington's planners must have pondered hard over the example of Mozambique. Here, by refusing to budge an inch, the Portuguese rulers had set up the ideal conditions for a successful revolution. Inflexibility had fashioned Frelimo into perhaps the most impressive radical liberation movement on the continent. Would a similar pattern now develop in Zimbabwe and Namibia, and eventually in South Africa? As the anti-colonial wars intensified, the guerrillas needed more and better arms and training: as only the communists would oblige, the West's influence declined correspondingly.

In May 1977, Vice-President Walter Mondale met Vorster in Vienna to inform him of the new White House policy. The Afrikaner Nationalists were required to be flexible. Mondale put forward some suggestions for change: the abolition of the pass laws, job reservation and Bantu Education, and the end to persecution of political dissidents. Questioned at a Press conference, he insisted that what he wanted was 'one man, one vote'. But the State Department, in a more considered response, subsequently toned down this demand.

Perhaps the real clue to the aims of Western policy came from Andrew Young in an interview with *Playboy* magazine (banned in South Africa on 'moral' grounds). White South Africans can only survive, he said, if they separate capitalism from racism and 'involve blacks in decision-making and in economic participation'. In that event, he foresaw a situation in which 'the blacks may control the politics but whites still run the economy'.

Young had exposed the crucial difference between the two countries. They both wanted capitalism to survive, but Pretoria believed this was only possible under separate development, whereas Washington insisted that it would require the installation of a friendly black government. If black rule is for Vorster the penultimate step towards communist domination of southern Africa, for the Americans, apartheid and white rule must lead inexorably to a communist take-over. Small wonder that a year after the friendly Kissinger call, Vorster was saying that the end result of America's pressure on southern Africa would be exactly the same as if the country were subverted by Marxists.

This did not mean that the West wanted to drive the whites into the sea, it was simply that the security of the whites had become secondary to the need for a black government – an acceptable regime that would secure the vast wealth of the area from Russian control. Diamonds, uranium, platinum, chrome, nickel, antimony (for aircraft batteries), gold, all these and other metals and minerals abound in southern Africa as nowhere else, save in the Soviet Union. That this Aladdin's cave should remain in the 'right' hands is one of the bulwarks of Western security.

To this end, in February 1977, high-ranking British and American Government officials mixed with heads of multi-national corporations at a secret meeting of the Ditchley Foundation in England to discuss 'U S–European relations with the countries of southern Africa'. They were working on a co-ordinated strategy to protect their common interests.

The West can wage a 'peaceful' struggle for southern Africa because it has the right economic levers to pull. The communist East, with no traditional interests in the area, is left with no choice but to make its way by force of arms. There is no reason why Britain or America should not sell arms to the A N C. Public opinion at home might be disturbed by open involvement in a war against whites. But arms can be sold clandestinely, or through a third party, and the liberation movements would then be grateful for the help; perhaps even shift their allegiance slightly westward. But the fact is that the West does not want a revolutionary victory. And the British rightly fear for the security – and profitability – of their extensive interests in the subcontinent.

But Washington retains a substantial degree of influence among the whites. It can talk, and act, tough because its investment in and trade with apartheid (1600 million dollars through its companies in mid 1977) are nowhere as high as that of Britain or even West Germany. Reprisals against foreign firms for 'playing politics' would not frighten Americans too much. In the meantime, the White House has begun a modest policy of encouraging bankers and industrialists to contain, or even reduce, their involvement in apartheid.

Since Soweto, and more especially since the crack-down on black consciousness, commercial bank loans have been drying up, and new investment declining. The Bank of America, the country's largest, announced in March 1978 that it had made no loans to South Africa for several months, while Chase Manhattan has become extremely cautious. One investment officer at a large bank explained: 'We have a strict prohibition on any general purpose loan – long term or short term – to the South

African Government. Moreover, our bank will make absolutely no loans to the homelands, border industries or Namibia.'

However, loans are still made. A consortium of banks lent R200 million to E S C O M (the State electricity supplier), but only because it was considered to be in the public interest. And despite public pressure, the Export-Import Bank, an autonomous American government agency, still provides insurance for short-term trade credits extended by commercial banks. South Africa has also become the International Monetary Fund's third largest borrower. The I M F does not budge without the approval of the U S Treasury.

Still, the fact that the gnomes of Wall Street, not renowned for over-sentimentality about the oppressed, have been persuaded to curtail their acquisitive instincts in the name of ethics, is a remarkable advance.

In the same way, American companies in South Africa are pumping in very little fresh money. Much of it is reinvestment of profits, and that often represents commitments made before Soweto. Don McHenry, deputy American Ambassador to the U N, explained recently that 'the question of what government does in encouraging or discouraging is almost becoming moot. Private investment has looked into the situation in South Africa, taken note of the fact that the economy has been in real trouble, taken note of the new level of profits, taken note of the political situation there and they obviously have decided that they are not going to put anything in there right now.'

Britain, inhibited by 300 companies in South Africa and a dependence on mutual trade, has not been able to make the same readjustments. Since the 1974 House of Commons code of conduct on the treatment of black workers employed by British firms, there have been modest improvements in factory conditions and pay. But these barely touch the real problems. It is pointless to talk about 'equal pay for equal work' when the great mass of desirable jobs is reserved for 'whites only'. Dr Owen, the Foreign Secretary, admitted British limitations when he declared: 'British subsidiaries in South Africa are South African firms, subject to South African law.'

The troubles in Soweto – and the strikes in particular – did bring some British firms face to face with a new and worrying reality. When at first Department of Trade and Industry officials had attempted to discuss the workers' code with parent companies in Britain, they were invariably given little co-operation. By the second half of 1976, however, the same executives were only too keen to be advised on how to reform their ways so as to remain in South Africa when the 'storm has blown over'. Midland Bank, bowing to pressure from church groups, stopped lending to the South African Government and its agencies, but continued to finance trade credit.

The select committee recommendations are toothless. There is no way of forcing companies to publish the facts if they do not wish to do so, so that many prefer to keep quiet or to supply inadequate or misleading information. Very often, top management is staffed by South Africans who are incapable of changing the habits of a lifetime whatever head-office in London may decree. Nor can the Department of Trade and Industry be expected to police the behaviour of firms in South Africa while at the same time trying to encourage trade with the country.

The only action by foreign business which could really damage South Africa is disinvestment. An estimated R20,000 million is invested from outside. It is, admittedly, difficult for a multi-national corporation like British Leyland, with factories and fixed plant worth many millions, to sell out all at once. But they, and the other mining, oil and motor giants – not to mention Pepsi Cola and the state-owned British Steel Corporation – could at least initiate a programme of selling, say, 10 per cent of their shares a year to local buyers.

Even if they have to sell at a discount, their actions would be viewed favourably in the Third World. And this is where even the British Tories could be persuaded that friendship with South Africa is bad for business. With British exports to Nigeria alone climbing over the £1000 million mark in 1977, there is a spectre of sanctions by black Africa against countries trading with apartheid. The South African market (less than £600 million in 1976) may one day seem expendable.

The Third World is united over two issues only: a more equitable distribution of the world's wealth, and hostility to apartheid. Each banning, 'riot', or thoughtless remark by an Afrikaner politician promotes this hostility in Africa and Asia. After the Biko inquest headlines, the West was unable to veto a United Nations resolution on a mandatory ban against arms for South Africa. France, apartheid's prime armourer during the decade and a half of 'voluntary' arms embargo, even announced that she would not deliver four warships destined for the South African navy that were nearing completion in her shipyards. By then, however, French planes, helicopters and military vehicles were being built under licence, deep in the Transvaal. As a result, South Africa will have the means to defend herself for some years to come.

There can be little doubt that recent events have brought forward the day when the West finds itself unable to veto a UN resolution calling for an economic embargo of South Africa. A dozen years of sanctions-busting by friends of Rhodesia do not encourage the belief that a boycott will be watertight. It would need concerted action by the West; and that means an air and sea blockade, accompanied by searches of suspicious vessels. For a brief period after UDI the Royal Navy boarded ships sailing towards Beira, in Mozambique, which were suspected of carrying cargo for Rhodesia. The prospect is fraught with the gravest possibilities. The South African navy and air force would not stand idly by. It might be better, then, for searches to be made by the United States, rather than the Soviet navy.

Oil tankers would be the primary – and most easily identifiable – target of an embargo. The Arabs did impose a boycott in 1973, but it has been nullified by the Shah of Persia's friendly ties with Pretoria. (His father, exiled in South Africa in the Second World War, is buried in Johannesburg.) With so many urgent problems awaiting solution in the Middle East and the Horn of Africa, the world is unlikely to force Iran to toe the line. In preparation for just such a day, however, South Africa has been stockpiling oil in disused coal mines, as well as extending facilities for extracting oil from coal. But a concerted oil embargo, in which the petrol companies were ordered by their governments to conform, would eventually have South Africa tottering.

One instant effect of Soweto has been the drop in immigration and the rise in emigration. In 1975 there was a net gain of 40,000 settlers. Two years later, despite the steady trickle of new arrivals from Rhodesia, the process had gone into reverse, with a net loss of more than one thousand. Television had had much to do with it. In the old days, whites would turn to the sports and fashion pages of their newspapers to keep themselves abreast of world affairs. But now, though S A T V's reporting of current affairs is propaganda of the most obvious kind, it cannot ignore war, politics, and the isolation of the country caused by its race policies. Viewers look at the little bioscope and realize that they have a political problem which will not go away.

In the border war, S W A P O guerrillas may not be able to defeat the South African army, but they do kill regularly enough to remind white mothers and fathers that the defence of their privileged way of life demands a sacrifice. A stream of white youngsters are departing to avoid military service, now extended to two years for every white school-leaver. Some of them go because of principle, but most simply do not see much future in a country where whites have to kill blacks in order to survive. Others are concerned at the extended period of economic stagnation. Prosperity is what interests the English, who have left political management of the country to the Afrikaner. If they cannot make profits, then the sun will not seem so warm nor the playing fields so green. A significant number of middle-class Afrikaners is to be found in this exodus, but the English-speakers leave more easily, and are often entitled to immediate British nationality under the patrial rule.* Those with exportable occupations – doctors, dentists, engineers – are going to the United States and the Commonwealth, while the business-men who have nursed their Swiss bank accounts long and sagely enough are welcome almost anywhere.

The departure, in droves, of the Jews is a sign of the times. Numbering only 125,000, Jews have played a disproportionate role in business, professional and academic life. Some have been active in radical politics. Many have gone along all too happily

*The Afrikaners call the English '*sout piels*', or 'salt cocks' – feet stretched so widely between South Africa and England that their private parts trail in the sea.

with the laws and conventions of apartheid. In the middle ground, the Progressive Federal Party (the official opposition is an amalgamation of the original Progressive Party and periodic refugee groups from the, now extinct, United Party) gains much support from liberal Jewry. As the young leave for Israel, America and Britain there is a rekindling of the anti-semitism which has lain dormant since the victory of Afrikanerdom in 1948. This in turn will spur even greater emigration.

A visit to the South African Government immigration offices in the Barclay's Bank International building in Trafalgar Square is a graphic reminder of the effect that Soweto has had on the recruitment of British settlers. The man in the lift complains that about midway through 1976, his job suddenly became one of the quietest in London.

Since the early sixties, Britain has supplied about a quarter of a million new settlers for apartheid, well over half of all new arrivals. It was not so much the numbers which Pretoria wanted, as their skills. After all, even if immigration returned to the annual high of 35,000 during the early seventies, black births would cancel them out in a mere three weeks. Ten years ago, a South African official estimated that immigrants, who cost the Government £77 a head to bring in, contributed £90-million worth of skills annually – the cost of training 7000 tradesmen and 3000 professionals. Now these jobs will have to go to blacks –if there are any skilled enough to do them.

These settlers have not always played the game with Pretoria. Only one in four ever takes out South African nationality. And even if they have done so, they would still be entitled to recover their original citizenship, should they feel safer at home. Potential settlers will not be encouraged by a new Bill before Parliament by which immigrants under the age of twenty-five will automatically become South African citizens after two years. They will then be called upon to defend their new homeland on the battlefield.

Does this steady departure of emigrants suggest a crumbling of white cohesion? There are signs since Soweto that morale is flagging. The black assault on the Afrikaans language had much to do with it. One conscience-stricken Afrikaner, Professor

Dreyer Kruger, wrote an article just before the uprising which declared that his people were doomed – and deserved to be. 'The Afrikaans culture, as it is now conveyed by parents, teachers, professors, leaders of the *volk* and Afrikaans church ministers,' he wrote, 'is primarily the culture of the strait-jacket in which we are held and prevented from developing our humanity.'

The psychological state of the Afrikaner was viewed with some seriousness; at one stage the National Party placed a full-page advertisement in *Die Transvaler* to cheer up the rank and file. 'Things are not so dark in South Africa as some well-meaning and enemy commentators put forward', was the soothing message from Connie Mulder. The ad. quoted the Prime Minister as well: 'If you don't have confidence, how do you expect others to have confidence? If you don't believe, how do you expect others to believe?'

In October 1977 Vorster called an election. Its purpose, he said, was to show the world who ran this country – South Africa or the interfering West. In the course of the campaign, Kruger banned the whole of the black consciousness movement and a cluster of white churchmen, sweeping into illegality a giant section of non-communist political resistance. The bannings angered Western governments. But the voters were impressed with the show of *kragdadigheid* (power or, more especially, white power), and that is what mattered. The Nationalists emerged with a record majority. And, importantly, they had won over, for the first time, half of the English-speaking voters.

The apartheid bulldozer drove all before it – quite literally, in the squatters' camps around Cape Town, where thousands of homes were razed in the middle of winter. With two million blacks out of work a new law planned to dispatch 'idle Bantu' to labour camps. The compass of Afrikaner nationalism veered hardly a minute off its true course – the establishment of more 'independent' Bantustans, then the ultimate aim of making every African a foreigner in the land of his birth (incidentally, making Soweto a city inhabited entirely by foreigners). As Bophuta-tswana followed the Transkei to 'nationhood', its citizens found that nothing had changed for them. Separate development was now seen for what it was: an attempt to alter the facts of South African life by redrawing the map but without touching the harsh social, economic and political realities.

Mr Vorster postponed plans to set up a multiracial Cabinet Council with representatives from separate white, Coloured and Indian 'parliaments'. The Coloured Labour Party had rejected the concept because urban blacks would be excluded and, thus, the whites – probably under President Vorster – would continue to rule. Even so, a Government spokesman had to reassure voters that Coloured and Indian 'cabinet ministers' would not live in Bryntirion, the Pretoria suburb where white ministers have their official residences.

The ebullient Connie Mulder replaced the dour M. C. Botha at Bantu Administration (leaving three Bothas in the Cabinet – Piet, defence, Pik, foreign affairs, and Fanie, labour and mines). Though no less right-wing than his predecessor, Mulder, who retained his portfolio of Information, attempted to remove some of the more emotive labels of apartheid. He abolished 'separate development' for 'plural democracy', and changed the name of his department to the Ministry of Plural Relations. The word 'Bantu', he explained, was no longer acceptable to the black. (He might have said the same of apartheid.) The Minister of Plural Relations did not say whether there would now be plural pass offices, a West Rand Plural Administration Board, or plural beer. In keeping with this mood of semantic daring, 'homelands' became 'self-governing states'.

All this only serves to highlight the vast gap between what the blacks demand and what the whites are prepared to give. To the Afrikaner, the admission of a black man into a white rugby club is an act tantamount to revolution. To the youth of the townships, now talking the language of majority rule, nothing less than the vote in the Cape Town Parliament is acceptable. And if the minute intellectual wing of Afrikanerdom known as 'verligte' is more pressing in its calls for 'change', all that it really intends is an end to such discrimination as is not essential to white supremacy.

Yet in Namibia, Judge Marthinus Steyn, the administrator-general appointed by Pretoria, scrapped the Immorality and

Mixed Marriages Acts, and showed that 'petty' apartheid could be jettisoned without the sun stopping in its tracks. Though a calculated attempt to win international acceptance of Turnhalle-style *uhuru*, it did pose the question: 'If it can be done in our old fifth province, why not here in the Republic as well?'

Mr Vorster is a prisoner of his people. He is elected to office by that entire nation – trade unionists, working women, farmers, urban commuters and the growing might of Afrikaner capitalism. Liberalization in any of these sectors would result in a shift to the right and votes for the flat-earth policies of Dr Albert Hertzog's HNP (Reconstituted National Party). The tens of thousands of white women who run the lower echelons of the public service hold their positions solely because of the colour of their skin. It would be simple to throw these jobs open overnight to all races without lowering standards. But black civil servants don't have votes in elections.

Since coming to power in 1948, this rural people has embraced the materialism of the age with much dexterity. At the summit of society, cabinet ministers had to be scattered to far-flung consul-generalships to cover up their dubious business deals. They have packed the boards of para-statal organizations running enterprises such as the railways, airlines, electricity, steel, oil-from-coal and many others. The mediocre are found jobs in apartheid's voracious bureaucracy – Bantu (Plural) Administration, Bantu Education, Coloured Affairs, Indian Affairs, Group Areas, Community Development. Others have joined the vast Afrikaner raj administering the Bantustan empire. As the Bantustans near 'independence', the Afrikaner bankers, engineers, military experts and economic advisers arrive. Should apartheid end, such people would be wondering where the next pay-cheque was coming from.

The white police force, which secures the sanctioning of apartheid, has, if anything, hardened in its attitude towards black activists since Soweto. This is not surprising for the police come mainly from the lower slopes of Afrikaner society, and their position would be threatened by a dismantling of racial discrimination. Yet these are the whites who play a critical role in shaping race relations. At the Police College in Pretoria they are taught from a textbook which explains the 'Bantu way of thinking'. 'They cannot talk logically', it says. 'They do not think in an abstract way, but concretely, according to what they can feel, see or hear.' Their way of thinking is 'full of contradictions'. There is no alternative to apartheid: 'it is our only safeguard.'

Speaking at a Nationalist women's meeting, the Prime Minister's wife, Tienie Vorster, regretted the destruction of family life, the attack on law and order, and the devaluation of truth. Mrs Vorster must surely know that hundreds of thousands of families are destroyed by the migrant labour system in her own country, through the policies of her husband. Perhaps she thinks that only whites are entitled to a family life. The inability to credit black people with a humanity similar to their own is the dangerous blind spot of Afrikaners. Surveying the world around him, Dr Daniel Malan, the inventor of apartheid, once said: 'Our history is the highest work of art of the architect of the centuries.'

There is room for disagreement over the architectural merits of the Voortrekker Monument, the granite mausoleum overlooking Pretoria, which is the holiest shrine in Afrikanerdom. Built, in the words of its mortal architect, 'to last a thousand years', the monument enshrines the most basic spiritual and political motivations of the Afrikaner people. Inside the building, encircling the Hall of Heroes, a carved marble frieze 300 feet long recalls the epic moments of the Great Trek. Panel twelve of the frieze has the Voortrekker pioneer, Piet Retief, signing a 'treaty' with the Zulu King Dingaan, by which much of Natal was to be handed over to the Boers. On panel thirteen, Retief and his seventy followers are massacred by Dingaan's *impis*. The message is unmistakable – 'Never trust a kaffir.' The memory of Dingaan's 'treachery' is a crucial psychological barrier to the settlement of today's race problems.

Afrikanerdom still resists tenaciously. At the moment, its soldiers are fighting the SWAPO guerrillas in northern Namibia. When eventually they withdraw to within the borders of South Africa, they will know better how to defend the laager. The one weapon of incalculable value in their armoury is the knowledge that if they lose, there is nowhere else to go. The Dutch, if Holland is viewed as a potential bolt-hole, do not care for them. And even so, the Afrikaners know well enough that their language, traditions, everything that makes them unique, are in jeopardy away from '*die aard*'. Times are not favourable for an Afrikaner diaspora.

But the very knowledge that there is no Afrikaner homeland could well have a salutary impact on their long-term behaviour. As the regime slides deeper into friendless isolation; as foreign investment dries up and technical know-how is withheld; as the English slip away and the black birth-rate soars; as township rebellion becomes permanent insurrection and white casualties increase, a moment could well arrive when the *bittereinders* decide that the game is no longer worth it. This built-in paradox offers some small hope for the survival of Africa's only white tribe.

But in Soweto, life continues much as before ... WRAB, the West Rand Administration Board, built a record low of 422 houses in 1977. It also rejected plans to electrify the township because the cost of £40 million was too great. The *makgotla* tribal elders announced that they would *sjambok* (whip) any girl under eighteen years of age found in the streets after eight at night. A £30 fine or ninety days in prison became the standard sentence for violations of the pass laws.

In elections to the new, Government-sponsored Soweto community council, 460 (out of a population of 1½ million) cast their vote. Only two of the thirty wards were contested, and another nine candidates were returned unopposed. Plural Relations Minister Connie Mulder hailed them as 'the democratically elected leaders of Soweto'.

Not one of Soweto's 27,000 secondary school students wrote their end-of-year examinations in November 1977. One third of the standard-five (the final year in primary school) pupils wrote their exams, and nearly all were successful. When the academic year began in February 1978 half the secondary schools remained closed. The Department of Bantu Education was renamed the Department of Education and Training.

Connie Mulder promised to turn Soweto into the most beautiful black city in Africa ...

Bibliography

Black South Africa Explodes, Counter Information Services, London, 1977.

Black Reviews, 1972–5, Black Community Programmes, Durban.

Davenport, Terence, *South Africa: A Modern History*, Cambridge Commonwealth Series, Macmillan, London, 1977.

Dugard, John, *The SWA/Namibia Dispute*, University of California Press, 1975.

Hepple, Alexander, *Verwoerd*, Penguin Books, 1967.

Horrell, Muriel, *Bantu Education to 1968*, South African Institute of Race Relations, 1968.

House of Assembly Hansards, 1976.

Johnson, R.W., *How Long Will South Africa Survive?*, Macmillan, London, 1977.

Lawrence, Patrick, *The Transkei: South Africa's Politics of Partition*, Ravan Press, Johannesburg, 1976.

Moore, Basil (ed.), *Black Theology*, C. Hurst & Co., London, 1973.

Reeves, Ambrose, *Shooting at Sharpeville*, Gollancz, 1960.

Rogers, Barbara, *Divide and Rule: South Africa's Bantustans*, International Defence and Aid, 1976.

Survey of Race Relations, South African Institute of Race Relations, published annually.

Thompson, Leonard, and Butler, Jeffrey (eds.), *Change in Contemporary South Africa*, University of California Press, 1975.

Troup, Freda, *South Africa: An Historical Introduction*, Penguin Books, 1975.

Troup, Freda, *Forbidden Pastures*, International Defence and Aid, 1976.

van der Merwe, Hendrik, and Welsh, David (eds.), *Student Perspectives on South Africa*, David Philip, Cape Town, 1972.

Wilson, Francis, *Migrant Labour in South Africa*, South African Council of Churches and SPRO-CAS, 1972.

Index

Absentees, non-payment of wages by employers, 50, 54

Ackerman, N.C., 156, 163

Africa, development of independent states, 50, 54; possible sub-continental war against white supremacy, 51, 235; socialist credo, 79; Western world and its successive disasters, 164–5

African Congregational Church, 70

African National Congress (ANC), 38, 51, 52, 125, 231; anti-pass law campaign, 29–30, 31; declared unlawful, 31–2, 82, 117, 149; release of leaders, 33; military wing, 34; arrest of underground leaders, 36; and Bantu Education, 86; and student rebellion, 166, 176, 231; and British NUS, 231n; and armed struggle, 231–2; ideological problems, 233; admits non-Africans, 233; communist infiltration, 233, 234

Africans, definition, 12n, 25; tribal lands limitations, 38; prohibited from striking, 38; residential prohibitions, 38; and separate development, 38–9, 50; industrial demands, 39–40, 95–6; expulsions through 'endorsing out', 40–41, 44; position of 'borners' and 'section-ten' people, 40; position of wives and children, 40; rooting out of 'superfluous appendages', 41; 'bachelor' designation, 44; abolition of labour-tenant category, 44–5; excision of 'black spots' from rural and urban areas, 45; numbers living in homelands and municipal townships, 46; creation of jobs in or near reserves, 46–7; population figures (1970), 47; control by labour bureaux, 48–9; employment in arms industry, 55; demonstrations of industrial strength, 59–60; unrecognized under industrial laws, 59; movement into semi-skilled work, 60; position of 'temporary permanents', 61; diminished effect of wage rises, 61; made to think themselves inferior, 69, 101–2; overall areas of grievance, 79; and education costs, 87–8; language instruction, 93–5; and white labour market, 95–6; operation of floating colour bar, 96; sent to 'ethnic' colleges, 96; inappropriate text books, 99–101; precede Dutch in SA, 103–4; white ignorance, 108–9; housing leases, 135–6, 173; restrictions on travel and public places, 136–7; bear brunt of recession, 140–41; method of taxing, 141–2; Government policy on hostel dwellers, 176–7; marriage and moral prohibitions, 186; HSL living standards, 217; numbers appearing in court, 227; psychological effects of Soweto, 229; nationalist–communist relationship, 233

When black teenagers marched through the streets of Soweto in June 1976, they were met with a hail of bullets from Mr. Vorster's policemen. The confrontation shattered the illusion that South Africa could peacefully maintain a system based on institution-alised racial inequality. At least 500 were dead; 4,000 more in detention; but, led by their children, the millions of blacks living in townships like Soweto had made it clear that *apartheid* would not be perpetuated without a struggle.

Denis Herbstein witnessed the events in Soweto and elsewhere at firsthand. He has written an account that is remarkable for its immediacy and depth. He describes the life of the township dwellers with sympathy, skill and vigour, drawing on many inter-views and conversations which enable his readers to understand the grim paradox of being black and living and working in Africa's richest 'white' cities. He sets the people and the events in a wider historical and ideological context; he exposes the fraudulence and ruthlessness of the South African government towards its black citizens, the uncaring mouthing of promises never intended to be kept. He shows how the ideas of Black Consciousness grew and spread in the townships, especially among the youth, arming them with a philosophy for which they were ready to risk all.

After Soweto, with the *cordon sanitaire* of Mozambique and Angola gone, and white supremacy in Rhodesia and Namibia under siege, South Africa stands at bay. This book is essential reading for those who wish to understand the historical backdrop to the tragedy and the people who are doomed to act it out.

Denis Herbstein's anger is tempered with irony, his sense of outrage modulated by an understanding of how South Africa has come to the brink of disaster. A well-informed and timely book, it is written with a sympathy that brings home the terrible dilemma of the men and women involved, as well as the depth of feeling which separates them.

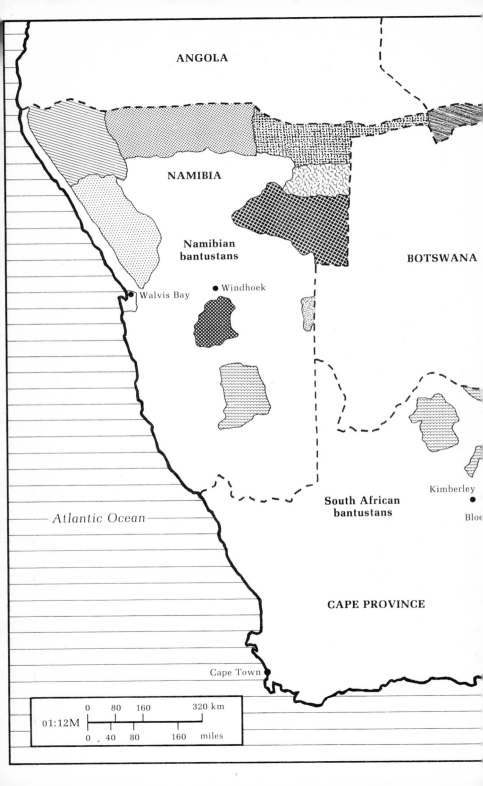